Science, Society and Power

In this book, James Fairhead and Melissa Leach bring science to the heart of debates about globalisation, exploring the transformations in global science and its contrasting effects in Guinea, one of the world's poorest countries, and Trinidad, a more prosperous, industrialised and urbanised island. The book focuses on environment, forestry and conservation sciences that are central to these countries and involve resources that many depend upon for their livelihoods. It examines the relationships between policies, bureaucracies and particular types of scientific enquiry and explores how ordinary people, the media and education engages with these. In particular it shows how science becomes part of struggles over power, resources and legitimacy. The authors take a unique ethnographic perspective, linking approaches in anthropology, development and science studies. They address critically prominent debates in each, and explore opportunities for new forms of participation, public engagement and transformation in the social relations of science.

JAMES FAIRHEAD is Professor of Social Anthropology at the University of Sussex and MELISSA LEACH is Professorial Fellow at the Institute of Development Studies, University of Sussex. They have jointly authored *Misreading the African Landscape: Society and Ecology in a Forest-Savanna Mosaic* (Cambridge University Press, 1996) and *Reframing Deforestation: Global Analyses and Local Realities – Studies in West Africa* (1998).

'To date, the discourse on "Science in Society" has focused mainly on the industrialised world. In this timely book, Fairhead and Leach redirect our attention to the discourses around scientific forest management in West Africa and the Caribbean, where they effectively demolish persistent stereotypes associated with science, governance, development and globalisation. Instead of the usual caricatures of heroes and villains, we are presented with carefully contrasted case studies elaborating the complex interplay of science and policy among communities, governments, businesses, and NGOs that constitute the multi-scale institutional vortex of "Tropical Forest International". *Science, Society, and Power* presents a rich and detailed narrative accompanied by insightful analysis. It should provoke a much-needed re-evaluation of the "Risk Society" hypothesis, which characterises community engagement with science as a peculiarity of late modernity.'

Steve Rayner, Director, ESRC Science in Society Programme and Professor of Science in Society, University of Oxford

'A remarkable and fascinating book. Fairhead and Leach combine the ethnographic study of two "developing" countries with a thorough grasp of wider theoretical debates over science and society. They bring a much-needed anthropological perspective to issues of scientific governance and the social relations of science and policy. Our understanding of the international and local dynamics of environmental practice is accordingly transformed. This book has significant implications for both social scientific understanding and the development of future forms of governance. At a time when the interaction of social life and scientific practice is more important than ever, *Science, Society and Power* addresses crucial issues and deserves a very wide readership.'

Alan Irwin, Professor of Sociology, Brunel University

Science, Society and Power

Environmental knowledge and policy
in West Africa and the Caribbean

James Fairhead and Melissa Leach

CAMBRIDGE
UNIVERSITY PRESS

PUBLISHED BY THE PRESS SYNDICATE OF THE UNIVERSITY OF CAMBRIDGE
The Pitt Building, Trumpington Street, Cambridge, United Kingdom

CAMBRIDGE UNIVERSITY PRESS
The Edinburgh Building, Cambridge, CB2 2RU, UK
40 West 20th Street, New York, NY 10011–4211, USA
477 Williamstown Road, Port Melbourne, VIC 3207, Australia
Ruiz de Alarcón 13, 28014 Madrid, Spain
Dock House, The Waterfront, Cape Town 8001, South Africa

http://www.cambridge.org

First published 2003

Printed in the United Kingdom at the University Press, Cambridge

Typeface Times 10/12 pt.   *System* LATEX 2_ε [TB]

A catalogue record for this book is available from the British Library

ISBN 0 521 82874 0 hardback
ISBN 0 521 53566 2 hardback

Contents

Figures

Maps

Tables

Preface and acknowledgements

When we visited Trinidad and Tobago in 1999, the country was gripped by the staging of 'Miss Universe' which appeared to be holding up the execution of drug baron Dole Chadee and eight accomplices. The country has been trying to deal with the increasing use and trade of cocaine. On the islands drugs are also cultivated on many scales, including within forested state land, reserves and wildlife sanctuaries. The illegal drugs fields are protected by trap-guns operated by tripwires, their threat creating no-go areas for foresters and hunters alike given frequent media reports of those killed or maimed. People living near these areas are concerned that they are out of their control and influence; were they permitted access and use, they argue, they could assist policing. A radically contrasting vision was driving scientific inquiry and policy deliberations around the same protected areas. The country is under pressure from foreign donors and international environmental agreements to expand its protected areas and their zones of exclusion. Legislating for and implementing a national parks system had become a 'green conditionality' for a series of international development loans, on the grounds that this would benefit both the environment and the eco-tourism economy.

Earlier that year we had re-visited West Africa's Republic of Guinea. The European Union had been financing the establishment of a vast new national park. In keeping with international orthodoxies around participation and community conservation, the park was working experimentally to support local hunters and their organisations to regulate wildlife use and protection. This peaceful community-focus was to contrast with the paramilitary forest guards who had been at the sharp end of Guinea's earlier repressive approach to conservation. Yet with civil war raging in Sierra Leone and Liberia, bringing refugees and the threat of an expanded regional crisis, hunters also aired a radically different conception of themselves: as the nation's second army, the bush counterpart to the government soldiers based in town.

Emergent international policy debates and the sciences enwrapped with them, stood, in both countries, in contrast with a multiplicity of alternative concerns and framings, at times as stark as in these examples. Over the previous decade, our earlier research in Guinea had exposed equally stark disjunctures between the perspectives of those living close to the land, and those considering it through grids of Science, Administration and Policy. Where the latter treated islands of forest around villages as last relics of a diminishing tropical forest, the former spoke of ways they and their ancestors had established them in earlier savannas (Fairhead and Leach 1996). Where the latter interpreted large forest areas in relation to natural history – natural climax vegetation – the former considered them in relation to social history – as ancestral lands once farmed, then depopulated by war (Fairhead and Leach 1994, 1998). The very land use practices and the social world framing them which the scientific and policy world had considered so problematic could, and as we argued should, be thoroughly re-cast.

It is such experiences which have come to drive our focal concern with the practices of science in contemporary society, and their relationships with policy and power. In particular they problematise the ways in which increasingly internationalised scientific and governance regimes engage with national practices, shaping in turn the ways in which these engage with particular localities. These are the processes we explore in this book. While in some senses, it is about the environment, we are not considering the nature and extent of particular environmental problems, but rather, how environment comes to be problematised, and international dimensions to this. And while this book is in some senses about African and Caribbean states and localities in a contemporary world order, our focus on science and policy shows how conflicting visions exist at each of these levels, and how alliances continually emerge across them.

A comparative, multi-sited work of this kind incurs many debts of gratitude. First, we should like to thank those involved in the comparative research project of which this is a part. In particular, Kojo Amanor from the University of Ghana at Legon not only conducted a parallel study in Ghana, but also shared with us some important moments of fieldwork in Trinidad and Guinea, many hours of discussion of the findings, and much mutual learning. In Trinidad, we would particularly like to thank Thackwray Driver of the Ministry of Agriculture, Land and Marine Resources for introducing us to the island's scientific and policy worlds, and for his research collaboration, and Keisha Charles for her invaluable research assistance. We were affiliated to the Sustainable Economic Development Unit (SEDU) of the University of the West Indies, St Augustine, and would like to thank Denis Pantin and his colleagues for their warm welcome and hosting of seminars. At the government Forestry Division, we would especially like to thank the Chief Conservator Narine Lackhan and the head of FRIM, Anthony Ramnarine, as well as the staff of the North-Eastern and South-Eastern Conservancies who gave so generously of their time and opinions during our field visits. We are equally grateful to the many donors, NGO staff, farmers and hunters who spoke with us.

In Guinea, special thanks are due – once again – to Dominique Millimouno, our longstanding research collaborator, and to Ibrahima Boiro and his colleagues at the Centre d'Etudes et de la Recherche en Environnement (CERE) at the University of Conakry to which this research project was formally affiliated. Numerous national, prefectoral and local forestry and environment staff, as well as members of donor and non-governmental organisations, farmers, hunters, teachers and others spoke with us – often at length – during our interviews and field visits, and we are grateful to them all.

In Europe, we should like to thank the staff of the Forestry Department, United Nations Food and Agriculture Organisation (FAO) in Rome; of CIRAD in Montpellier, France, and of the Department for International Development (DFID) in London who discussed science and policy issues with us. The Washington-based Conservation International supported our participation in their West Africa biodiversity priority-setting exercise, while numerous other individuals and organisations responded generously to our e-mail inquiries. While we are grateful to everyone we interviewed during this research, we have sought to preserve their anonymity in what can be such sensitive scientific and policy fields by citing interviewees only by position, rather than name. Nevertheless in an arena of study of this kind, and given the tightly-interconnected policy worlds both internationally and in the focal countries, those involved will still be able to identify individuals. Realising that this would be the case, we endeavoured to make all those we interviewed in the course of the research aware of its aims, context and possible implications. It is also research that focuses on aspects of people's lives that are already in the public domain. Nevertheless as a study exploring the political and social dimensions to knowledge and practice, it may well play into personal and professional sensitivities. We apologise if this is indeed the case, and of course take full responsibility for any errors of fact or interpretation which may have influenced our analysis. Our hope is that those involved – as well as the wider constituencies to which they speak – will find the book interesting and useful.

The research for this book was funded by the Committee on Social Science Research (CSSR) of the UK Department for International Development, as part of our research project on 'Forest Science and Forest Policy: Knowledge, institutions and policy processes' (1998–2001). We are very grateful for this support, although it should be noted that opinions expressed here remain our own, and are not attributable to DFID. Several of the chapters have been presented in earlier versions at seminars, conferences and international meetings, where we should like to thank participants for their numerous doses of constructive criticism. We are particularly grateful to colleagues in the IDS Environment Group for their shared interests in and stimulating discussions about environmental policy processes over the years, and to Alan Irwin, Steve Rayner, Brian Wynne and anonymous reviewers for commenting on the draft manuscript. Lastly, special thanks are due to Cassandra, Rory, Xanthe and Francesca for the stages in this work that they shared, and to Elisa Eade for making this possible.

For Cassie, Rory, Xanthe and Cesca

1   Science and society: an ethnographic approach

Introduction

With science now shaping anxieties as much as destinies, poverties as much as opportunities, tracking its conduct and conductors is ever more pressing. Much has been said of economic globalisation, and the effusion of global media, desires and morals. Much less, however, has been said of the 'globalisation' of science, especially as experienced in poorer countries. Perhaps this is because the defining claims of science have long been portrayed not just as global, but universal: not just modern, but eternal. Yet there is a peculiarity to the sciences of any place and era and to the values they embody, and current patterns in the globalisation of science are no exception. It is these which this book sets out to explore.

Contemporary powers and power blocs are grappling to secure their worlds within a voracious global economy, and to tame the global media to their concerns. Yet they must also engage with globalised science, whether natural or social. International conventions, agreements and the deliberations leading to these – whether around climate change, biological diversity or trade – are increasingly important in shaping national policies and international engagements. There are now over two hundred international environmental regimes and supra-national organisations which manage them. Each is co-established and co-evolves with scientific committees.

Within this new world, there is an emerging role for science – a certain kind of it at least – in international governance. In as much as the operation of international regimes depends on particular negotiated, scientifically authenticated truths, the politics of their operation is conducted through the practice of science. There is a negotiation through science: through the determination of key questions, analytical frameworks, methods and monitoring. As negotiations are between governments, the deliberations give new impetus to the idea of 'government scientists', and to negotiators speaking simultaneously in the name of government and of science. Concurrent with the proliferation of international regimes is a tendency towards establishing supra-national regional blocs which can negotiate common interests in international agreements; a necessity within the international system. Regional political unions are being shadowed by regional scientific unions, with regional inquiry shaped in articulation with global debate. The co-production of science with policy, and the political and economic forces shaping it, has never been clearer.

Yet contradictory tendencies seem to run counter to this increasing internationalisation. The presence of non-governmental organisations, public pressure groups and 'indigenous people' in the streets, on the television and at times in the negotiation chambers of international deliberations defies simplistic pictures of nation states and their scientists forging international orders. Complex alliances and oppositions link elements of international research and policy organisations with citizen's groups and private enterprises. These tendencies seem to signal a greater role for 'voices from below' in the shaping of international science and governance. Similarly, political decentralisation, the claims and protests of social movements and citizen action have been associated with new engagements with science in national and local settings. Publics are increasingly unwilling to place unquestioning trust in formal expertise and public institutions. Citizen action is now frequently articulated through 'citizen science', and curious alliances have formed in appreciation of 'indigenous knowledges' and 'ethnoscience'. The questions begged by these terms are certainly interesting– what constitutes science and citizenship, and what differentiates indigenous knowledge, citizen science, and 'normal' (non-citizen?) science. But the terms do capture something of the way that science has ever more visibly come out of the laboratory, field station or university to be conducted, contested and authenticated in society, in politics and in the law courts; something of the way the conduct of science is becoming important to moral and economic contestation. Indeed to the extent that social and moral debates and dissent are being conducted through science and its media mediation, it is possible to speak of the structuring of social life in relation to the practices of science, and the ways in which they choreograph relationships with commodities, kin, religion and authority.

As this book argues, however, these apparently contradictory trends between globalising and localising forces of science in governance are rarely so opposed. First, they can be united by shared problem-framings: the local concerns or forms of knowledge which come to be represented in national and international debates frequently share dominant, globalised questions (for instance about what is happening, and which trends need to be arrested or modified), while alternative framings and their implications drop out of view. Indeed such local-global links are often fostered explicitly, whether from below (when local groups appeal to the authority and economy of global discourses) or from above (when international institutions appeal to the authority of locality and participation). In this sense, even the most distantly 'local' actors and their everyday lives may be caught up in the vortex of global debate – although with highly unequal capacities to shape its terms.

Second, an apparent polarity between globalising and localising forces obscures important 'intermediate' processes operating within national settings: the complex, historically-embedded relations between politics, bureaucracies, institutions and research traditions which articulate with and shape the engagement of local and global pressures. This is, in part, the field of national governance and science. The so-called civil character of 'non-governmental organisations' (NGOs) does not mean dissociation from this field. On the contrary, the alliances forged between different NGOs, government departments and research organisations within countries are powerfully constitutive of it. Switching the focus from institutions to the processes of science and policy, as we do in this book, helps discern these alliances and the ways different publics become involved in them, in ways which transcend conventional dichotomies between state and society, expert and public, global and local. It is not just 'the state' that sees (cf. Scott 1998), and states embody antagonistic forms of expertise.

Shared problem-framings, and the institutional complexity within which analysis is conducted, must qualify arguments that located, everyday activities and cultural expressions are excluded or distanced from the global networks which orchestrate political and economic power (Castells 1997). Rather, how local activities are incorporated into such networks is a central research question. As we shall explore, this complicates and compromises calls for change which imagine that 'participation' or 'social movements' will enable local knowledges to challenge global perspectives in a straightforward way. Rather, it becomes necessary to understand the links between science and policy, identifying the circumstances in which citizen critique (or at least expression of alternative, located perspectives) can be forged, and the conditions in which it can be effective.

To discern contemporary relationships between science and society, then, will require a multi-sited and ethnographic approach (Marcus 1995), extending from international organisations and networks, through national bureaucracies, scientists and activists and their local staff and activities, to the complexities of everyday life. This is the complex task that this book undertakes. One needs to focus on the processes by which different strands of science and policy come to shape each other, and gain authority, but also do so in the broader social field of which they are a part.

Science and society: comparing issues and settings

'Hi-tech' science, tropical forests and conservation

Public engagement with science has never been a simple enchantment. The killing of scientists in Mao's China, and the suppression of genetic science and politics in the former Soviet Union or fundamentalist religions in the United

States, underscore the extent to which the conduct of science is part of social and moral struggle. Nevertheless, several commentators have discerned a new moment of heightened moral concern and transformed public engagement with science. In what Beck (1992, 1995) would describe as reflexive modernity and Giddens (1990, 1991) as late modernity, and as elaborated by Lash (1996, 2000) and others (e.g. Adam 2000, House of Lords 2000), there is seen to be a new mood of anxiety with 'expert' institutions and their knowledges, new forms of personal and cultural engagement with science, and increasing public critique and demands for new sorts of dialogue.

Yet this contemporary writing on science and society is imbued with a sense of here and now; the here which is high-tech Europe and North America, and the now which is the right now of 'post-modernity'. This sense is conveyed in the examples used: genetics, biotechnology, new reproductive technologies, nuclear physics and so on.[1] Anxious publics question the values and risks linked to rapid technological change, and the capacity of established forms of expertise to deal with them. Techno-economy increasingly determines both bodies – farming and food, immune and reproductive systems – and the social world, configuring communication, vocabularies, fears and fortunes.

This book looks at very different domains: the science and policy surrounding rural environments, land and forests. It does so in very different places: in West Africa, and in the Caribbean. The broad concerns of contemporary science and society debates apply here, but are manifested quite differently and carry different implications. In the histories and social relations of these once-colonised regions, environmental questions are central to policies and programmes exerting control over the rural world. Deliberations at the intersection of science and policy have been central to the shaping of social categories, identities and oppositions: to ideas of gender, ethnicity, citizenship, criminality, and so on. Land, trees and ecologies have also been central to the social lives and livelihoods of publics in these places, although frequently for very different reasons, and understood in different terms. Thus rural environmental issues have long been points of contest between citizens and the state, and indeed between patternings of social coalition and alliance which make mockery of this simple distinction. In engaging with such issues, this book links contemporary debates on science, technology and society with the concerns of environmental and development anthropology, showing how the latter can be enriched and rejuvenated through an ethnographic approach to science and policy.

Moreover the last two decades have seen a massive increase in international attention to the rural environments of tropical countries, and in particular forests. These have been re-positioned on an international stage as repositories of global value: as sinks of tradeable carbon, stores of biodiversity wealth, and symbols of cultural alterity. As will unfold, this new internationalism, its science and governance now intersect with national and local social relations of science whose institutions, practices and debates have been shaped by earlier colonial experiences. At the same time, the domination of much of the policy arena that falls under the rubric of conservation and development by certain disciplines (notably conservation biology) and by international perspectives has shaped and inflected critical debate, and at times, as will become clear, enabled the production and deployment of what are often experienced locally as highly coercive practices. Claims to liberal and participatory approaches have come to characterise forms of conservation intervention that often seem to disavow the colonial past only to reproduce its practices in another guise. This book explores the politics of knowledge in such contemporary, liberal managerialist conservation, and alternatives to it.

Sciences focusing on forests may not be icons of modernity, and the sense of rapid technological advance and associated risks which preoccupy contemporary science and society debates is often absent. Nevertheless, the lens of tropical forests is compelling for an anthropology of science first, because it focuses on a discursive terrain strongly inflected by exigencies of environmental crisis, and the assorted disciplinary and policy positions associated with this. It invites critical reflection on how the environment comes to be problematised, when and by whom and with what implications. Second, forest ecology has, for a number of years, been on the cusp of major reconceptualisation in its core assumptions. Different views emerging from a variety of disciplines offer opportunities for discursive coalition with different policy and land user interests, revealing how perspectives and debates in science interlock with questions of material and social control.

First, forests have long been analysed as if they were stable and equilibrial: as vegetation communities specific to climatic and other conditions which reproduced themselves, and if disturbed would eventually revert to their original form. Models for applied management from colonial times onwards were based on these assumptions, and hence on the view that vegetation succession could be directed for economic or environmental ends. While such core assumptions of stability always had their dissenters, since the latter decades of the twentieth century they have become more thoroughly challenged by research in several disciplines.[2] Analyses of climate and vegetation history suggest major fluctuations in forest cover and quality over recent centuries and millennia (Maley 2002; Tardy 1998). Work in ecology underscores this, and suggests the importance of disturbance events and path dependency to forest dynamics, quality and species distributions (e.g. Hawthorne 1996; Sprugel 1991). At the same time, studies in social anthropology and history show the long term shaping – in some circumstances enrichment – of vegetation through local practices, and highlight the relationship between landscape, memory and resource claims (e.g. Amanor 1994; Fairhead and Leach 1998). Emerging work thus suggests that vegetation patterns reflect the real historical legacy of many interacting influences, human and other, over many, overlapping timescales; what one might term a 'dynamic landscape perspective' on forests. Second, questions and analytics around tropical forests have been reconceptualised in relation to new concepts, such as biodiversity, which themselves reflect new social meanings, desires, and uses, particularly in the arena of conservation.

The world of tropical forests can thus illuminate powerfully the contemporary shaping of relations between different scientific traditions and governance, allowing one to address important questions about which strands of debate become pursued and embodied in policy at different times and which do not, and why this might be. Equally the very existence of a multiplicity of perspectives on the nature and value of forests gives forest science a particular quality; something recognised by many practising foresters who, acknowledging that their work intrinsically involves social questions concerning people and resources, frequently reflect on it as 'more of an art than a science'. This has always been the case, but is now more pronounced than ever. So as a science, forestry might be considered a 'weak' one – similar perhaps to psychology or criminology – in which the social implications are particularly visible (cf. Foucault 1980).

Moreover, the stakes are high. Debates in forest science intersect starkly with resource interests. Diverse conceptualisations of forest problematics are intimately related to claims over forest stewardship and resources. In their different ways, forests and their resources are valuable, economically and symbolically, to local users, to administrations, to corporations, to nations and to the globe. Issues of forest control lie at the heart of both local political economies, and global interests. The political economy of timber extraction and forest conversion for commercial farming and ranching, and the national and trans-national interests in these, are key dimensions of these dynamics; ones which much conservation-oriented research and policy aim to tackle in the avowed interests of environmental and social justice. Yet these environment and conservation efforts themselves involve political economies, and it is on these that we largely focus. There are many local forest governance initiatives which link forest exploitation with conservation, invoke community control, participation and decentralisation, and involve varied relationships with local state representation. At the same time, forests are now embroiled within international conventions and deliberations concerning biological diversity, climate change, desertification and sustainable use. The lens of tropical forests, then, is peculiarly apt for comprehending and theorising the interrelationships between the apparently contradictory forces of globalising and localising governance, and their politics.

These concerns around tropical forests indicate why science and society issues are not just a concern of the hi-tech high-latitudes, and why tropical countries' experiences of science-society relations cannot be captured within an analytical fascination with the hyper-modernity of the hi-tech. They remind us of a much longer engagement between the shaping of science, governance and the social world, and of a world of unequal economic and political power; an engagement which this book sets out to explore.

Addressing public engagement with science

That the place of scientific expertise in colonial, fascist and democratic regimes is very different raises sharp questions concerning how publics relate to 'scientific expertise'. Who has the capacity to establish certain questions and agendas as legitimate foci of study, and to carry these through? Is this confined to specialists in laboratories or projects? Or open to citizen participation – and if so, by whom? What are the dynamics of ordinary people's engagements (and confrontations) with experts? Linked to these issues are the ways in which science is becoming important to moral and economic contestation.

These questions have been a central concern in emergent debate on science and society in Europe. Indeed they have been core to celebrated depictions of a new social order, and a resurgence of 'grand theory' about it. Central here is the work of Beck (1992, 1995, 1998) whose 'Risk Society' thesis suggests that publics are increasingly concerned with risks that are no longer 'external', but continually thrown up by the processes and systems of industrial technology and its governance. This engenders a critically reflective attitude among a wider public to expert institutions and their knowledges, and a growing lack of trust. Yet for Beck, science not only creates the problems, but also the analytics required to recognise them; 'the pre-requisite for "overcoming" the threats for which it is responsible itself' (Beck 1992:162). That this reflection is also enwrapped in science plays down attention to alternative knowledges, sciences and forms of social order in the public realm (Wynne 1992, 1996).

It is precisely these alternative framings that have been the focus of two very different research traditions, one concerning 'citizen science' (conducted largely in Europe and North America) and the other 'ethno-science' or indigenous knowledge (conducted largely in low income countries, and among 'indigenous peoples').

It is critical engagement by publics with the perspectives of expert institutions either through funding or orchestrating their own scientific investigations, or lobbying to transform research questions, that has been dubbed 'citizen science' (e.g. Irwin 1995; Irwin and Wynne 1996; Fischer 2000). This is associated with both a crisis of legitimacy in science among lay publics, and a critique of the view that this just reflects a 'deficit' in public knowledge that good science education could fill. Public understandings of science have been shown to be more sophisticated and nuanced than they had been given credit for, focusing not just on the content and methods of science, but also on forms of its institutional embedding, patronage and control (Wynne 1992). Work on citizen science has now documented many cases where lay people have explicitly engaged with and contested science and its advice by conducting their own investigations and experiments (for instance in 'popular epidemiology' around issues of toxic waste pollution, see Brown 1990; Brown and Mikkelsen 1990; Hofrichter 1993). The emphasis has thus been on citizen science as alternative science, conforming with its broad categories, more than on the ways in which public's knowledges develop in an embedded relationship with local social processes and differences, concepts and moralities.

In contrast, rural environmental issues in Africa, Asia and the Caribbean have more usually been addressed through a very different theoretical vocabulary, concerned with indigenous knowledge (IK) and its relations with development. This tradition is rooted in social anthropological work from early in the twentieth century, which detailed 'knowledge systems' concerning issues such as health, agriculture and ecology in the context of broader ethnographies of society and culture (e.g. Richards 1939; Evans-Pritchard 1937). It thus emphasised how knowledge and beliefs about 'technical' issues were largely inseparable from ideas about cosmology or local religion on the one hand, and the maintenance of social order and prevailing relations of authority on the other.

IK has been seen in ambiguous relationship with 'western science' in its modernist guise, sometimes depicted as a valuable and complementary resource to be repackaged in the terms of modernising, expert scientific institutions (Brokensha *et al.* 1980; Warren *et al.* 1990), and by others as rooted in incommensurable concepts and framings, necessitating a more comparative framework of analysis (Fairhead 1992; Scoones and Thompson 1994). Whilst it shows how dispute and debate over agro-ecological issues in 'localities' are locked into struggles over control of resources, and over socio-political authority, this work, however, has been largely silent on engagements of contestation with 'expert' science – in stark contrast with the citizen science tradition. Works in the anthropology of development have tended to describe distrust in development expertise as manifested in withdrawal from, and resistance to its effects, rather than active engagement with the science underlying development interventions (e.g. Crush 1995; Fairhead and Leach 2000).

Thus while works on citizen science show how science has 'come out of the laboratory' in the sense of being conducted within wider social relations, works in the IK tradition suggest that some forms of science have never been in it. Emerging in very different parts of the world, it might be argued that each of these analytical traditions relates to the particularity of its settings. Yet in imagining a shift from modernity to more fragmented and critical public reflection in 'late' or 'reflexive' modernity, analysts may be over-emphasising past acceptance of scientific expertise (Lash *et al.* 1996; Latour 1993), and hiding the experiences of certain social and cultural groups. Equally, analytical traditions emphasising the non-integration of indigenous knowledge and expert science have been questioned as overplaying the coherence of each (e.g. Agrawal 1995; Last 1980). A comparative ethnographic approach is necessary to 'dig beneath' these different analytical traditions to see how far these respectively more autonomous and more engaged modes of public interaction with science take place in different settings. Comparative analysis can also consider such differences between countries, as opposed to aligning with particular social constituencies, positionalities and issues which may cross-cut inter-country distinctions.

Environment and tropical forests in Guinea and Trinidad

The comparative ethnography in this book focuses on the Republic of Guinea in West Africa, and Trinidad within the twin-island Republic of Trinidad and Tobago in the Caribbean. This is an appropriate choice of countries for several reasons. In common, both share important similarities of environmental setting and tropical forest ecology. In each, too, environmental policy concerns run high, and turn on similar issues – especially on the conservation of biodiversity and on ensuring sustainability of timber production. In contrast, however, Trinidad is a middle income, industrialised and urbanised country, while Guinea is a very low income country with much higher dependence on agriculture and rural livelihoods. In line with this, Guinea is far more dependent on donor aid than Trinidad, a difference which influences how each country's scientific and policy institutions relate to the international world. Perhaps most significantly, different patterns of public engagement with science appear to dominate in each country. As will become clear, Trinidad has stronger traditions of public participation and critique through national politics, the media and citizen science. In Guinea, by contrast, indigenous knowledge and 'traditional' local institutions appear much stronger and more vibrant.

In these respects, then, patterns in Trinidad appear closer to those identified by science-society analysts for Europe and North America, while those in Guinea would appear to typify those identified in Africanist analytical traditions. The analysis in subsequent chapters will trace how and why these seemingly different patterns have emerged, and their implications; however it will also show that these apparent dichotomies turn out to be more complicated than such simple stereotypes, obscuring some important commonalities of experience between particular groups of people in each country setting.

Inflected by these country contexts and animated by the international world, a cacophony of voices now speaks of 'forests' and 'environment' in both Guinea and Trinidad. In Guinea, French bacteriologists researching nitrogen-fixing leguminous trees justify their work as 'to minimise the environmental impact of refugees'. Much European, German and World Bank-funded assistance to Guinea's rice farming, coffee cropping and even bee-keeping is financed by

Figure 1.1   Processing the upland rice staple in a Guinean village

environmental programmes. Curiously, it is environmental programmes which have the funding to provide schools, bridges and wells, as inducements to villagers to transform their land management ways. All three Guinean universities are altering their structures to respond to 'environmental' questions, and to the international funding these are attracting. The only PhD programme in the country is in environmental studies, not agriculture, geography, history, politics, mining, or economics as one might expect. The environmental research centre is a stunning oasis of Canadian funding in an otherwise near-destitute institution. Foreign researchers – even at times in their very critique of environmental anxiety – animate the debate. At the other end of the educational scale, primary school teachers' latest and glossiest handbooks are not for mathematics, science or history, but for environmental education.

There has been an efflorescence of environmental messages in popular culture and mass-media. Indeed, environment is now pivotal in the shaping of media forms as well as content. A European Union environment programme funds a local language newspaper and the establishment and running of rural radio. Alongside print and radio media, environmental projects are working with Imams to green Islam and the Friday prayer, and with Christian preachers to green their sermons. They are working with hunter's brotherhoods to green and groom rural society into international environmental conformity, and with theatre groups and praise singers who now eulogise the trees as much as chiefs and ancestors.

The relative wealth and urbanisation of Trinidad may contrast with Guinea's poverty and rurality, but the cacophony of environmental voice rings equally loud. Government departments in Trinidad and Tobago vie for turf in the stewardship of forest lands and their contemporary symbolic and financial values. An Environmental Management Authority with glamorous professionalism and smart logos now eclipses a workhorse forestry department in publicising environment. It rewards journalists, activists, communities and businesses with awards for conservation as well as for addressing the environmental impact of Trinidad's oil and petrochemical industries. It calls forth essays from school pupils which eulogise forests as a well-spring of life and spiritual solace in the hustle and hassle of modernity. Tourism has become the eco-tourism which private entrepreneurs, NGOs, government departments and donor agencies promote. Publicity and plaques identify communities through their conservation and tour-guiding activities. All this fills column inches, air time and web-space in a highly newspaper, television and internet-literate society.

For many, the mountains of Trinidad themselves speak of their denudation. Looking up from the urban-industrial corridor inland of the capital, Port of Spain, the partially forested Northern Range annually disgorges smoke and floods, evoking concern and provoking reaction in fire control and repeated attempts to restrict land-use. The University of the West Indies, set in these foothills, has a history of natural history, now repackaged to address biodiversity. Social sciences have established new environmental units and programmes. Consultancies in conservation, planning and environmental impact assessment for government, businesses and donor funded programmes offer lucrative opportunities to university staff and graduates alike. Foreign researchers, whether representing conservation biology or participatory natural resource management, animate discussion and are enrolled into environmental politics and controversies.

In both settings, knowledge and deliberation concerning the environment provide a potent lens through which to discern how national and local social relations of science and policy have been shaped by international animation, and how this process re-shapes broader society. A comparative approach can reveal

Figure 1.2 View over Port of Spain from Trinidad's forest-clad Northern Range

how a massive expansion and emerging set of configurations – the organisations, deliberations, research and funding linked at an international level which we call 'Tropical Forest International' – has nevertheless had very different effects in different locales.

Analysing science, policy and society: approach

The relationship between science, policy and society can be explored in many theoretical contexts, with each posing very different questions with different methodological implications. Reviewing these will locate the particular ethnographic approach that we take. The study of policy processes and the study of science each have their own genealogies. Our concern here is with analytical traditions which help integrate these.[3]

In anthropology, early concerns with science asked how it differed from magic and religion,[4] and how scientific research, technological investment and advance could contribute to imperial expansion and the administration of expanding national populations and colonies. This fed the idea that administration was rooted in impartial science, lending a legitimacy to 'rational and just' colonial administration, just as it now provides legitimacy in international regimes.

As the fieldwork tradition in anthropology progressed, it explored comparatively how far other societies are 'scientific', considering this in relation to science as defined through western philosophical traditions.[5] When ethnographers eventually turned their fieldwork attention to laboratories, however, it became clear that philosophy was less of a guide to the conduct of science, than was the history of specific practices, and the political, economic and cultural forces that shape them (e.g. Latour and Woolgar 1986).

Anthropologists and sociologists began to ask how practices of science related to social and political values. Their work was frequently motivated by frustrations that their own concerns, or those for whom they spoke, were marginalised, misconstrued, delegitimised or silenced by science, along with economic and political claims relating to them. This is the case, for instance, for feminist critiques of science and social science (e.g. Haraway 1988, 1989; Harding 1986, 1991, 1998), responding to frustrations that, 'An androcentric picture of nature and social life emerges from the testing by men only of hypotheses generated by what men find problematic in the world around them' (Root 1993). The same can be said of class interests, exposed in Marxist critiques of scientific practice, and 'ethnic' interests exposed in anti-colonialist writings dating back to the 1930s if not before (e.g. Levy 1932). And this has motivated our longstanding interest in the subject; in the ways agricultural and environmental sciences have delegitimised the knowledges of West African land users (Fairhead and Leach 1996, 1998).

Work on the social shaping of scientific knowledge now recognises that 'nature cannot speak alone' (even in recognising that 'society' cannot speak in separation from the 'natural' and technological processes in which it is embroiled; Latour 1993, 2000; Haraway 1991, 1997). Scientific knowledge is inevitably created by people and institutions with particular situated and partial perspectives, and asks partial questions responding to partial interests. Some research questions find funding, others do not. Again, what is shown is that ideals concerning objectivity and scientific method may be bad guides as to how scientific knowledge is actually made (Haraway 1988).

It is this embeddedness of science, its constitution within a social, institutional and political field, that we find interesting and choose to explore ethnographically. It means that to define 'science' or 'policy' at the outset of this study, or to depict their essential characteristics would be to presuppose a priori what it is that we are examining empirically. Dispute over whether a finding is, or is not 'scientific' or 'good science' is common to policy debate. The practice of a philosophy of 'science' becomes part of the social field to be studied.[6]

Our analytical approach to science and policy draws from the intersection of two traditions: Foucauldian approaches to power and knowledge, and the ethnographic approaches to scientific practice, actors and networks originally associated with Latour and others.

In total contrast to those working in Durkheimian, Marxist and Structuralist traditions, who were refining their social and human sciences, Michel Foucault began to ask how the evolution of modern human sciences is constitutively interdependent with the evolution of practices for the surveillance, discipline, administration and formation of populations. To capture this co-evolution of forms of knowledge with institutional practices he uses the shorthand *pouvoir-savoir* (power/knowledge). To capture the singularity of the field of inquiry and institutions he refers to it as 'discourse'. He came to explore how discourse does not merely act on individuals but also produces its subjects, through a combination of external subjection and internal subjectification, shaping desires.

Foucault deliberately chose what he called 'dubious' sciences, such as psychiatry and criminology, where the interweaving effects of power and knowledge could be grasped with greater certainty. In contrast with theoretical physics or organic chemistry for example, these are linked with a whole range of institutions, economic requirements and political issues of social regulation (Foucault 1980). As we have suggested, the same can be said of the environmental and forest sciences that we study in this book.

Latour, and the 'Paris School' in science studies more broadly (e.g. Callon *et al.* 1986; Callon 1986), were worried by the methodological scepticism of Foucauldian analytical traditions. They questioned the divisions between the 'social', the 'natural' and 'commentary on them' enabled by this and other analytical traditions. As Latour put it: 'The ozone hole is too social and too narrated to be truly natural; the strategy of industrial firms and heads of state is too full of chemical reactions to be reduced to power and interest; the discourse on the ecosphere is too real and too social to boil down to meaning effects' (Latour 1993: 6). To proceed, he suggests, one should follow the liberating, ethnographic approach of anthropology to expose links between cosmologies/ethnosciences, material practices, and political, domestic and economic structures, and then transpose this approach to the scientific laboratory. Yet, he notes, such an anthropology risks falling into social constructivism; being constructivist where nature is concerned, but realistic about society. The only solution is that combined 'natures-cultures' become the object of inquiry and of reflexivity. To capture the continual boundary crossing, Latour speaks of 'actor-networks' in which actors may be people, institutions or hybrid objects combining elements of culture, nature and technology. Any analysis of power must consider the intellectual and institutional configuration that obscures this hybridity, as well as the strength and reach of constructed networks. For Haraway, similar reasoning rooted in feminist, post-empiricist science leads her to the metaphor of a 'cyborg' to capture the simultaneity and non-distinction of social, natural, technological and discursive attributes in objects, systems and texts about them (Haraway 1991). As Haraway puts it the problem is 'how to have *simultaneously* an account of radical historical contingency for all knowledge claims and knowing subjects, a critical practice for recognising our own "semiotic technologies" for making meanings, *and* a no-nonsense commitment to faithful accounts of a "real world" ' (1991: 187). Rather, knowledges are to be understood as situated, partial perspectives, and a new objectivity requires that the partiality be constantly interrogated and reflected upon.

Foucault's call to history, and attention to the constitutive interdependence of science and governance, and Latour's (and others') call to ethnography provide the basic grounding of the approaches that we pursue. Nevertheless, it remains the case that Foucault's methodological scepticisim leaves his analysis open to Latourian critique as social constructivism. Reciprocally, in the 'particularism' of ethnographic accounts of science as practice, Foucault's insights into the broader relationship between science and governmentality can be lost. It is important to integrate the insights of both.

Combining Foucauldian perspectives on knowledge and power with an ethnographic perspective on science and policy as practice enables us to engage with, but also move beyond, a number of further traditions in the analysis of science and policy processes.

Drawing explicitly on Foucauldian perspectives, some anthropologists have treated international development as discourse (Escobar 1984, 1995; Hobart 1993; Ferguson 1994). They ask how institutional structures and their 'scientific' analytics emanate from and reproduce the power of states and their international sponsors, and how these play into highly political struggles for control over the rural world, while frequently hiding these political operations in a technical, managerial discourse (Ferguson 1994). Institutional theory in science and technology studies considers international dimensions to science in similar terms (Schrum and Shenhav 1995).[7] It asks why structurally similar forms of science are found throughout the world, relating this to the power of assumptions concerning the universality of science, and its necessity for modernisation. Practices, processes, and national policies are adopted, transformed and reproduced, not necessarily because their technical superiority has been demonstrated, but owing to participants' beliefs in the efficacy of certain ways of doing things. Institutional alignment promotes comparability and compatibility, but not solutions to local problems.[8]

Yet both these traditions of critical work on international dimensions to science and policy are rooted in a structurally-focused analysis, which tends to present science, policy and discourse as somewhat monolithic. This is problematic, obscuring the diverse views, actions, interactions and everyday dilemmas of scientists and administrators, and the ways that scientific and policy change may reflect the agency of particular people.[9] These are precisely the aspects highlighted in more ethnographic approaches to actors and their practices.

Actor-oriented approaches in the sociology of development, for instance, ask about the knowledge and intentions of state and non-state actors, and how they actively strategise to represent issues in certain ways and forge alliances in promoting them (e.g. Long and van der Ploeg 1989; Long and Long 1992). They ask particularly how policy processes are shaped by the activities of 'frontline workers' (such as forestry extension agents or local NGO staff), and the interfaces through which they exchange knowledge with members of rural communities.

Certain political scientists and analysts of public administration similarly ask about the strategising behaviour and agency in the policy process of 'policy entrepreneurs' (elites who take advantage of the opening of policy spaces to effect change; Grindle and Thomas 1991), or 'street-level bureaucrats' (Lipsky 1979). Such works also ask how particular actors interpret directives, deal with contradictory instructions and ideas, take initiative and exercise discretion. It firmly undermines any notion of policy as a linear process proceeding from agenda-setting through policy-making to implementation. Rather, local 'bureaucrats' can be *de facto* policy-makers,[10] while the interlocking of intended plans with the diverse social and political agendas of the numerous actors involved produces multiple, and unintended outcomes.

Others ask how policy communities, networks and advocacy coalitions link shared interests across divisions within governments, pressure groups, business interests and so on (e.g. Jordan 1981; Coleman *et al.* 1997; Sabatier 1988). Hajer (1995) asks how the outcomes of argumentative interactions between people with different views and positions lead certain discourses to become and remain dominant, and how 'discourse coalitions' are formed, linking previously independent practices in common political projects.[11] Scaling up further, Haas asks how trans-institutional networks of people who share common analytical perspectives become 'epistemic communities' which strategise to bring about international agreements (1990, 1992). Each of these approaches foregrounds agency, and calls for situated, empirical inquiry.

Similarly in science and technology studies, ethnographic approaches ask what scientists actually do in day-to-day laboratory or field settings, and how their practices draw on and reproduce established cultures of scientific conduct (e.g. Pickering 1992: 2). Actor-network theory asks how scientists create facts through closing controversies, boxing-off ('black-boxing') uncertainties and assumptions away from further scrutiny, and extending the reach of locally-specific knowledge (i.e. derived from particular field sites or laboratory experiments) through enrolling actors and institutions in broader, even globalised, knowledge networks (Latour 1987). Knorr-Cetina – questioning an over-emphasis on individual agency in some ethnographies of science – asks how the 'machineries of knowledge construction' (1999:3) arise; how particular framings of the problem, research technologies, social configurations of scientists, funding contexts and laboratory settings combine to form 'epistemic cultures', 'amalgams of arrangements and mechanisms – bonded through affinity, necessity, and historical coincidence – which, in a given field, make up how we know what we know' (1999: 1).

Many of the processes to which Knorr-Cetina draws attention (problem-framings, funding contexts and so on) are also highlighted in work on the co-production of science with policy (see Jasanoff and Wynne 1997). This asks how scientists contribute to the framing of policy issues by defining what evidence can be produced and its policy significance. Reciprocally, it asks how those working in policy frame scientific inquiry by defining areas of relevance, and pertinent questions for investigation. Thus emerges a field of mutual construction or 'co-production' which can become self sustaining.[12] [13] Whilst work on co-production has frequently been associated with 'critique', it also offers theoretical ground to ask how the field of co-production could be reconfigured to be socially inclusive, rekindling trust and confidence in it.[14]

These analytical approaches treat the conduct of science and of policy in broadly ethnographic terms, avoiding essentialising and instead focusing on particular practices, contexts and histories. However, they differ in how they conceptualise practice, agency and structure, and this strongly influences the depiction of context. Whereas some foreground the intellectual dimensions of making and contesting knowledge, others highlight how knowledge is practical as well as discursive, and schemes of perception and action are learnt – at least in part – through practical engagement with the world (Bourdieu 1990).[15] Our approach in subsequent chapters shares this general ethnographic emphasis, and draws on a number of particular concepts and insights from these works – including the co-production of science and policy, the notion of discourse coalitions, and the value of focus on the action of field-level agents. We integrate these by combining a Foucauldian discourse analytic with attention to the particular scientific and policy practices and forms of agency which both give rise to and sustain, but may also challenge dominant discourses over time. Our approach also differs from many previous works which have focused either on international, national or local settings, by explicitly traversing them to explore their interconnections.

Thus in the chapters that follow, we have as a first principle endeavoured to treat 'science' and 'policy' as constellations of component practices and procedures enacted by people and institutions, but also used to structure their choices. We have considered the emergence of such practices historically. Ideally, this perspective allows each practice – each workshop, meeting, report, legislative decision, funding flow and so on – to have its own biography and sedimentation of meanings which at once contributes to 'policy' without conforming to any particular totalising narrative of its evolution, enactment, or meaning. Practices that are 'scientific' also have their own specificity (reviewing species lists, characterising ecological zones, listing the forces leading to degradation . . .), and need not conform to any totalising narrative of scientific method and scientific advance.

Second, specific practices, viewed in this way, become linked: for instance when national workshops and funding flows from donors lead Guinean university researchers to carry out species inventories in proposed national parks. Specific practices which are linked within institutional and interpersonal networks, whether intentionally-forged or more circumstantial, structure subsequent meanings and agendas, coming to frame problems and approaches to them in certain ways. The co-production of science and policy thus occurs through such shifting clusterings of scientific and policy practices. In turn, such framings can become encoded in institutional organisation and networks of collaboration, or in objects such as landscape features (e.g. 'watershed protection reserves' 'fire curtain reserves' or 'permanent sample plots'). Certain practices and analytics may endure and be reproduced through their enaction in policy, its networks and quasi-objects, while other ideas, less integrated into policy processes, become rather different phenomena.[16] Thus taking a practice-based approach encourages us to pay attention not only to co-production (of science and policy) but to co-endurance and co-validation.

Third, today's practices can build in a sedimentary way on earlier ones. The authority of the embodied practices in what today's scientists are doing is shaped by the conduct of earlier scientists. The meanings of these practices are shaped in relation both to old practices and new imperatives. The reconfiguration under new political and economic circumstances and in conjunction with new practices shapes the contemporary production of knowledge, but shapes it in dialogical relation to the past.

Attributing authority to particular sets of practices, and drawing boundaries between these and others, can be a process of active, discursive construction. Key, here, are the ways some sets of practices come to be construed as 'Science', and at its 'cutting edge', excluding others as impoverished or non-science, ethnoscience or indeed as 'culture'. In this way, one can examine, ethnographically, what comes to be construed as Science (and policy), by whom and when, and how a composite of practices comes to acquire the authenticated signature of 'Science'; an ethnography of boundary work (Gieryn 1995: 394).

Fourth, we examine the ways that international, national and local sets of practices interlock with each other. Tracing these processes requires the type of multi-sited ethnography outlined by Marcus (1995). As he suggests, this does not merely involve the contextualisation of a locality within a wider world, but conducting research at different sites, and exploring their connectivity – through following metaphors, following stories, following people, following finance, and following networks across them.[17]

Fifth, our analysis traces specific links between scientific and policy practices, political and administrative struggles, and social objectification. This makes clear that science and policy are not practised on the margins of society, but are central to the unfolding of wider social configurations. In extending the field inquiry 'beyond the citadels' of research and policy institutions (Martin 1997), we also trace how scientific and policy practices are mediated with wider society not only in politics, but also in popular mass-media and education. Our analytical reflections therefore extend to wider questions of public engagement with science, with media and education, and to the historical conditions shaping these.

In taking a multi-sited approach, our research in Trinidad and Guinea combined broader discussions of forest research and policy with case studies of research/policy initiatives. Three months of fieldwork in Guinea in 1999 built on our decade-long engagement with the region and its issues (Fairhead and Leach 1996, 1998), and a longstanding working relationship with a Guinean researcher, Dominique Millimouno. Three months fieldwork in Trinidad, in contrast, was conducted in a context new to us, and thus relied more heavily on close collaboration with resident researchers, most notably Dr Thackwray Driver as well as research assistance from Trinidadian graduate Keisha Charles. In both countries, fieldwork involved interviews in ministries, universities, NGOs and with forest users, both in the capital, in regional and field level offices and in villages. We made field site visits to locations important to the cases, in interaction and discussion with government and project staff, and participated in meetings. We also analysed policy, research and project documents, and educational and media materials.

Research in 'international' locations aimed both to track scientific and policy processes explored in the two countries, including the international processes which influence them, and to explore configurations of science/policy debate as conducted amongst organisations operating internationally. The strategy was, first to gauge the positions, recent activities and interconnections of a range of influential organisations,[18] and then to focus on certain scientific and policy debates of high contemporary relevance both internationally and to Guinea and Trinidad. In this we combined documentary analysis (published, 'grey' and website materials), with follow-up interviews with staff in certain organisations, and participant-observation in a number of international meetings.

The unfolding of environmental knowledge and power: structure

This conceptual approach and set of methods are deployed in a set of chapters focusing on different issues as they play out in Trinidad and Guinea. By cutting the analytical cake by issue rather than by institution, project or programme, we are better able to discern the coalitions, networks, oppositions and exclusions that form. By devoting separate chapters to each country, we are able to locate their unfolding scientific and policy stories within their particular social, historical and political settings. By pairing the Guinea and Trinidad chapters according to issue, we are able to highlight how the same international concerns have played out in very different ways in these different country settings.

Chapters 4 and 5 focus broadly on biodiversity, now one of the most prominent international concerns with tropical forest. In Guinea, we explore the various sets of practices deployed as researchers and administrations have grappled to define and implement this concept. In Trinidad, we explore how biodiversity-related research and governance have become embroiled in debates over the establishment of national parks. In Guinea, the focus is on the variety of discourse coalitions which have formed around biodiversity concepts and practices, and their effects in shaping social and moral categories. In Trinidad, the focus is on a particular unfolding policy story, considering how particular scientific concepts and practices have been part and parcel of it. In part, the difference of approach in each chapter is driven by the nature of debates in each country, yet it enables the two chapters to spotlight complementary dimensions of contemporary scientific and policy processes: their shaping in articulation with international processes, and their national and local politics.

The particularity of debate in each country also inflects Chapters 6 and 7 addressing a second tropical forest issue: sustainable timber production. Again, this is a preoccupying international concern. In Guinea, the promotion of village-based 'forest groups' has recently come to be seen as a key means to achieving sustainable forest management. We explore the processes through which this policy change has come about, the scientific and policy practices and institutional relationships which it involves, and their social effects. In Trinidad, the sustainable forest management case focuses on government-controlled forest reserves. It examines the evolution of a system for managing 'natural' forest for timber production, and the scientific and policy practices involved in its construction and maintenance. Again, the chapters complement each other in analytical approach. In Guinea, we pay particular attention to how different actors narrate and experience the scientific and policy processes and practices, showing how an apparently unitary 'policy' can actually mean very different things to different people. In Trinidad, we focus particularly on the tension between whether 'natural' forest management is dealing with a stable system, or with far less predictable social and ecological processes, and how scientific and policy practices serve to maintain an image of stability in the face of uncertainty.

Despite these differences, each case gives analytical attention to a common set of themes. First, each addresses the practices and interactions of diverse forest users: local government and NGO staff; researchers; national administrations; international organisations and consultants. Second, each case exposes how scientific and policy processes interplay with struggles for control over the rural world, and shape particular patterns of resource control. Third, each case is located in its historical context, showing how contemporary practices build on and acquire meaning in relation to earlier activities, practised within other agendas. Fourth, each case shows a variety of ways in which ecological processes themselves intervene in and are comprehended within scientific and policy practices and debates. Finally, each case shows how scientific and policy processes draw on and play into the objectification of social categories. The cases thus examine how national and local social relations of science and policy are shaped by international animation; and how this is shaping contemporary society.

To understand this animation, and our cases within it, we need first to examine the ways in which science and policy around forests have come to be configured internationally. This is the focus of Chapter 2. It shows that the production of knowledge about tropical forests, and attempts to govern them are now subject to a globalisation with a dynamic of its own; a vortex into which researchers and those involved in policy are drawn whether through finance, obligations to regimes, interest, relevance, epistemic community or critique. Although the sheer mass of what we term 'Tropical Forest International' is too vast and complicated in its networks to grasp in any totality, we attempt to outline and exemplify key trends, linkages and rivalries in the way that forest and biodiversity issues are approached in the nexus of international conventions, United Nations and other international organisations, multilateral and bilateral donors, transnational corporations, international NGOs, international research centres, and the research community more widely.

We argue that local experiences are drawn into (or drawn up by) this vortex in ways which frequently generate consensus and conformity in knowledge and management of the forest, but which also shape opportunities to challenge, critique or express alternatives to dominant international discourses. In exemplifying the processes and procedures through which this happens, we are able to reflect on the interplay between self-referentiality in Tropical Forest International and the construal of locality/experience within it.

Yet as our case chapters show, these international scientific and policy processes play out in very particular ways in national and local settings. These differences need to be understood not only in relation to the specifics of scientific and policy practices in each country, but also the broader political and economic histories and settings which shape these. In Chapter 3, we set out this comparative context, treating each country on its own terms, but drawing out some axes of difference that become relevant in understanding their contrasting engagements with Tropical Forest International.

Different country settings and histories have also shaped the evolution of and constituencies for environmental education and mass media. This comes to the fore in Chapter 8, where we expand our conceptualisation of scientific and policy processes within a broader social field. We focus on the mediation of relations between science and society through newspapers and radio, schools and adult education. With media and education frequently co-produced with the institutions of science and policy, these disseminate and embed their particular messages about forests and environment in everyday life and wider public consciousness. At the same time, they provide forums for critique, dissent and commentary. Just as earlier chapters show how science and policy interlock with broader ideas or constructions of morality and objectification of social categories, so in this chapter we examine the extent to which media practices and their rhetorics and stylistics of authority contribute to, affirm, amplify or question these processes.

As we discuss in Chapter 9, the cases show how new international configurations of science and policy fit into struggles for authority between political and administrative institutions nationally, and struggles for control over the rural world and its resources. They become integral to processes of enrichment and legitimation for some, and impoverishment and disqualification for others. The ways in which science and policy become integral to processes of social objectification, stigmatisation and dissent, and their relationships with forms of media and education, are important elements in discerning this.

With the analytical focus on the co-production of knowledge and policy, a set of power relations come into view which cross-cut 'governments', 'international organisations', 'NGOs' and local 'communities', and question the analytical salience of these popular distinctions. Cutting the cake in a different way discerns how alliances form around particular issues and positions in scientific and policy debate. That governance and science are increasingly internationalised, but also apparently localised in the forms of claims to decentralised governance, means citizen voice and local participation no longer appear as a contradiction. Rather, more salient distinctions are made between the types of management, regulation, order and control sought through the practices of science – or indeed how they are used to escape this, and pursue alternative paths.

It is easy to be cynical about the capacity of international deliberations and agreements to have any serious direct effect. Yet by tracing the broader, more indirect ways they shape epistemic communities and coalitions around the ideas they embody, the book shows how the institutional aspect of these agreements is only a small part of a much more extensive field of transformation. In the field of environment, international deliberations in articulation with national scientific and policy communities alter the questions that are posed about the environment. Globalised science influences the social categories through which it is understood, serving to naturalise and stabilise those social categories within readings of nature and livings of a landscape.

Those who argue that 'environmental policy is about politics, not science', or that 'scientific research is divorced from the realities of policy-making' – contentions voiced by some of our interviewees, as well as common in media and academia – overlook these ways that the social and ecological categories and logics deployed in political debate are themselves shaped by and shape scientific inquiry. In this vein, studies of the public understanding of science have tended to focus on how publics think about the contents and methods of 'science' and its forms of institutionalisation, patronage and control (Wynne 1992). They can overlook how the practices of science and its mediation with wider society contribute to the production of social and natural categories in which people frame any such reflection. The metaphor of a vortex captures this alignment of a broader field, bringing even those who are hardly involved and barely sense the operation of the institutions at its centre into the patterns of its circulation.

Our conclusions reflect on these issues, and through them engage critically with contemporary debates on risk, science and modernity. We consider how scientific and policy processes operate in social objectification, stigmatisation and the shaping of new social subjectivities; in shaping forms of inclusion and exclusion, and in shaping the work and politics of national and trans-national institutions, in ways which sometimes constrain effective public critique and expression of alternative perspectives, but which also create opportunities for new forms of public engagement and transformation in the social relations of science and policy.

Notes

1. A few among numerous possible examples of such work are Martin 1994; Rabinow 1996; Miller 1999; GECP 1999; Irwin 2000; Prior 2000 and Rose 2000.
2. A transformation is exemplified in the rewriting of P.W. Richards' classic textbook *The Tropical Rainforest.* In the first edition of 1950, analysis was grounded in ideas of climax vegetation, but the 1996 edition (Richards 1996) embraced far less equilibrial notions.
3. In anthropology, focused study of policy processes is relatively recent. Thus when Shore and Wright edited their volume on *The Anthropology of Policy* in 1997, they were able to call their introduction 'Policy: a new field for anthropology' (Shore and Wright 1997). Yet as they make clear, the study of these issues has long been foreshadowed, without a policy process or science label, in political anthropology and its general concerns with power (e.g. Gledhill 1994). 'Policy' has been a much longer-established focus of inquiry in other disciplines, notably political science and public administration.
4. Thus in the mid-nineteenth century, Tylor (1871) proposed that science would vanquish myth and ritual, and Frazer (1911–1915) supposed that this could be built into a frame for social evolution.
5. Classic works ranged from Malinowski's *Magic, Science and Religion* (1925), to Evans Pritchard's *Witchcraft, Oracles and Magic Among the Azande* (1937), to Levi-Strauss' *The Savage Mind* (1966), and Horton's *African Traditional Thought and Western Science* (1967).

6. This perspective contrasts with those rooted in Marxist and Durkheimian traditions which simultaneously highlight how science is a social activity, while presupposing a form of 'higher science' through which one could realise this. For Marx (e.g. in *The German Ideology*, Marx and Engels 1964) ideology is a socially embedded system of representation that can be opposed to (revealed by) the higher truth of 'science'. Althusser, while arguing that ideology – at the level of unconscious generative structures attributable to modes of production – is an inevitable medium in the production of human subjects, nevertheless retains the idea of science as a radically separate subjectless process, able to discern the unconscious.

7. There is a vast, interdisciplinary literature on science and technology in 'less-developed' countries, which links with an even larger literature on theories of development. We refer only very selectively to such works here. Shrum and Shenhav (1995); Agnew 1982; Shrum *et al.* 1993 and Yearley 1988 are among a number of useful reviews.

8. Works such as those by Eisemon 1982 and Schwartzman 1991 do, however, emphasise the importance of considering practices shaped by regional and national traditions.

9. These and related problems are the subject of a growing anthropological literature critiquing and refining 'development as discourse' perspectives: see, for example, Grillo 1997; Harrison 1995; Gardner 1997; Fairhead and Leach 2000; Sivaramakrishnan and Agrawal 1998.

10. Joshi (1997) provides an example in the forestry field, showing that forest extension workers were in fact the prime-movers in a major policy shift from state-controlled to devolved forms of forest governance in the case of Joint Forest Management in West Bengal.

11. Particular argumentative interactions might in turn form part of the broader 'fields of argument' which Fischer (2000, following Willard 1996) proposes as a unit of analysis for the study of what he terms 'policy epistemics'. This would focus on 'how different professional groups and local communities see and inquire differently, and the ways in which differences become disputes' (2000: 255).

12. A clear example of this is presented in Shackley and Wynne's (1995) work on the reliance on general circulation models in climate change research. This illustrates how policy needs certain types of information or prediction; scientists set out to create them; scientists claim that these types of prediction are doable (and more work will refine them), reinforcing the idea that policy can and should rely on these.

13. In general, work on co-production reveals the inadequacy of analysis couched in terms of distinct 'research communities' and 'policy communities', and how the interface between them might be improved; a premise embodied in the vast majority of works, for instance, on forest policy (e.g. Solberg 1997).

14. This brings concerns with public participation in science (e.g. Funtovicz and Ravetz 1993; House of Lords 2000) and a more longstanding tradition in policy (e.g. Drysek 1990; Chambers 1997 and Holland 1998 in development studies), to the field of science and policy, leading to a range of approaches to the democratisation of science, and to deliberative and inclusionary processes for decision making (e.g. Fischer 2000 and Holmes and Scoones 2000).

15. In something so apparently 'logo-centric' as science and policy, there is value in recognising that the production of ideas can be locked into an engaged knowledge

of the world that is practical, unthought and sensuous, accommodating perhaps an aesthetics as much as a logic of deduction.

16. Scientists might have disproved that the Sahara is advancing because of anthro-pogenic influence, for example, but the idea that it does lives on in the international Convention to Combat Desertification. If the idea of human induced desertification had never been practised there, its refutation would be a very different phenomenon.

17. This perspective questions any primacy to 'the global' or 'the local', in that all practices are 'located', whether in a meeting of people from different countries in a Brazilian city or in a village in Trinidad (cf. Murdoch and Clark 1994). Yet where international and local perspectives may differ strongly is in the strength and reach of their networks, and in the resources they are able to mobilise in scientific advance and its associated forms of governance.

18. As the next chapter details these include: the Convention on Biodiversity; the Inter-governmental Panel/Forum on Forests (IPF/IFF); the Forestry Department of the United Nations Food and Agriculture Organisation (FAO); the WorldWide Fund for Nature, (WWF); the United Nations Environment Programme and World Conser-vation Monitoring Centre (UNEP/WCMC); The World Bank, the UK Department for International Development (DFID); French CIRAD and the European Union.

2 Science and globalising governance

Introduction

The production of knowledge about tropical forests, and attempts to govern them, have become increasingly internationalised. Over the last twenty years, the number of scientific and policy organisations that are international or claim international reach has grown enormously. There is a lure of far higher financing than at present if those arguing that similar funds might be devoted to biodiversity conservation on Earth as to the Space Programme (looking for life elsewhere) ever win their case. This internationalisation shapes what we know about the environment and tropical forests (and what we don't), and the ways in which debates are conducted and manifested. In this chapter, we outline certain trends in the treatment of forest and biodiversity issues in the nexus of international conventions, the United Nations and other international organisations, multilateral and bilateral donors, trans-national corporations, international NGOs, international research centres and the research community more widely. We make the case that the sheer mass of organisations and the networks (and rivalries) which link them generates a dynamic of its own. This has the quality of a vortex into which people and organisations involved with research or policy – nationally and locally as well as globally – are drawn whether through obligations to internationally negotiated regimes, funding, interest, the need for work to have contemporary relevance, or as the audience for critique. It is impossible to research and describe such a mass in its entirety, so we attempt, in the first part of the chapter, to strike a balance between the encyclopaedism necessary to convey the true mass of contemporary institutions, and the sketching and exemplification of key interrelationships within it. We focus on particular international agreements and organisations, and consider a variety of other donors, NGOs and research organisations in relation to these.

The metaphor of a vortex captures something of the growing global coordination of science and policy, without orchestration by any particular international organisation, state or located institution. The sense is more akin to Hardt and Negri's (2001) characterisation of an 'Empire' dominating contemporary world politics, premised on an increasingly de-centred, de-territorialised form of global governance. Rosenau (1990) describes the growing importance (alongside states) of a world of transnational sub-politics, with dimensions including dominance of transnational organisations, transnational problems dominating the political agenda, transnational events, the development of transnational communities, and transnational structures such as various forms of network. Especially given the transformations wrought by information and communications technology, Castells (1996) argues further that dominant functions are increasingly organised through networks and flows which link them up around the world. None of these theorists of globalisation are explicitly concerned with science, let alone the perspectives from an ethnographic approach to it, yet their insights are relevant to comprehending the networks and flows of institutions and ideas which constitute the 'Empire' that we term 'Tropical Forest International'.

This vortex quality is important in the way it shapes the questions asked about tropical forests – and the terms in which debates are conducted. As subsequent chapters will explore, globalised 'framings' of scientific and policy debate have important influences on research and policy in Guinea and Trinidad – although in ways which are far from direct, as they are mediated by the histories and practices of science and policy in these particular national and local settings. The second part of this chapter outlines some key issues which have come to dominate deliberations amongst international organisations, and which are of particular significance in the country case studies covered in Chapters 4–7. We also consider how 'local' experiences and evidence give substance to these international debates. This is not least because within the international field, virtually all organisations and staff are now at pains to embrace local diversity and particularities, as well as to incorporate the perspectives and participation of 'the poor', 'the indigenous' and 'the marginalised', and the perspectives of poorer governments. That located experiences are critical to (and become connected to each other through) the tropical forest vortex modifies Castells' (1996) picture of globalised networks and flows, where value and power are produced and decided, as increasingly segregated from 'subordinate' people and locales. Nevertheless, the manner in which localised experiences are drawn into this vortex is a matter for empirical inquiry, as are the extent and ways in which consensus and conformity in knowledge and approaches to management of the forest are generated.

We begin with a brief contextualisation of the internationalisation of tropical forest concerns within more general trends in the internationalisation of environmental governance, its current configurations and links with science.

The internationalisation of environmental governance

Since the early 1990s there has been a transformation in the ways that environmental issues are addressed and governed. There is a growing presence of international negotiations and regimes to address the environment, a growth in the number and presence of NGOs, and new forms of coalition between NGOs, citizens and international players. These challenge any conventional picture of governance by states within an international order, yet how to characterise the emergent arrangements?

First, there are now several hundred international environmental regimes. Over the past twenty years a range of environmental issues with global or transnational causes and effects has been identified, and new international pacts, conventions and protocols have been negotiated in response to these (GECP 2000a; Porter and Brown 1991, Haas *et al.* 1993). These international regimes (collections of legal, institutional and political processes through which governance is conducted) are of increasing importance for framing national policies. Certain global players (or coalitions) are well placed to enforce other countries to become signatory to such regimes, and eventually to comply. This signals an attenuation of the era of national sovereignty, or perhaps better put, a transformation in patterns through which national sovereignty is alienated – especially for certain countries.[1] Consequently, those either seeking to shape their own national policies, or to influence those in other countries (as donors or lobbyists perhaps), need to engage with the international conventions.

Science plays a new role in this international governance (e.g. Jasanoff and Wynne 1997). The environmental regimes are co-established and co-evolve with scientific committees which inform their political deliberations. In as much as the operation of international environmental regimes depends on particular scientifically-authenticated calculus, then, the politics of their operation is conducted through the politics of science. Competitors negotiate through this science (e.g. Boehmer-Christiansen 1996; Taylor and Buttel 1992). Concurrent with the proliferation of international regimes, then, is a tendency towards establishing supra-national regional blocs which can negotiate common interests in international agreements. Such regional political unions are being shadowed by regional scientific unions, promoting specific regional perspectives. International funding flows are shaping these networks (e.g. Vogler and Jordan 2003).

Second, and linked to this growing intensity of international governance, it is possible to discern an 'era of policy' in international co-operation. Rather than direct technical assistance through interventions and projects, budgetary and other support to ministries, policies and policy-making capacities have become primary foci of bilateral and multi-lateral donor assistance. Concomitantly, discussions in international arenas are led by a new sense of the capacity to influence other state's policies, whether to harmonise them (generate conformity across nations and with international regimes and 'best practices'), or to assist them to become more 'rational' or 'participatory'. In this context international agencies have been engaged in funding and assisting 'policy reviews', and co-ordinating these in regional programmes.[2] Such reviews provide opportunities for international leverage over national agenda-setting, not only in the elaboration of policies, but also in the capacity subsequently to hold countries accountable to them.

Third, a range of non-state, and 'intermediary' actors and organisations are playing new roles in brokering relationships between international environmental regimes, funders, governments and citizens (Newell 1999). NGOs have become involved with international environmental regimes in a variety of ways. Certain NGOs are accredited with having representation at meetings of international regimes or the NGO fora which take place alongside them. Others engage in less formal but no less visible protest demonstrations. NGOs have also become involved in regime processes through engagement with and lobbying of the organisations managing conventions and protocols, and those shaping the regimes and their analytics, such as international political institutions (United Nations system) and international financial institutions (e.g. the World Bank/IMF, Regional Development Banks). NGOs can have a major influence on international policy processes through their conduct of science, shaping the framing of international deliberations. Where relationships are more supportive than critical, the distinction between NGOs and official international institutions can become hazy. Thus the WorldWide Fund for Nature is in official agreement with the World Bank in developing forest policy, while Conservation International has a similar agreement over biodiversity.

While the variety of NGO stances precludes generalisation, many claim to represent national or regional perspectives, or those of particular people and groups – often the poor and otherwise marginalised. Some have emerged as trans-national or international, becoming active in forging networks and alliances between certain local groups, bringing them to international prominence and shaping their public representation in the process: for example in taking 'indigenous people' ('non-government' people par excellence) to international conventions.

NGOs are also engaged in lobbying transnational corporations, which can appear to have become more important than governments in environmental impact (Fabig and Boele 1999).[3] Business corporations have also become significant funders of environmental initiatives involving NGOs and international organisations, as agendas for 'corporate social and environmental responsibility,' and the need for 'green' practices, image or both, have become more important. So, while there are often intense divisions between large corporations and the international brokering and financial institutions, on the one hand, and NGOs on the other, in other domains there is evidence of processes of co-operation, congruence and coalition which unite NGOs, governments and international business players.

These current engagements confound many of the conventional boundaries which have been drawn around NGOs and other types of organisation. First, conventionally, strong distinctions have been drawn between organisations which have global mandate and formal representation of (and accountability to) different countries, and organisations which claim international/global scope, such as many large NGOs. Those within the United Nations (UN) system, in particular, can at times be dismissive of NGOs who 'may work internationally, but cannot represent governments internationally'.[4] Yet, shared perspectives, funding and so on render the distinction between many NGOs and official international institutions hazy. Second, NGOs have usually been strongly distinguished from government. Yet international regimes undermine the very government sovereignty (or at least the pretence of it) underlying this distinction. At the same time, NGOs and governments frequently find themselves in alliance, either against corporations and 'oppressive' international agreements, or as the joint vehicles through which internationally-agreed priorities should be enacted. It thus becomes easier for particular NGOs and government departments to work together, and for NGOs to be staffed by government employees, and vice versa. Third, distinctions between what have conventionally been characterised as 'international', 'national' and 'local' NGOs also become blurred through these engagements. At the least, the ways in which organisations representing distinct constituencies may become allied through common perspective, cause or funding comes to require empirical analysis.

'Tropical Forest International'

Internationalisation of governance and science, and trends in the interrelationships between types of organisation, are well illustrated in the case of tropical forests. Recent decades have witnessed a massive expansion in the number of organisations which deal with tropical forests and the networks and alliances linking them.[5]

The United Nations Conference on Environment and Development in Rio, 1992, provides an appropriate entry point for discussion. It established three conventions relevant to forestry: those on climate change, on desertification and on biological diversity. It also adopted non-binding Forest Principles and negotiated Agenda 21 which remains the responsibility of the United Nations Commission on Sustainable Development.

During and since Rio there has been considerable dispute over the question of a legally binding Forest Convention. Put crudely, many countries of the 'north' (although notably not the US) were in favour, and many of the 'south' against, largely because a convention would specify conditions of sustainability and its monitoring, and these could be achieved in the north but not in the south, so limiting developing countries' marketing opportunities for forest products. Only non-binding principles could be agreed upon. Since then there has been a range of alternative, UN-co-ordinated initiatives. In 1995, the UN Commission on Sustainable Development established an 'Intergovernmental Panel on Forests' to address a wide range of forest-related issues.[6] Its proposals for action were formally endorsed at a United Nations General Assembly Special Session which then established the 'Intergovernmental Forum on Forests'. This was to promote implementation of the Panel's proposals; consider outstanding issues (those pressed by successful lobbyists, including analysis of 'underlying causes of deforestation', and 'traditional knowledge'), and consider international arrangements and mechanisms (such as a legally binding convention) to promote the management, conservation and sustainable development of all types of forest.

This last question was pursued in a series of inter-sessional meetings. As ever, negotiation occurred through the powerful alliances or 'bloc players' of the UN system, including the G77 representing 'the south', and the European Union. Yet after four meetings no legally binding arrangements could be negotiated. Instead, a new forum (the UN Forum on Forests) was proposed which would promote 'National Forest Programmes', provide a forum for policy development, and enhance co-operation, so that parameters for a legal convention could be developed over time.

The Rio conference, the Intergovernmental Panel and Forum processes (conducted by world forest ministers), and the regional power-bloc meetings of government representatives to strategise and orchestrate negotiating stances have spawned a vast documentation by governments and international institutions: strategy documents, sector overviews, case study analyses, and so on. As offering potentially crucial leverage into international – hence national – policies, the process attracted wider interest, not least from NGOs keen that the results of international deliberations should reflect their particular interests – such as those of minorities and 'indigenous peoples', or of conservation as opposed to timber production. Thus, although a convention has not been established to date, international policy deliberation has been strongly animated and shaped by its ever-present possibility. This has fuelled deliberation over goals and a cacophony of stated approaches to achieve sustainable forest management and conservation, reflecting diverse ethical, economic and international political commitments.

A similar vortex for analysis and deliberation has been generated around the Convention on Biological Diversity (CBD). This has as objectives the conservation of genetic, species and ecosystem diversity, its sustainable use, and the equitable sharing of its benefits. The Convention's work is dictated by the original convention agreed at Rio, and the cumulative decisions of each meeting of its Council of Parties which sets out the topics on which advice is required. This is delivered by a scientific committee, which is multidisciplinary and composed of competent government representatives (in the case of forests, members of government forest departments, training institutes and so on). There are provisions and procedures for accredited NGOs to participate. Regular inputs are also provided by the Centre for International Forestry Research (CIFOR).

CBD deliberations concerning forest biodiversity have themselves been shaped by the possibility of a forest convention. Initially the CBD deferred to the Intergovernmental Panel on Forests on forest issues, and sought to feed into it, especially in advising on the relationship between indigenous and local communities and forests. Forest biodiversity became a topic of special priority, and a dedicated work programme on forest conservation and analysis of use trends was established. It urged countries, international and regional organisations and other relevant bodies to collaborate in carrying out its tasks.

The CBD is huge and wide-ranging. Signatory countries have been required to develop national biodiversity assessments, strategies and action plans to implement them. The CBD sets the broad parameters which national exercises should follow, but they are expected to be elaborated to suit national and local conditions and priorities. Funding for the Convention, its work plans and operational and research projects are provided by a Global Environmental Facility (GEF) that was agreed at Rio. This is managed by the World Bank and paid for by industrialised countries.

Government negotiators from low-income countries such as Guinea and from small island Caribbean states are disconcerted by the dominance of Euro-American representatives in both the Council of Parties and inter-sessional meetings, and indeed by the abilities of richer and larger countries to come prepared following major preparatory conferences.[7] In response, international NGOs and donors have become involved in orchestrating the funding of attendance from developing countries, and preparatory meetings. So, for example, the WorldWide Fund for Nature organised preparatory meetings in Côte d'Ivoire, drawing together West African delegates to co-ordinate a common position (MLCVE 1998).

Direct NGO involvement in the UN system deliberations is highly regulated. Within the Inter-governmental Panel/Forum process NGOs were largely barred from the negotiations. Only accredited NGOs can attend CBD meetings. Accreditation requires procedures which deter all but the larger international NGOs. In practice smaller (and southern) NGOs gain attendance only through international NGOs, who become gatekeepers. NGOs have, however, lobbied successfully to participate in particular initiatives, such as on the underlying causes of deforestation, which informed the Intergovernmental Forum.

They worked with governments in a series of inter-sessional regional meetings (e.g. ICA 1998), leading to a global conference which exerted pressure not to establish an intergovernmental negotiating committee on a legally binding instrument on forests until progress had been made to redress the imbalance between trade and other international agreements.

NGOs have also been instrumental in forging alternatives to UN-led processes. The lack of a firm position on forests at Rio, and dissatisfaction with deliberation within the UN system (not least the exclusion of non-governmental voice) has spawned other international agenda-setting exercises. Most notable was the World Commission on Forests and Sustainable Development (WCFSD), an initiative of former Heads of State and Ministers. Twenty-three independent commissioners comprised politicians, and a number of major figures in the international and NGO world of forestry. The Commission was closely linked with the Woods Hole Research Centre in Massachusetts, USA, which co-ordinated its establishment and recruitment. While describing itself as an independent non-governmental process set up to examine issues of forests and sustainable development (WCFSD 1999), it risked being seen through the Woods Hole link (and through the several US-based foundations which funded the Commission's work) as aligned with US interests in envisaging alternatives to a convention.

International dialogue concerning forests is linked with longer established UN programmes addressing forest issues, most notably the Forestry Department of the UN Food and Agriculture Organisation (FAO) and the UN Environment Programme (UNEP). FAO serves as an international forum and secretariat for forestry matters, answerable to governments at a Committee on Forestry which meets every two years, in which other international organisations participate (and some NGOs now observe). Six 'Regional Commissions' (e.g. the African Forestry and Wildlife Commission) hold regular meetings which feed into and complement the Committee. FAO has also chaired the inter-UN agency Task Force on Forests, and co-ordinated the contribution of other UN organisations to the work of Inter-governmental Forum on Forests. It has been lead organiser for several aspects of these processes, contributing to the preparation of agenda setting Secretariat notes, and organising conferences and workshops (FAO 1999a). FAO also supports the National Forest Programmes, which build on earlier massive planning exercises that the FAO led: the Tropical Forest Action Plans (TFAP) of the mid-1980s and the National Forest Action Programming of the early 1990s (FAO 1999b). One critique of the earlier TFAP process, which generated dozens of forest project outlines for many countries, was that the projects were generated outside 'coherent policy frameworks'. The cart was before the horse; the project before the policy. On the basis of such arguments, by the late 1990s support was being given to forestry 'policy reviews' in each country.

As staff point out, the FAO Forestry Department is not a research organisation, but it does act to facilitate research and international co-operation in this: 'We do not do research in-house; we work with other researchers and institutions who have credibility'.[8] In this, it has served to strengthen the globalisation of forestry research. The perceived need to strengthen the global forestry research system has also been concretised in recent years by the establishment of the Indonesia-based Centre for International Forestry Research (CIFOR) and the Kenya-based International Centre for Research on Agroforestry (ICRAF). These are International Research Centres of the Consultative Group on International Agricultural Research (CGIAR), mandated to conduct strategic and applied research at a global level (Souvannavong 2000). In 1998 FAO, CIFOR and the International Union of Forestry Research Organisations (IUFRO) collaborated on an international consultation on research and information systems in forestry which urged the setting-up of a global forum to unite policy makers, funders, research agencies, scientists and other stakeholders to guide forestry science initiatives in the context of global initiatives. At the same time FAO has been involved in strengthening regional research systems, facilitating the establishment of a Forestry Research Network for Sub-Saharan Africa (FORNESSA) broken into subregional networks supported by different donors. The rationale for this is cast explicitly as assisting globalisation of the research system, on the grounds that:

National Research Systems play an essential role in the global research system . . . International research programmes would have limited impact without appropriate participation and complementary research by national institutions. Developing countries do not have the adequate capacity to participate in international research projects and to capitalise, adapt and transfer results to the local level. Strengthening national research systems in order to link them effectively to both the international research community and local users will remain an issue of great importance (FAO 1999c: 1).

The 'global research system' is by no means a neutral field. Not only are there rivalries between international organisations over authority, but these rivalries also play into (and are interpreted as playing into) broader geopolitical disputes, in which science and the institutions that conduct it become a vehicle for international politics. Nowhere is this clearer than in global forest monitoring. The importance of monitoring has heightened through debates surrounding carbon accounting linked to the Kyoto protocol of the Climate Change Convention, and opportunities for putting real costs and tradeable values on carbon emissions and carbon-absorptive forests. Scientific debates over monitoring methodologies, technologies and findings are therefore bound up with the political economy of carbon control. This is in addition to ways that monitoring feeds into debates and claims over biodiversity loss and human impacts on forest, with the potential to attract heavily-funded conservation initiatives.

Several organisations have become involved in monitoring forest status and assessing forest cover change, leading to overlap and rivalry. FAO has long been central to the production of global statistics on forest resources and cover, and since 1980 has conducted a decennial Forest Resource Assessment, and a more frequent report on the 'State of the World's Forests' (e.g. FAO 1999d). Yet several other organisations, including the UN Environment Programme (UNEP) and the Washington-based World Resources Institute (WRI), have also taken up global environmental and forest cover monitoring, and inter-organisational competition is now shaping the ways in which assessments are conducted and are seen to be conducted.

For example, the FAO Forest Resource Assessment for 2000 adopted a new approach, incorporating transparency of data sources, electronic maps and analytic reviews of deforestation processes.[9] This was driven explicitly by awareness of competition from other organisations: the need to 'make a good show' and to 're-establish FAO as the leading forestry information organisation'.[10] Key to the FAO's new claim, and its desire to conduct a 'World Forest Survey' is that its mandate assures neutrality, positioning it to conduct a 'singularly objective survey' (FRAP 1999: 1), concerned that 'other institutions may bias information to fit their own agendas and constituencies . . . [for example] the World Resources Institute has an agenda related more to Washington than to the real world'.[11]

The World Resources Institute has long produced the annual World Resources report, and is involved in global monitoring of forest extent and change,[12] drawing on data from FAO, UN, the European Union and NASA. Other initiatives have included the Forests Frontiers initiative (Bryant et al. 1997) which drew on 'expert opinion' worldwide to map areas of 'remaining' forest cover, and Global Forest Watch which monitors current forest use activities. It has also provided the location and impetus for an 'autonomous' Millennium Ecosystem Assessment, with an independent secretariat. In 2000 this received US support for satellite images of global forest cover.[13] WRI also teamed up with the World-Wide Fund for Nature in a study which critiqued FAO's 2000 forest resource assessment, arguing that any apparent slow-up of deforestation which it showed was an artefact of methodology. It argued that FAO should focus on what it can do and collaborate with other, better-resourced organisations (implicitly WRI) to improve.[14]

UNEP also conducts resource assessments, including forests, and has recently incorporated the UK-based World Conservation Monitoring Centre (WCMC) which itself has conducted independent major tropical forest assessments in the past. It produces maps of potential original forest cover, current forest cover and protection – including global, regional and country-level statistical analysis – and forest biodiversity. It also produces 'analyses and syntheses of forest data to facilitate policy and decision-making', which now include priority areas for conservation in relation to climate change (Forests in Flux); trends in forest area and forest ecosystem status in the last thirty years (Living Planet Index), defining priority areas for forest restoration, and putting development and forest conservation in context using poverty indicators (Poverty mapping).[15]

Organisations within the UN system may argue that their mandate is special: as an FAO staff member put it 'there are international organisations and organisations that work internationally'.[16] Thus FAO is not seen to be in competition with WRI and other international NGOs because it has an official mandate to represent countries, which NGOs do not; 'thus they have no way to bring people together at government level'.[17] Another staff member expressed the perception that FAO's real competition is with UNEP, casting it as 'a bad message and a bad concept',[18] as its very existence gives the impression that other UN organisations are 'non-environmental'. There is also some competition with international forestry research organisations.

Bilateral and multilateral donors are also important players in this 'Tropical Forest International'. While they are involved in technical co-operation projects, policy advice and conditionality leverage in particular countries, they also develop broader forest policy frameworks and strategies alongside these. Within this field there are increasingly strategic links between particular donors and international NGOs, both at a high level in policy formulation, and in operational projects. This both serves NGO funding needs and offers mutual credibility and interdependency. The World Bank, for example, has been developing a Forest Policy Implementation Review and Strategy with support from the International Union for the Conservation of Nature.[19] It orchestrated a long stakeholder consultation process to build consensus on a global strategy for preserving and managing forests in the context of sustainable development and poverty alleviation; to identify issues that impact on forests, and to assess stakeholder perspectives on the Bank's comparative advantage. The World Bank has also linked up with WWF in a major forest conservation initiative for West Africa.

The EU funds biodiversity support projects under its Environment and Tropical Forest budget lines, as well as through the European Development Fund. Tropical forestry projects are a major focus of biodiversity activities. For example, its 'Biodiversity in Development' project has involved collaboration between the EU and the British Department for International Development, with the International Union for the Conservation of Nature as executing agency.[20] This is providing a strategic framework for agencies to implement sustainable development activities.

Each of these donors (and the many others) have broad strategies orchestrating their approach to development, and have married obligations to international processes such as the biodiversity convention with their existing policies. New analytical concepts are generated in the search for alignment. For example, when the British Department for International Development conducted a review of its biodiversity strategy programmes (Koziell 2001: v), it coined the term 'bioquality' to merge natural science perspectives on biodiversity with the organisation's overriding emphasis on poverty reduction (see also DFID 2001, Koziell and Saunders 2001).

As 'Tropical Forest International' has grown, it generates fields not only of common interest, but also of mutual critique, which is often vitriolic. The configuration of institutions is partly shaped by the need to manage this critique, in which multilateral institutions such as the World Bank forge strategic links with vocal and powerful NGOs, or expand their consultation processes. As a senior forest policy advisor in a rival organisation put it, 'The World Bank . . . is being participatory in this way because they are exposed to criticism from NGOs etc. They need to prove that policy has been discussed with all the world.'[21]

Many donors are involved in funding research programmes around tropical forest issues. These include the research of international organisations such as the Centre for International Forestry Research, established in response to global concerns about the social, environmental and economic consequences of the loss and degradation of forests. It researches forests and livelihoods, environmental services and sustainable use of forests, and forest governance. It conducts its research agenda through a variety of collaborative arrangements with partners in many countries. An important element of the Centre's research agenda is to improve the scientific basis for international action, feeding into the UN deliberations and conventions.

There is also a large variety of other internationally-collaborative research programmes, many of which receive funding from donors involved with forest policy. The European Tropical Forest Research Network lists over 500 European institutes involved in tropical forest research, many of which are running large programmes, covering all aspects from the technical and ecological to the social and historical. Such programmes also usually involve collaboration with institutions based in tropical countries, whether forest research institutes, government departments, universities or NGOs. They therefore provide a further means by which researchers from tropical countries are drawn into the vortex of internationalised forest science and policy. They join other means of incorporation: the promotion and funding of networks of research organisations within and between tropical countries and the forging of information networks linking forest conservation and management programmes on the ground. Research is not only conducted by research organisations, but is now integral to most projects and programmes. Many projects are self-styled as 'pilot' or experimental, or have research components. Staff become 'scientists', at times appearing to work more in extended laboratories than in development projects. Through a grey but often glossy literature, and the co-ordination of donors and international NGOs, project experiences are networked into the global policy and research community.[22]

The sheer mass and complexity of 'Tropical Forest International', and the multiple nodes through which science/policy is conducted, has, for many, created an impossible arena of overlap, competition, multiple terminology for similar phenomena and confusion. Attempts at harmonisation and co-ordination are frequently made. They spawn a whirl of international meetings, new projects, secretariats, organisations, commissions and websites – nodes of nodes in international networks. For example, the Interagency Task Force on Forests was an 'informal' inter-UN agency, helping people to harmonise. A so-called 'landmark project in harmonisation' was a joint project with the European Union, International Union of Forestry Research Organisations and FAO on information systems in African, Caribbean and Pacific countries, which was (at least initially) to be a 'one stop information shop' for global forest information. Another is the Ecosystem Conservation Group, which is convened by the UN Environment Programme and brings together assorted international organisations and NGOs[23] to provide an avenue through which science and technology relating to ecosystem conservation can be brought together in the design of policies, strategies and programmes. Much has been spent on harmonisation, arguably with little reward. Difficulties reflect fundamental political differences between organisations: a politics which is to a significant extent conducted through science. Harmonisation attempts nevertheless have other effects. Harmonisation in international agreements has become little but 'a by-word for deferral' as one British negotiator put it, stalling any momentum. Nevertheless, attempts proceed and already globalised organisations are thus integrated in further layers of globality. Tropical Forest International multiplies itself as if in a hall of mirrors.

Contemporary debates in 'Tropical Forest International'

To exemplify briefly how particular debates around tropical forests are configured within this international vortex, we shall focus on two themes that are central to current discussion and initiatives, and which echo through later chapters: first, biodiversity debates concerning where to prioritise, and what approach to take, and second, debates around timber production and sustainable forest management, concerning both how to conceptualise sustainability, and how to achieve it – particularly through involving forest users. Within the mass of organisations involved with each particular theme, there is rivalry and competition, both institutional and conceptual, and attempts at harmonisation.

Biodiversity

Within the broad concern with forest biodiversity established and promoted within the CBD, several organisations have become involved both in setting priorities for where biodiversity conservation efforts should be concentrated, and in debates over how such conservation should be achieved.

Priority-setting for biodiversity conservation

The International Union for the Conservation of Nature and its members have aimed to expand the worldwide network of protected areas to 10 per cent of all terrestrial ecological regions.[24] By 1993, 5 per cent had been achieved and the expansion of national parks and protected areas remains their priority. In recent global analysis concerning how to allocate international resources for global biodiversity conservation most efficiently, West Africa and the Caribbean feature prominently.

Since the mid 1990s a number of international organisations have launched priority-setting exercises for conservation relevant to forest biodiversity. Birdlife International has conducted prioritisation of areas of endemic and threatened birds (Stattersfield et al. 1998). The WorldWide Fund for Nature has developed the Global 200 Ecoregions, in which ecoregions are defined and selected to represent major habitat types (Olson and Dinerstein 1998; WWF 1997, 1999). Conservation International (CI) has developed an approach based on biodiversity 'hotspots' (Mittermeier et al. 1997, 1998, 2000).

These exercises are regional in scope, responding to the arguments of conservation biologists and others that isolated protected areas are insufficient to ensure the protection of species and their habitats (Soulé and Terborgh 1999). Eco-regional approaches therefore scale up, going beyond the national systems plans for parks and protected areas which dominated conservation during the 1970s and 1980s and well beyond the localised community based approaches which became popular in the early 1990s. In so doing, they play into arguments for transfrontier parks and the promotion of inter-state co-operation in regional conservation agendas.

Scientific exercises are linked with different institutions. They all depend, in different ways, on drawing in 'expert scientific opinion' both in designing broad prioritisation criteria, and in the application of these criteria in particular regions. Science and policy become inter-linked in the common aim of establishing principles by which choices may be made in the targeting of conservation – given that resource constraints and competing land uses necessitate selectivity. Priority-setting exercises and the glossy publications and maps drawn up to summarise them are also geared to garnering broader support and financing for biodiversity conservation, from donors, governments and their constituent publics. There are strong distinctions between approaches. Distinctiveness is partly a facet of the very mass of organisations now involved in such work, as different approaches create 'trademarks' that organisations can subsequently trade on in attracting further funding and building up organisational programmes.

The Conservation International Hotspots approach and the WorldWide Fund for Nature Ecoregions approach can illustrate such distinctions. First, the CI approach inevitably focuses on the tropics as it characterises hotspots as areas of high biological diversity which are under human pressure; where only 10 per cent of 'original' habitat remains. The diversity of tropical ecosystems dwarfs that of temperate ones so there is a tropical focus. The WWF approach by contrast defines ecoregions as relatively large units of land or water characterised by their distinctive climates, ecological habitats and species distribution, and thus adopts greater relativity, with 200 ecoregions encompassing Arctic tundra and desert as well as tropical forest. The approach is thus geared to protecting representative samples of all types of habitat.[25] Second, CI's hotspots are defined at regional scales, with the Upper Guinea forest zone, for example, constituting a single hotspot, although forest fragments within these are also ranked in priority. The approach is explicitly geared towards promoting regional and trans-boundary co-operation in conservation efforts. In contrast the ecoregions approach is nested, identifying vegetation patterns and biogeographic processes at regional scales, then stratifying down to national scales and priority habitat examples in-country on the basis that conservation operates at a national level. Proponents of the latter approach argue that the former is impractical (e.g. Whitmore 2000).

Priority-setting conceives of localities within an explicitly global, as well as regional frame. Locations are examined and prioritised with respect to their global significance for habitat or species conservation and sustainability, and any actions on the ground which follow, no matter how 'participatory', are framed by such extra-local concerns. As illustrated in Chapter 5 where a CI priority-setting workshop for West Africa is traced ethnographically, this has particular consequences for the ways in which science/policy processes in such exercises proceed, and local people-forest dynamics come to be construed.

Approaches to biodiversity conservation

Since the mid-1990s a particular 'ecosystem approach' to biodiversity conservation has been developed as the primary framework for action under the CBD, to balance and integrate the Convention's three objectives of conservation, sustainable use and equitable sharing of benefits. In this, 'ecosystem' means a 'dynamic complex of plant, animal and micro-organism communities and their non-living environment interacting as a functional unit'.[26] There are strong similarities with approaches used by other organisations, including the bioregional approach of IUCN (McNeely and Miller 1984; McNeely 1999). However, while this appears to represent an increasingly strong international consensus about approaches to conservation, tensions are also evident between organisations, which play into different scientific traditions and lines of inquiry and debate.

Some commentators see ecosystem approaches as having emerged from past policy experience; the evident failure (on grounds of both practicality and equity) of conventional approaches to conservation which protected 'nature' from people. In contrast, in placing greater emphasis on sustainable use, ecosystem approaches claim greater potential to address people's social and economic concerns along with biodiversity conservation, and thus generate greater sustainability through local support. By focusing on 'functional units' conservation integrates biological, physical and socio-economic processes, considering that humans, with their cultural diversity, are integral to ecosystems. The approach is seen not to preclude other management and conservation approaches, such as biosphere reserves, protected areas, and single-species conservation programmes, as well as other approaches carried out under existing national policy and legislative frameworks, but to provide an overarching framework within which these could be integrated.

An emphasis on integrated approaches to conservation planning was found twenty years ago in the World Conservation Strategy (IUCN 1980), and was reinforced in subsequent meetings such as the 1992 Fourth World Congress on National Parks and Protected areas in Caracas, Venezuela which devoted an entire session to the bioregional scale of landscape conservation (McNeely 1992, 1999). Following the establishment of the CBD in 1992 a series of meetings held within its broad ambit, though co-ordinated by various agencies, helped develop the concept and delineate practices to implement it.

Many donor agencies and NGOs have been developing practical approaches to integrating conservation with economic and social development. These range from various forms of Integrated Conservation and Development Project (ICDP), usually incorporating zonation into strict nature reserves (with no settlement), buffer zones and further zones where rural development is geared to providing alternative livelihood opportunities; to various forms of extractive reserve; community-based use and management of wildlife and ecotourism resources, and discussion (though little implementation) of new landscape approaches modelled broadly on European national parks (Franks 2001). These approaches vary, not least, in the extent to which they rely on protected areas as opposed to biodiversity use in 'lived-in-landscapes', and the nature and degrees of resource and decision-making control assumed by local users. The wide field of experimentation through projects on the ground has generated a mass of literature reflecting on such experiences, drawing lessons and attempting to define best practice (e.g. IIED 1994; Wells et al. 1992; Ghimire and Pimbert 1997; Bass et al. 2001).

There are underlying philosophical and disciplinary tensions between broadly 'ecocentric' positions (advocating the protection of 'nature' for its own sake) and those emphasising social values and people's involvement; and between those advocating sustainable use, and those seeing it as a threat to the real

business of protecting species and habitats. Such tensions both divide organisations, and different groups within particular organisations (e.g. Jeanreneaud
2001). Indeed evidence of apparent implementation failures of conservation-
with-development and community-based approaches have fuelled a backlash
against the entire conservation-with-development enterprise, led by conservation biologists who advocate a return to the values and practices of strict nature
protection (Oates 2000; Terborgh 1999). While funding for conservation was
locked into development agendas, however, dissent and backlash was curtailed.
Yet major new funding, more exclusively for conservation, has enabled these
agendas to be pursued with greater vigour, most notably in response to Conservation International's $6 billion programme from public and private sources
pump-primed by a $240 million donation from a private foundation. In this
context, eco-regional approaches have become more than mere ways to set
priorities for conservation, coming to represent a new era of biologically-led
and supra-national initiatives responding to the urgency of biodiversity protection, overcoming the problems of inefficient or failed states, and justifying
major funding through scientifically-led strategic plans (Brosius 2002). The
momentum in this scientific and policy movement could eclipse conservation-
with-development approaches, especially as it sits alongside other decidedly
non community-based approaches such as 'conservation concessions' where
loggers are outbid for timber concessions.

While much conservation literature presents 'ecosystem approaches' considering people within them, as socially liberating, the idea of managing nature
and people together in 'functional units' has a longer and somewhat murkier
genealogy. It stretches back to the ideas of 'holism' characterising ecology in
the USA and in South Africa early in the 1920s and 1930s where they fed
into political debate, naturalising and legitimising policies of segregation and
reservation. Such tensions are still evident today, with the notion of integrated
biological and cultural diversity sometimes providing a justification for cultural
protection through a 'cultural apartheid' of indigenous people within protected
areas. This is sometimes drawn on by 'indigenous people' themselves to gain
rights to resources.

Most debates about protected area management have been framed by a view
of equilibrium or balance. Sometimes this is a balance in 'nature' as a baseline against which to assess (and restrict) human disturbance; sometimes –
as in much discussion of community-based natural resource management and
indigenous peoples – a functionally-integrated balance of society and nature
which might be preserved or restored. However, less equilibrial scientific perspectives have also been raised. A strong theme in the ten or more international
conferences that led to the elaboration of CBD's ecosystem approach, was a
recognition of non-equilibrial ecology; a recognition that change is inevitable,
and that management objectives are a matter of social choice – rather than able

to be pegged to a notion of baseline 'natural' vegetation. Moreover, incomplete knowledge and inherent uncertainty in ecosystem dynamics have been embraced, and adaptive management approaches incorporating 'learning-by-doing' advocated. In this vein McNeely (1999) emphasised the 'experimental' basis of ecosystem approaches as – based on 'best available science' – they continually adapt to new knowledge, as well as to fluctuations in ecosystems themselves. Nevertheless, eventual agreement on a set of guiding principles on the approach incorporated divergent, even contradictory emphases; ideas around non-equilibrium and adaptive management sitting alongside more static emphases on conservation of ecosystem structure and functioning.

Thus in the meetings and practices which have shaped the 'ecosystem approach', two dominant strands of thinking – one emphasising managerial functionalism, the other uncertainty, adaptation and 'experimentalism' – have co-existed, somewhat uneasily. Both acknowledge a key role for the 'sciences', whether in defining parameters for functional units, or in monitoring the unexpected. While much is said about local/indigenous expertise, with principles of the approach emphasising the importance of paying attention to multiple forms of knowledge and expertise, including 'indigenous knowledge', the assumption is that it is drawn on 'downstream' in more operational stages. This is encapsulated in the imperative that ecosystem management needs to 'think globally but act locally'. In the meantime, the persistent urging at international meetings to generate more case studies provides a route by which local experiences are drawn up into and reconfigured within the frames and styles of international 'ecosystem approach' impetus. The impression is of incorporating knowledges within an overarching managerialist framework, with less attention to ways that alternative scientific or local perspectives might dispute this vision itself.

Sustainable timber production and forest management

Timber production remains central to international deliberations around tropical forests. Research and policy have focused on ways to reconcile this with other uses and users, most notably conservation and socio-economic benefits to local communities. This has come to be discussed within the vocabulary of the 'Criteria and Indicators' by which 'sustainability' can be assessed and measured, and as part of debates about centralised versus decentralised and community-based forest management.

Criteria and Indicators

Two alternatives are envisaged in seeking to reconcile timber production with other forest values. The first would set aside natural forest for conservation, and focus timber production on plantations. The second anticipates integrating timber production and other values through sustainable natural forest management.

'Natural forest management' has received high profile in recent international forest policy debates, at least in its ideal as a sustainable use for forest profitable enough to prevent conversion to other uses (e.g. Harcharik 1997). Nevertheless reviews of experience raise a variety of questions (Rice *et al.* 1999). Some concern its economic viability and profitability compared with alternative land uses and conventional management (Davies & Richards 1999). Others concern the sustainability of silvicultural management itself. Policy reviews accept that 'No tropical forest has been managed for substantive periods of time and therefore nobody knows for sure whether the best management practices employed are in fact sustainable' (FAO 1999e: 6). Nevertheless, 'it is generally believed that the results obtained to date have provided a reasonably solid basis for effective silviculture in humid tropical forests' (Dupuy 1999:9; FAO 1999e).

Hopes for sustainable forest management have stimulated international dialogues surrounding the criteria to define it (the range of forest values to be addressed), and the quantifiable indicators to measure and monitor it. Several research organisations are pursuing research within the Criteria and Indicators debate, and their research has been conducted through, and serves to shape, an intense series of international and regional processes.

Initiated by the International Tropical Timber Organisation (ITTO) in 1992, there have been at least eight intergovernmental processes covering different regions to discuss the scientific and policy aspects of sustainable forest management.[27] FAO's Forestry Department catalysed or assisted all these (FAO 1999). Numerous regional technical committees have been established to 'ensure scientific soundness of approach' (ibid). These processes have been linked with research by international organisations. For example some research initiatives have focused on criteria and indicators at 'forest unit level'. Some embrace social and economic as well as ecological aspects of sustainability. Some encourage local planning around similar 'criteria and indicators for sustainability', which whilst conforming with higher level criteria, make sense in relation to the local site (topography, forest type), society and economy. The ideal, here, is that national-level criteria and indicators speak to laws, policy and regulation, whereas those at the level of local forest management units help adjust management to meet established national goals. Debate also has moved towards the ideal of a globally-harmonised system which could become the background for a Forests Convention (or alternatives to it) and globally-standardised quality control for sustainable timber production (FAO 2000). Convenors of separate processes initially resisted this move, some of whom have been concerned about the capacity of poorer countries to negotiate their interests.[28] Nevertheless influential international organisations have endorsed a set of common principles, summarised in Box 2.1:

Box 2.1
WWF/World Bank criteria for forest sustainability (Simmula and Oy 1999)

The WWF/WB Alliance believes that a common set of principles that should under-score any standard for improving forest management should include: (a) compliance with all relevant laws; (b) clear definition, documentation and legal establishment of tenure and use rights; (c) recognition and respect of the legal and customary rights of indigenous peoples to own, use and manage their lands, territories and resources; (d) maintenance and enhancement of the long-term social and economic well-being of forest workers and communities; (e) efficient use of the forests multiple products and services to ensure economic viability and a wide range of environmental and social services; (f) maintenance of the ecological functions and integrity of the forest; (g) a written, implemented and updated management plan with long-term objectives of management and means of achieving them; (h) appropriate monitoring and as-sessment of the condition of the forest, yields of forest products, chain of custody, management activities and their social and environmental impacts; (i) maintenance of natural forests including primary forests, well developed secondary forests, and sites of major environmental, social and cultural significance, and (j) appropriate design and management of plantations.

International tension between those seeking to assure sustainability through a 'Forests Convention', and those who advocate market mechanisms has informed the debate. For the former, Criteria and Indicators provide a mechanism for international harmonisation which is compatible with a Convention. For the latter, Criteria and Indicators are seen as a way to provide benchmarks for timber certification, as a market-based mechanism to improve forest management. Several national initiatives (e.g. in Ghana) have been undertaken, balancing price premiums to be gained through certification, and the market restrictions that non-certified timber would face. Overall this has provided the impetus to harmonise national Criteria and Indicators with globally and regionally agreed ones (WCFSD 1997).

Several international organisations have emerged and grown in conjunction with these debates. The Forest Stewardship Council is already the major inter-national organisation involved in certifying timber for trade. It emerged out of pressure from green consumers in northern countries, and lobbying by NGOs, such as the WorldWide Fund for Nature. This encouraged some timber coun-tries and governments to regulate their timber supplies – or at least make claims to do so. From 1990, there were calls for a system of independent timber certi-fication, to bring order to what had become a 'confused and confusing market place' (Dudley *et al.* 1995: 143). NGO lobbying led the World Bank to advo-cate systems of timber eco-labelling in its 1991 forest policy. The same year, the Forest Stewardship Council was established as an independent non-profit NGO to evaluate and accredit certifiers, as well as to develop certification initia-tives worldwide. The dominance of certification concerns (despite claims that

Criteria and Indicators address forest management more broadly) is illustrated by the point-for-point similarity of the WWF/World Bank criteria with those of the Forest Stewardship Council,[29] from which they were derived (Simmula and Oy 1999). More recently, the World Commission on Forests and Sustainable Development has advocated the establishment of a Forest Management Council, to establish and monitor sustainable management standards in countries and assist their international harmonisation.

Although certification is a market-based approach, it is linked to a strongly bureaucratic and managerialist regimen, requiring the establishment and maintenance of detailed forest management plans. That these impose costs – additional to the payments required to certification organisations – have led to questions about their appropriateness to developing countries, and particularly to small forest projects within them (Carter 1996: 272). The benefits of certification to a country also depend on the extent to which it is exporting a significant quantity of produced timber (as opposed to using it domestically), on national structures of forest control, and on the extent to which access to markets paying a premium for certified timber can be guaranteed and sustained. Each is problematic for many low-income countries.

Decentralisation and community forestry

The need to address local forest users' concerns has been a pervasive theme in recent international discussions of forestry and forest conservation, conforming with the ethos of participation and community involvement which have become strategic objectives for donor agencies, NGOs and governments alike. Small-scale projects linking 'communities' with NGOs or donors have also been joined by an array of new partnerships between local users and the state and/or private sector organisations. A variety of terms have evolved to describe these arrangements, with overlapping meanings, whether community-based forest management; joint forest management (particularly in the Indian context); collaborative forest management, forest co-management or participatory forest management. Whatever the term 'the thrust of the approach lies in the assumption that collaboration between communities and other partners might lead to better management while ensuring sustainable livelihoods for forest-dependent people' (Dubois and Lowore 2000: 1).

The move to participation/decentralisation has emerged from a powerful convergence of at least four dimensions, including a critique of past experience of centralised forest management and its ineffectiveness in assuring sustainability; decentralisation in the broader structuring of government; traditions of community-based development in other fields, and approaches or social movements demanding equity, empowerment and rights. Decentralisation and participation are being incorporated as key principles within international agreements addressing forestry or biodiversity more broadly. For example participation, decentralisation and recognition of traditional rights and tenure are key principles within the National Forest Programmes recommended by the Inter-governmental Forum on Forests. Agenda 21, agreed at Rio in 1992, strongly advocated a combination of government decentralisation, devolution to local communities of responsibility for natural resources held as commons, and community participation (Holmberg *et al.* 1993). Principle 2 of the Convention on Biodiversity's Ecosystem Approach is that 'management should be decentralised to the lowest appropriate level' noting that the 'community' is often the appropriate functional unit and that 'empowerment of local stakeholders' should accompany it.[30]

This has become a vibrant field for applied social science research, with international forest policy research institutions sometimes providing umbrellas for funding and publication. Numerous studies have appeared from diverse disciplines, and with academic or donor funding but claims to policy 'use' which explore, elaborate and critique concepts and applications of community management in forestry.[31]

Because experiences of community-based forestry are inherently 'local', international debate has been heavily informed by the commissioning of overview studies, and by workshops which collate experiences and attempt to draw general lessons from them. The World Bank and FAO, for instance, commissioned a review of community-government partnerships in the forestry sector in Africa (Dubois and Lowore 2000) to contribute to the FAO's Forestry Outlook Study for Africa and to the World Bank's reform of its regional forestry strategy. The then ODA undertook a review of 'key factors, best practice and ways forward' in sharing forest management (Bird 1996; ODA 1996). International NGOs have also prepared overviews (e.g. Kerkhof 2000). Several international networks aim to collate and disseminate experience with community-based approaches in forestry. This was, for example, one aim of the Forests, Trees and People Programme managed by the Community Forestry Unit of FAO in Rome until recently (e.g. FAO 1997). Participatory and co-management approaches have been major themes of the Network Papers and other publications of the Rural Development Forestry Network managed by the London-based Overseas Development Institute (e.g. Brown 1999).

Although there is convergence, internationally co-ordinated reflection nevertheless reveals tensions between those emphasising benefits for managerial efficiency and those placing greater emphasis on local empowerment (and state disempowerment). In international agreements, such tensions have been accommodated in the co-existence of somewhat contradictory principles. Equally, there are tensions between 'managerialist' perspectives identifying the common structuring with 'design principles' for successful community forestry, and those emphasising local specificity and dynamism as all-important. For the latter, all situations are said to be different, precluding generalisable principles and arguing for their replacement with more flexible 'navigational aids' (Dubois and Lowore 2000). The process of developing and enacting community forest management is also presented as dynamic and unpredictable, requiring a 'learning process approach' (ODA 1996: 15) both overall and for each step. The need for flexibility to adapt to year-to-year changes – for instance in climatic or market conditions – is seen to make formal long term plans inappropriate (Kerkhof 2000). CIFOR, for instance, has been undertaking comparative case study research on 'Adaptive Co-Management', which aims to develop models, tools and strategies to enhance the ability of management systems to be 'self-improving', recognising this as necessary given the dynamic ecological and multi-stakeholder settings encountered in tropical forest environments.[32]

Nevertheless these emphases on uncertainty dovetail with a further recurring image in international discussions: of community forestry initiatives as 'experimental'. International reviews of experience themselves have the effect of imaging the cases they draw on, so frequently boxed as examples, as 'test cases' from which lessons can be drawn, within an international field of learning and comparison. Lowore and Dubois elaborate explicitly on the centrality of 'project' experiences in this respect:

As 'experimental laboratories', projects are often authorised to try innovative arrangements. . . . Indeed, it is mainly via projects that success stories on CNRM [community natural resource management] are known and reported beyond the local level. . . . This does not mean that success stories occur only in the context of projects. In many instances, they happen without being noticed by outsiders. Nonetheless, projects often seem to play a catalyst role in good CNRM. Yet, this privilege may stem precisely from their artificial, non-political and limited (both in time and scope), hence non-threatening character vis-à-vis existing power structures in the 'real world' (2000: 44).

Extending this suggestion, one might argue that it is through this process of laboratorisation, that non-project community forestry – and indeed broader society and forest use – are being imagined as if they were actual or potential projects, and thus de-politicised.

In these ways, international research and networking – co-ordinated by some key international organisations – have provided a frame that at the same time justifies and lends legitimacy to local initiatives, but also feeds off them, in doing so coming to represent them in very particular ways.

Conclusions

This chapter has briefly sketched out a transforming international context within which science and policy are conducted, and some emerging relations between them. The multiplication of internal forums and organisations dealing with environmental issues coincided with a proliferation in non-governmental organisation and business interests in environment, and new forms of alliance between these. The international 'machineries' (Knorr-Cetina 1999) producing knowledge about tropical forests are constituted within the activities of these organisations, and the meetings, funding flows, networks and forms of documentation which link them.

It is clear that international policy deliberations are interlocked with the conduct of science in a variety of forms of co-production. Particular forums within which policy deliberations take place have developed relationships with particular scientific institutions. On the one hand there is plenty of overlap, and studies carried out for one forum prove useful to others. But on the other hand there are tensions between these which are shaping imagery and reputability.

The sheer mass of institutions and organisations involved can be examined as self sustaining, generating around itself a vortex into which researchers and organisations influencing policy are drawn, producing a community of broadly common focus if not of common interest and approach. Important parts of the vortex around 'Tropical Forest International' – and those of particular focus in this book – concern biodiversity and sustainable forest management, each of which has come to attract its own community of theorists, researchers, advocates, programmes and funding.

Linked to this internationalisation of the machineries of knowledge production has been an internationalisation of the frames of reference in which environment is understood and debated. One aspect of this is a focus on global dimensions of tropical forests; their implications for global environmental change, global biodiversity, global carbon emissions and so on. A second is the establishment of internationalised terms and questions through which local dynamics are conceptualised, problematics discerned and policies/programmes elaborated; whether in the terms of community forestry and co-management, best practice in ecosystem conservation and so on. In this, local experiences are drawn on and up into international vortices through specific routes, and filtered through particular institutional frames and their conceptual lenses.

The science/policy processes in particular countries which we later explore in specific cases cannot be understood without considering how national political economy, social processes and scientific traditions interplay with such stereotyping internationally, and with experiences of this vortex.

Research and policy, even when conducted amongst international organisations, increasingly attempts to embrace local diversity and particularities, as well as to incorporate perspectives of 'the poor', 'the indigenous' and 'the marginalised', and the perspectives of poorer governments. Yet these concerns have developed in ways which mean the production and incorporation of 'locality' is structured and circumscribed to generate consensus and conformity in knowledge and approaches to management of the forest in ways that are beyond the influence of any individual or organisation. One dimension of this is the creation and reproduction of a range of social stereotypes within the vortex: from the slash-and-burn farmer to the eco-friendly indigenous person; from the deforesting migrant to the well-organised traditional community; from the rapacious logger to the responsible 'green' business; from the corrupt government official to the noble conservation professional. In these ways, there has been a 'globalisation' of the local, as localities are configured within the international vortex, coming to be seen in terms of the common currency of global scientific and policy arenas.

Later chapters, conversely, examine how the concepts and ideas dominant in 'Tropical Forest International' become practised and transformed in their enaction in particular settings. They will illustrate the numerous routes through which international scientific and policy processes are animating those in national settings. These include influences on national policy and agenda-setting through international conventions, donor conditionalities and policy reviews; the creation of 'nodes' in national governments which are responsible for attending/negotiating with international organisations and conventions; obligation, encouragement and finance to produce national strategies and action plans to implement international agreements; short and longer-term work by international advisors in countries; internationally-funded programmes and projects; donor-funding to universities and research institutions, and more broadly, the setting of intellectual and practical agendas to which national academics, government departments and NGOs come to speak. At the same time national processes are inflected by their subordination to new forms of regionalisation; through regional policy reviews, regional priority-setting, and regional policy and scientific networks.

Sayer once lamented that 'The real problem with placing nature conservation in the hands of big international bureaucracies is that conservation can only succeed if it is based on a thorough understanding of local ecological, social and economic conditions. Big international organisations are not good at this. They like simple, standardised solutions to problems' (Sayer 1996:1). He goes on: 'The best national personnel have all been assigned as counterparts to the experts . . . All the money and best people are involved in writing plans or strategies and the persons responsible for managing the resources on the ground are marginalised' (Sayer 1996: 6).

Nevertheless these processes intersect with the histories and practices of science and policy in particular countries, and by no means always by subordinating them to international homogeneity. An important aspect of the cases is to consider how 'independent', 'critical' research in universities, and alternative framings in local knowledge, or a combination of these in citizen science, comes to engage with wider scientific and policy processes, and how the configuration of science and policy, and the practising of knowledge is implicated in social and intellectual marginalisation where this does occur.

In respect of their location within internationalised scientific and policy processes, there are major differences – and yet similarities – between West Africa and the Caribbean, and Guinea and Trinidad within them. It is to these comparative national settings that the next chapter turns.

Notes

1. Whilst it is often stated that there has been a shift in resource governance from national to international, regional and local, this may be overly characterising past governance as 'national', overlooking the ways that 'nations' have always been part of international and regional worlds, and have always been composed of localised factions; the stuff of real politics. So we should be cautious in portraying the present 'global world' in contrast to a 'nationalist' myth of an independent past. But whilst all these levels of influence may have been relevant, they have certainly changed in shape.
2. A number of such internationally-supported policy reviews have been conducted around forest issues in West Africa and the Caribbean, including FAO (1998).
3. This trend was highlighted by the head of Greenpeace campaigns who explained that during an international summit 'over 100 governments discussed the protection of the ozone layer [while] just twelve companies made the gases that destroyed it' (Rose 1996: 31, in Fabig and Boele 1999: 59).
4. Interview, senior forestry advisor, Food and Agriculture Organisation, Rome, 31 May 1999.
5. In sketching out key dimensions of these networks we do not attempt focused analysis of how particular organisations have developed their agendas, as shaped by their histories and organisational sociologies. Others have attempted such analyses: good, relevant examples include Wade's study of environmental policy at the World Bank (Wade 1997) and Brechin's organisational sociology of forestry activities at FAO, the World Bank and the NGO CARE (Brechin 1997).
6. *http://www.un.org/esa/sustdev/ipf/htm*, 25 June 2000.
7. E.g. Interview, Biodiversity co-ordinator in National Environment Directorate, Conakry, 15 March 1999.
8. Interview, senior forestry advisor, FAO, Rome, 31 May 1999.
9. *http://www.fao.org/forestry/*, July 1999.
10. Interview, senior FRA 2000 staff member, FAO, Rome, 31 May 1999.
11. Ibid.
12. Pilot Analysis of Global Ecosystems, PAGE.
13. *http://www.wri.org/wr2000/forests_page_execsumm.html*, July 1999.
14. *http://www.wri.org/press/fao_fra5.html* 9 June 2001.
15. *www.wcmc.org.uk/biodev/*, 20 June 2000.
16. Interview, senior forestry advisor, FAO, Rome, 31 May 1999.
17. Ibid.
18. Interview, Forestry Division staff member, FAO, Rome, 31 May 1999.
19. http://wbln0018.worldbank.org/essd/forestpol-e.nsf, July 2000.
20. *www.wcmc.org.uk/biodev/* 20 June 2000.
21. Interview, senior policy advisor, Forestry Division, FAO, Rome, 1 June 1999.

22. Examples of such networking/communication activities include the Overseas Development Institute-managed Rural Development Forestry Network; the former FAO co-ordinated Forests, Trees and People programme, and the WWF co-ordinated Tropical Forests Portfolio.
23. These include FAO, the UN Development Programme and UNESCO, the World Bank, the International Union for the Conservation of Nature, the WorldWide Fund for Nature and the World Conservation Monitoring Centre.
24. World Conservation Union, 3rd World Congress on National Parks and Protected Areas, Bali. Bali Action Plan.
25. *http://www.hp.com/ghp/features/wwf/index2.html*, June 2000.
26. Article 2 of the Convention.
27. These include the ITTO; Pan-European, Montreal, Tarapoto, Dry Zone Africa, Near East, Central American; African Timber Organization (ATO), and WWF/Forest Stewardship Council processes and initiatives. CIFOR and other international forestry research institutions are conducting their own related research programmes.
28. Interview, senior forestry advisor, FAO, Rome, 5 June 1999.
29. *www.fscus.org*, 15 July 2000.
30. *http://www.cbd.org*, July 2000.
31. This large literature includes, as just a brief selection of examples, discussions around the 'design principles' for successful community forestry (e.g. Ostrom 1999); the notions of ecology or community deployed (e.g. Leach *et al.* 1997, 1999; Guijt and Shah 1997; Western, Wright and Strum 1994; Li 1996), and discussions and critiques of assumptions about participation or accountability (e.g. Sharpe 1998; Ribot 1995, 1999).
32. *www.cgiar.org/cifor/research/projects/Adaptive.html*, 26 March 2000.

3   Science and policy in Trinidad and Guinea: comparative settings

Introduction

This chapter lays out the ground for this book's comparative project. It provides a background to each of the countries, to contextualise the cases explored in subsequent chapters. We consider common elements, showing the sense in examining Trinidad and Guinea together, and the contrasts which make this comparison useful; dimensions of difference which will be important when deliberating the social relations of science and their effects. Thus we lay out the different settings – ecological, political, administrative, social and institutional – in which practices of science and policy unfold in Guinea and Trinidad. Such settings and structures are themselves shaped and re-shaped by scientific and policy practices, in ways which the subsequent cases will illustrate.

Forest ecological settings

The Republics of Trinidad and Tobago, and of Guinea, each have extremely diverse ecologies. Nevertheless, there are some important similarities between them. First and foremost, each has extensive areas of humid tropical forest. Neither the island of Trinidad nor the forest region of Guinea has true 'rain forest' however, at least as defined by Richards (1999), because they have drier, more pronounced seasonal climates, although modified in their montane areas. Second, there are areas of savanna fringing on these forests in each country, where debates concerning their status have focused on whether they are natural (edaphic) or anthropogenic.

   Both locations have featured in theoretical debates concerning the status of tropical forest plant communities. When Beard developed his own classificatory scheme in his classic *The Natural Vegetation of Trinidad* (1946a) it was in critical engagement with the leading ecologists of the time, Tansley, Chipp and Clements (see, for example, Tansley and Chipp 1926; Clements 1936). Beard was concerned with the relationship between 'climatic climax' (the type of plant community with the most complex structure and richest flora that can exist in a given climate) and the status of differentiations according to soil and

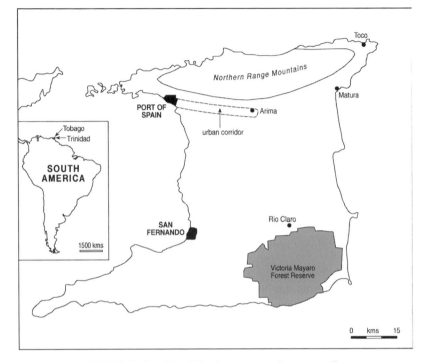

Map 3.1 Trinidad and localities important to the case studies

topography.[1] Similar questions were considered by leading French colonial botanists and ecologists for Guinea and its French West African neighbours (most notably Chevalier 1911; Aubréville 1949; Adam and Schnell 1949; see Fairhead and Leach 1996, 1998).

In Guinea, forest in the administrative 'forest region' came to be characterised as semi-deciduous forest (e.g. in South West Macenta prefecture) or as a mosaic of forest and savanna of the transition region (e.g. in Kissidougou and Gueckedou prefectures). The forests belong to the 'Upper Guinean Forest' (see Map 3.2). In Trinidad, Beard distinguished between the montane evergreen rain forests of the Northern Range, and assorted forms of seasonal evergreen forests covering much of the island such as that dominated by a single species, *Mora excelsa* (see Map 3.1). The vegetation is characteristic of the South American mainland, from which Trinidad has only recently been separated. That the silk cotton tree, *Ceiba pentandra*, has been the subject of reverence, and an indicator of historic settlement in both countries underscores their similar ecology, as does the economic importance each has given – at times – to tree crops suited to this ecology such as cocoa and coffee.

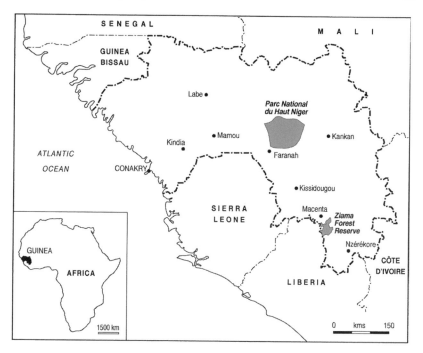

Map 3.2 Guinea and localities important to the case studies

The loss of forest cover, and its impacts on soil and climate (and on tree crops) became colonial preoccupations in both regions. Indeed, the reputed 'first forest reserve in the Western Hemisphere' was declared in Trinidad's twin-island Tobago in order to 'protect the rains' in the eighteenth century. It was concern over climate and soil which led, in the early twentieth century, to policies of forest reservation in both countries – in Trinidad of lands already under state control, in Guinea of lands that were alienated from African control. Both countries continue to manage these reserves, and forest reservation is important to relationships between the state and rural inhabitants in each.

Early analysts considered the vegetation formations as stable and in equi-librium with their present environment: formations which, if destroyed and not subsequently disturbed, would reappear through a succession of particu-lar stages of secondary vegetation (e.g. Beard 1946a, although see Aubréville 1937). Although historical climatic variation was understood as important for understanding current vegetation distribution, it was not recognised as impor-tant for current vegetation dynamics. And whilst the capacity of pre-colonial (and pre-Columbian) populations to shape vegetation was at times considered (e.g. in Beard 1946a), this was minimised, especially given ideas of that time concerning low historic populations and their limited capacity to transform vegetation. Attempts were therefore made to describe the 'natural' vegetation in each country.

The forests of both countries lie, however, in regions where more recent research indicates that larger populations have lived at times during the past several centuries (e.g. Boomert 1984; Fairhead and Leach 1996, 1998), and that there have been deeper and more recent climatic fluctuations (Tardy 1999; Maley 2001). Yet while the latter have been explored in both regions, the research and its implications still remain marginal to policy processes. The case studies track why this is so.

These common elements of ecology, of early science and policy, and their linkage have interplayed with very different policy and scientific settings since the colonial period, so it is important to consider the policy settings in each country in terms of political and economic history, and contemporary administrative and social structures. These settings themselves have shaped some important contrasts in the structuring of contemporary scientific research, particularly in the ways that national structures interlock with contemporary global concerns.

Political and economic settings

Trinidad

Modern Trinidad is suffused with global connections, through media, commerce and diaspora. Yet analysts of Trinidad's contemporary politics, society and economy inevitably find themselves to be historians, as global connectedness interplays with the specific history of slavery and its legacies in shaping ethnicity, society and the control of capital and labour – or at least representations of these.

Trinidad was populous in 1498 (Newson 1976: 31), but exactly how populous remains the subject of some debate. Amerindian inhabitants were shifting cultivators of cassava, sweet potatoes, cotton and a great variety of other crops, and had been for almost two thousand years. Their economy was locked into wide reaching trade networks, the water-borne nature of which strongly influenced settlement patterns (Boomert 1984). Population estimates from the sixteenth century vary from a low of 35,000 to a high of about 200,000. Certainly, the substantial pre-Colombian population suffered catastrophically as European powers struggled for control and by 1634, it is estimated that there were only 4,000 Amerindians on the island (Boomert 1984; Newson 1976).

When Spain gained control, it found it hard to attract Spanish settlers, so the island soon became all but deserted. From the 1770s, Spanish authorities encouraged settlement by granting land to any French speaking 'refugees' from the French and Haitian revolutions who could bring slaves. When the British acquired the island by capture in 1797, followed by formal transfer in 1802, they took over this capacity to grant 'Crown' land. Land was granted mainly to those establishing plantations using slave labour imported initially from various parts of West Africa and then, after the African slave trade was abolished in 1807, illegally from other islands until slavery itself was abolished in 1838. Even at this date less than 5 per cent of the island was cultivated, and the 'Crown' controlled the rest. Crown land was not widely granted to freed slaves, forcing them to become wage labourers. Nevertheless, many former slaves preferred to squat illegally on state land. Thus the 'labour shortage' question initially resolved through slavery became one to be resolved in part through control over squatting (Pemberton 1996; Brereton 1981). These issues of labour supply and squatting intersected with debates concerning the destructiveness of African land use, environmental decline and forest reservation. In short – and in ways which Chapter 5 will consider more fully – limiting land access through environmental control could serve to maintain the labour supply to plantations.

Such control failed to solve labour shortages. Plantation owners therefore attempted to import further labourers from West Africa and North America, and then encouraged Portuguese and Chinese-speakers to come to Trinidad as indentured labourers. The majority of the latter did not continue in estate work, and many instead became involved in trading occupations where they were joined after the First World War by Lebanese ('Syrians') (Yelvington 1993). From 1845, a more decisive solution to the labour supply problem was sought in the import of indentured labourers from India. More than 144,000 arrived before the scheme ended in 1917. Although a return passage home was guaranteed at the end of a labourer's five-year contract, most chose to forego this in exchange for land. Thus to Trinidad's 'plantocracy' and to those of African ancestry, was added a third major population of South Asian origin. This history is reflected in current census statistics, however controversial, indicating 41% of people of 'Indian' origin, 41% of 'African' origin, 16.5% 'mixed' including Carib, Lebanese, and Venezeuelan, 1% white and 0.5% Chinese (Miller 1997).

Many analysts of the Caribbean have described how the divisions of labour in the nineteenth-century colonial economy established ethnic and gender-based forms of stratification which – despite important changes during the century – have left enduring legacies. Wilson (1973) argues for a pervasive cultural dualism which contrasts masculine ideas of 'reputation' (linked to anti-institutional and anti-hierarchical values and behaviour) with feminine ideas of 'respectability' (linked to hierarchy, church and domestic life; see also Abrahams 1983; Olwig 1993). Other analyses highlight class or ethnicity rather than gender. Thus for Trinidad, the social (and colour) relations of slavery are argued to have been reproduced now in the class relations of capitalism (Brereton 1981; Braithwaite 1975; Yelvington 1993), where the slave-owning plantocracy has come to occupy the apex of a capital-owning pigmentocracy. This stems from early nineteenth-century divisions when Europeans formed a plantation-owning and administrative elite; coloureds/creoles tended to be in intermediate or professional occupations, and people of African and Indian origin were slaves, agricultural labourers or smallholder-farmers.

When legal changes from the 1860s enabled crown lands to be sold to smallholders, many squatters purchased their holdings, as did many former Indian indentured labourers, creoles, West Indian immigrants (descendants of African slaves and creoles from other islands), and peons (immigrants from Venezuela). Taking advantage of the cocoa boom (1866–1920), they transformed much forest to tree crops. Among the workers who remained on the estates, those of Indian ancestry generally took over more of the labour-intensive estate tasks, while those with African ancestry moved into more skilled occupations (Yelvington 1993). Increasingly, though, many 'Africans' eschewed agriculture altogether, to become urban-based in and around the growing capital, Port of Spain. With most 'Indians' remaining in agriculture, especially in the centre and south of the island, there was geographical as well as social distancing between 'Indian' and 'African' populations. This, when combined with the colonial elite's justifications for the labour arrangements they depended on, encouraged the development of stereotypes about 'ethnic' character and behaviour; stereotypes which may have originated in elite oratory, but which became appropriated within broader society (Yelvington 1993). This has had an enduring influence in ethnic differentiation throughout the twentieth century, as labour markets and administrative capacities have co-evolved with ethnic stereotyping. This continually tempers the otherwise considerable occupational overlaps, syncretism and cultural borrowing between groups.

Compared with agriculture, timber was not central to Trinidad's early economy. In the nineteenth and early twentieth centuries Trinidad imported much of its timber, despite large timber resources on private land and on the half of the island which remained forested state land. In the 1930s the first major sawmill was installed but it did not operate at anything near the estimated potential annual production. Timber imports continued, largely from Guyana. The port and milling infrastructure had already grown up around it, keeping it profitable.

The cocoa price and economy collapsed in the 1930s, and many plantations were abandoned and labourers were laid off. Many turned to crop cultivation on abandoned cocoa lands as tenants or squatters, with the resulting land use conversion instigating concerns with deforesation and erosion especially in the steep hillsides of the Northern range. Elsewhere, abandoned cocoa plantations reverted to forest. The collapse of agricultural economies also accentuated a move to the towns, especially by 'Africans', and greater emphasis on sugar cane in the centre and south west of the island dominated by 'Indians'. By this stage, however, the oil resources which had been discovered both on and off-shore early in the twentieth century were making a major contribution to the economy, and stimulated the growth of petrochemical and other spin-off industries.

Political struggle against colonialism began from the early twentieth century or before, and culminated in Independence in 1962. Early anti-colonial movements tended to submerge ethnic differences, such as in the linked struggles of (largely black) oilfield workers and (largely Indian) sugar workers, in the context of the Caribbean-wide labour movements of the 1930s. However as Yelvington argues, the party politics after the Second World War led political candidates to make overt appeals to ethnicity in order to become elected – effecting an 'institutionalisation of ethnic politics' (1993: 12). The People's National Movement (PNM) led by radical intellectual Eric Williams attracted a largely black following. It was opposed in the 1956 elections by the People's Democratic Party, led by the leader of both the Hindu religious organisation and sugar workers union. The PNM led the country to Independence and throughout the 1960s and 1970s held power over a series of opposition 'Indian' parties.

The PNM extolled 'creolisation' and 'nationalism' to forge a new nation which, it claimed, would erase ethnic difference. The cultural symbols of nationalism – steel band, calypso and carnival – were, however, widely interpreted as African-derived, while many Indian cultural practices were labelled as racist and unpatriotic. Non-blacks were given government posts perceived as token, however prominent. This has left an enduring mark on the civil service which has subsequently been seen as 'African' dominated, but with certain parts, such as the Forestry Division, as exceptions. This itself followed particular colonial practices of staffing and training. Claims for a new non-ethnic politics and culture were also contradicted by the European models which many societal institutions retained (in schools, churches, courts, newspapers) and continued multi-national and white domination of capital and economy (Forte 2000).

High oil prices from 1973–83 were accompanied by a boom in employment and construction which enabled a shift in lifestyle and outlook for an emerging middle class and even for many of the poor. This distinguished Trinidad from the rest of the Caribbean which remained mainly dependent on tourism and agriculture, not oil. A consumer boom intensified material and cultural relations with the United States, and its characteristic fast food, shopping malls, TV and car-culture. At the same time oil exploration and the construction boom put increased pressure on Trinidad's forests (Figure 3.1).

The structural limitations to economic redistribution during the boom prompted a 'Black Power' movement in the 1970s (Oxaal 1982; Sutton 1983), forcing the PNM into a more redistributive mode. This made both the patrimonial and ethnicised character of the state more obvious. A discredited PNM eventually lost power to a multi-ethnic National Alliance for Reconstruction (NAR). Their election, however, coincided with oil price collapse and economic

Figure 3.1 Oil pipelines through Victoria Mayaro Forest Reserve

recession, and intensified appeals for state patronage on ethnic grounds splintered the party itself (Premdas 1993).

The collapse of the oil economy in the late 1980s left Trinidad vulnerable to the strictures of IMF-led structural adjustment, and a contraction in the government sector. The resulting crisis in state-led development underlay the new government's policy to promote private property and enterprise, the formation of non-governmental and community organisations, and economic diversification. Tourism was prominent in this, in a strategy which combined Tobago's beach tourism with Trinidad's carnival culture on the one hand, and its ecotourism potential on the other. Successive administrations have continued this strategy, including the Indian-led United National Congress (UNC) of Basdeo Panday from 1995 to 1999.

This history has shaped the current complex patterning of livelihoods in Trinidad. Official statistics indicate that only 10 per cent of the population is dependent on agriculture, which itself accounts for only 2–3 per cent of GDP. Still fewer have timber-based livelihoods (notably the 'woodworkers' who fell timber, and sawmillers who convert it). Of those farming, a high proportion are smallholders and labourers on government sugar plantations. Some entrepreneurial youth (stereotypically 'Indian') have more recently been investing in valuable emergent niche crops such as melons and cristophene. Larger scale farming of sugar cane, rice, coconuts, cocoa and livestock (also stereotypically 'Indian') continues. It is often said that 'Africans' eschew farming due to its historical associations with slavery, but many more still depend in some way on the land within diversified livelihoods, combining employment or income from remittances with 'backyard' horticulture, hunting and so on. The nearly three-quarters of the population living in urban areas – and others who commute from rural homes – engage with forests largely through recreation including hunting; some wealthier urbanites have acquired second homes in attractive coastal and forest settings. Many aspects of rural livelihoods operate on the margins of legality, or beyond it, whether amidst ambiguous land, hunting and timber rights, or linked to marijuana cultivation in secluded areas. In certain forest reserves drug cultivation has created no-go areas protected by 'trap guns' triggered by trip-wires.

New processes are fuelling ethnic identification. Increased competition for resources and social mobility in post-oil boom recession has been joined by opportunities and pressures to market (ethnic) cultural values through business and tourism. Examples include the invention of a new Carib community, (re)vitalising Amerindian ancestry but organised as a limited company capable of marketing cultural products and tourism. This is animated by the new valuation of indigenous peoples in international organisations, and their networks and funding (Forte 2000). Reconnection with diasporic and cultural links, or at least more confident public performance of this, also characterises contemporary 'rasta', 'Hindu' and 'African' cultures such as 'Orisha' worship which now emphasises West African Yoruba authenticity. Alongside the more globalised lives that 'Trinis' lead, with migration having created many diasporic links to the United States and Britain, these emergent identifications go further to weaken the centrality of the Trinidad state apparatus and its nationalistic appeals, while reinvigorating ideas of ethnic primordialism more generally. The ethnicisation of politics is also dynamised by the knife-edge electoral balance between parties appealing to African and Indian constituencies. The effect, some argue, is to generate a political populism and a reluctance to implement unpopular measures, as well as to magnify investments and promises in marginal constituencies.

Miller (1997) sees these re-vitalisations of ethnicity as part of a broader and more fundamental transformation, arguing that in the region's modernity, a 'particular consciousness of time, may challenge customary morality, and the given criteria by which life is judged, creating a new fragility in which people become more conscious of the processes of self creation, and the creation of the principles by which they judge themselves' (1997: 16). While to some extent this echoes Beck's (1992) portrayal of a transition to reflexive modernity, Miller argues that in the context of Trinidad a pervasive dualism remains. Transient values (ephemeral, fragmented, individualistic – so strongly expressed at carnival, in street culture and recreational 'liming') exist in tension with transcendent ones (in stable institutions, religiosity and descent – epitomised in Christmas festivals and indoor domestic life). Viewed in this way, 'much of the specific content of ethnic stereotyping [in academe and broader culture alike] and the contemporary experience of ethnicity is the result of the use of ethnic groups to objectify a dualism whose source lies elsewhere' (1997: 15). Whether or not one accepts Miller's argument about modernity, his analysis does emphasise the practised, performed ways in which social objectifications take place. As we show, scientific and policy practices provide similar contexts for the objectification of social categories such as ethnicity, although rooted in material processes and institutional turf battles, as much as in 'culture'.

Guinea

Guinea's current status as one of the poorest countries in the world contrasts with its earlier history. Much of its current territory lay at the heart of the vast, powerful and wealthy Mande empire in the thirteenth to sixteenth centuries, and provided a conduit for the major trade routes linking the Sahara and savannas with the Atlantic coast. Rice, fonio, cotton and cattle formed the mainstay of agricultural economies supporting populous landscapes, whether in the Mande heartland of what is now Upper Guinea, the Fouta Djallon or in what is now the south-eastern Forest region. Iron smelting and artisanal gold production date back more than a millennium. With the empire's decline, shifting political alliances intersected with struggles to control a vibrant trading economy, rich natural resources, and European trade in slaves, arms, iron and other goods.

Within this region, and extending across what is now Sierra Leone and Liberia, complex migrations and shifting alliances created polities that were frequently multi-lingual, bringing together and sometimes creolising speakers of the main language groups (Mande and West Atlantic) and their dialects (Dapper 1668; D'Azevedo 1962). Many cultural practices such as family histories and prohibitions, initiation practices, secret societies and relations with spiritual 'forces of nature', transcended language groups, although there were local variants. The idiom of 'primacy of arrival' in a territory as a source of authority over subsequent arrivals was an important fulcrum in local politics, their rhetorics of power and control over land and resources (Murphy and Bledsoe 1987).

Large areas were depopulated in the nineteenth century during wars linked with European and American 'colonisation' projects (Person 1968–75; Fairhead *et al.* 2003). Eventually, French colonising forces consolidated the territory and Guinea became a distinct colony within French West Africa (AOF). By the 1930s the relatively low populations in many regions, often in proximity to what were new wildernesses grown over abandoned farmland, enabled both colonial administrators and anthropologists to describe primitive, isolated and distinct peoples and cultures in some kind of engagement with 'natural' environments (e.g. Germain 1984; Paulme 1954).

The French divided the territory into regions corresponding to colonial perceptions of nature and of cultural and linguistic dominance: Upper Guinea in the Mande dominated savannas; Middle Guinea focused on the Peuhl dominated highlands of the Fouta Djallon; Forest Guinea in the south-east, inhabited by Kissi, Toma, Guerze; and Lower Guinea near the coast. Thus over the rather fluid political and cultural matrix, colonial divisions and administrative perceptions served to consolidate ethnic identities and cultural regions. To some extent, these did link with political fractures which had emerged by the late nineteenth century (e.g. between expansionist Peuhl and Mande polities, and around trade-linked alliances in Forest Guinea); yet colonisation helped to cement a multiplicity of more located tensions into power blocs of ethnic character.

Regions were divided into administrative 'cercles' overseen by French administrators, and cercles were in turn divided into 'cantons' according to French interpretations of extant political units and authority. African canton chiefs were appointed and increasingly had to combine local legitimacy with compliance. They were responsible for taxation in money, goods and labour, and for implementing colonial policy. The legal basis of occupation maintained 'customary' rights, including tenure over land and trees (Arcin 1908). Yet the French administration claimed the rights to reserve for the state lands which were – or could be – deemed vacant and without holders. As in other French colonies, this was the primary mechanism used to create forest reserves, often in depopulated areas (Fairhead and Leach 1998).

The colonial administration was ruthless in its recruitment of rural labour from the forest region for porterage and railway-building and to serve a developing plantation economy centred in regions more accessible to the coast. Nevertheless, from the 1930s until independence in 1958, smallholders in the more inaccessible forest region participated in a booming coffee and rice economy, whereas in Upper Guinea economic policy focused on modernisation and mechanisation of rice cultivation. The buoyant post-Second World War economy in the 1950s was associated with an increase in administrative capacity – and with increased Guinean opposition to it. The politics of independence had begun and the regime had to respond to internal dissent, organised movements such as the trades unions and the rise of opposition parties (Rivière 1974).

Whereas Guinea's francophone neighbours continued a strong association with France after Independence, Guinea's leaders took a radically different path. Under President Sekou Touré, the new Republic of Guinea pursued African socialism, forging links with the Cold War communist bloc. It pursued a series of campaigns in the modernist spirit of 'La Révolution': tractorisation, demystification and abolition of customary chieftaincies and secret society ceremonies; collective production, work brigades, and later state farms; and state attempts to control trade through a command economy. The experience – at least among most rural people – was of an extractive and impoverishing political economy, with the collapse of coffee and livestock profitability provoking large-scale emigration of people and cattle herds.

While promoting African nationalism, Sekou Touré's regime was also perceived by many as favouring Malinke-speakers (of which he was one) and their cultural symbols, discriminating against forest peoples and particularly the Peuhl. The regime thus fuelled regional ethnic rivalries already consolidated in the colonial period. Ethnic identities were also sharpened through language and religion. The five largest language groups were imposed as the media for primary, secondary and even some tertiary education. Religious differentiation came broadly to divide those following Islam (albeit syncretically with existing cultural practices), principally the Malinke, Peuhl and Susu, and those in the forest region more influenced by Christianity.

The gold mines which had financed the Mali empire and fuelled the French colonial economy turned out to be the tip of a Guinean mineral iceberg which gradually became apparent throughout the twentieth century, and included bauxite, iron and diamonds. Even at the height of Guinea's integration with the communist bloc, American mineral firm enclaves were established to export bauxite. Alongside multinational mining interests and their national partners, artisanal mining of gold and diamonds has continued. But the difficulty of regulating and taxing the trade of easily smuggleable diamonds has limited the contribution which Guinea's rich mineral resources have made to national budgets. They have certainly not provided the basis for a prosperous industrial economy comparable to oil in Trinidad. Yet these resources (and foreign aid) have enabled and maintained a political and economic field strongly shaped by patronage.

A week after the death of Sekou Touré in 1984, a military coup led by Lansana Conte instigated a military regime. In 1993, his 'Party for Unity and Progress' (PUP) won multi-party elections under a new democratic constitution. From the outset Conte's liberal political and economic regime gained considerable rural sympathy as it reduced rural exactions. The new regime encouraged foreign investment, foreign-funded development projects and foreign ministerial advisors – now mainly from Europe and the United States – and embraced a series of economic and legal reform programmes ('Structural Adjustment') to meet the conditionalities for IMF loans.

By the 1990s, policies of political decentralisation were in place, establishing elected officers for 'Rural Development Committees' (CRDs) that operate at the level of the sub-prefecture (within the Prefectures which superceded colonial cercles). By the mid-1990s, neo-liberal reforms had also led to lay-offs from the public service, the transfer of responsibility for many state functions from central to more local budgets, and an emphasis on private sector and NGO contracts to perform previous state functions. Most NGO staff had formerly worked within government institutions.

Currently most people in the forest region and Upper Guinea live in rural villages, deriving livelihoods from agriculture, natural resources and small-scale trade. While there is continuous outmigration, rural life continues to depend strongly on the land within technical, social and cultural framings which maintain strong continuities with past eras. Yet the towns and cities are growing rapidly, not only the coastal capital Conakry, but also regional towns and trading centres such as Kissidougou and Kankan. High urban unemployment means that back migration is also occurring, and even well-qualified people often find farming a more secure livelihood strategy.

The development of multi-party politics has accentuated ethnic tension. Despite policies to prevent parties forming along ethnic lines, they have done so. In particular the PUP is considered to represent the coast and forest, the Guinean Peoples Assembly (RPG) the Mande region, and other parties, the Peuhl of the Fouta Djallon. Both the 1993 and 1998 elections generated dissatisfaction with procedures and results, with many Mande suggesting that they were rigged. Those working as government employees are frequently interpreted by others as belonging to the PUP and its patronage networks. The political balance is delicate, but it has not led to political populism. This is partly because 'Politics' is not conducted with the electorate so much as in the shifting alliances between the multiple parties. Party politics remains remote from the lives of many voters.

Current political tensions are compounded by those over resource control, with resentment and conflicts over foreign-controlled and elite-mediated mining and aid enclaves and the granting of timber concessions with very little spin-off for local populations. In 2000–01, Guinea's forest region was engulfed in conflict linked with the protracted civil wars on its borders – in Liberia from 1989, and in Sierra Leone from 1991. Throughout the 1990s, Guinea was a major military presence in the international forces deployed in these countries. Many former emigrants have returned, while the country has also received hundreds of thousands of refugees. As the borderlands of Guinea have the diamond, gold and timber resources associated with conflict and warlordism across its

Table 3.1 *Comparative human development statistics for Trinidad and Tobago and for Guinea, 2000*

	Guinea	Trinidad and Tobago
Population	7.3 million	1.3 million
Human Development Index (out of 174)	162 (low)	50 (medium)
Life expectancy at birth	46.9 years	74 years
Infant mortality (per 1000)	124	16
Adult literacy (age 15+)	36%	93.4%
GDP/capita ($)	1,782	7,485
Agriculture as % GDP	22.4	1.8
Aid flows received	$359.2 (10.3%)	$13.7m (0.2%GNP)
Aid flows received/capita	$50.7	$10.4
Debt per capita	$3546	$2,193
Urbanisation	31.3%	73.2%
Traditional fuel consumption as % of total energy use	72.4%	0.8%

Source: UNDP 2000

borders, it faces an uncertain future, especially given its own internal political tensions.

Comparative issues

In comparing the processes of science and policy in Trinidad and Guinea we are clearly comparing two very different countries within very different regions. The comparative statistics in Table 3.1 summarise some contemporary contrasts, reflective, in some respects, of the political and economic histories that we have outlined.

Trinidad and Tobago thus ranks as a middle-income nation, with high rates of education, urbanisation, modern energy use, long life expectancy and low infant mortality. In contrast Guinea ranks as one of the poorest countries in the world with low indicators to match.

Apart from the very different political and economic histories, several particular contrasts emerge as important to a comparison of processes of science and policy in the rural environment field. A first concerns relative aid dependency. Development aid per capita is notably five times higher in Guinea than in Trinidad. Whereas in Guinea it can be argued that 'development', embedded in donor discourses and manifested in numerous 'development projects' is a dominant grid through which society, economy and policy are considered, this is much less the case in Trinidad. As Driver argues, in Trinidad '"development policy" has tended to be used as a shorthand for physical development control policy – i.e. land use zoning for construction of housing etc'. The term 'development' lacks its connotations more associated with Africa, 'reflecting the relative lack of influence over national policy of international lenders' (Driver 2001).[2]

A second key comparative issue turns on relative degrees of livelihood dependence on land and forests. Trinidad's much higher levels of urbanisation and lower national economic dependence on farming make related direct uses of forest resources significant to far fewer people than in Guinea, where the majority live on and from the land. This difference can be expected to influence not only research and policy practices around forest issues, but also forms of and opportunities for public engagement. Questions also arise concerning the comparative experiences of smallholder farmers and forest users in both countries, but as minorities in Trinidad, and as large majorities in Guinea.

A third, important axis of comparison concerns the nature of political representation. Both countries have a multi-party system which appears finely balanced, in which ethnic affiliations appear to loom large, and in which channels of patronage are important. In Guinea, however, active party politics is, for many, seen to be something that belongs to the capital (and inter-party negotiations), with rural political affiliations stably-shaped by broader regional and ethnic considerations. In everyday terms, party-political issues are generally only raised in interaction with representatives of the administration. In Trinidad, by contrast, party politics looms large in daily affairs. Moreover in Trinidad, engagement with policy debate is animated by higher levels of literacy, and greater access to news through papers, radio, TV, and the Internet as compared with Guinea – issues which we explore further in Chapter 8.

Policy and scientific settings: institutional structures and national-international linkages

We now consider in more detail the institutions involved with forests and rural environmental issues and policy in both countries, whether governmental, national NGOs, or major foreign donors and projects, and the institutional structures for training and research, including universities and non-governmental forums. While we highlight some characteristic features of these different institutions and their structural connections with international organisations, we withhold detailed discussion of their scientific and policy practices and engagements until later chapters.

Trinidad

There are now two important institutions in Trinidad creating policies concerning much the same forest lands and resources: the Forestry Division and the

Environmental Management Authority (EMA, since 1995). A proposed National Parks Authority would constitute a third. Each is generating overlapping policies with different methods, sources of finance and political support. Each has links to different international institutions. Producing policy in this context is part of very real battles for institutional turf and capacity claims.

The precursor to the Forestry Division, the colonial Forest Department, was established in 1901 following colonial and local concerns about forest cover loss and management, linked to concerns with regional climate and hydrology and broader colonial policy related to sound management of forest resources (Lackhan and Ramnarine 1996a and b). The Department had a conservation rather than a production orientation, and focused on state land and forest reserves. From the late 1920s financial pressure was put on the forest service to engage with production forestry to reduce timber imports and help generate exports. This led to experimentation in the management of natural forests for timber production, and the establishment of teak and later Caribbean pine plantations. The Forest Department acquired a reputation for plantation-focused silviculture, with its staff training and structures linked to this.

Tensions still exist between conservation and production, and between plantations and natural forest management. These have been joined by tensions between Forestry Division control over lands and resources, and community control. As our case studies will elaborate, these tensions shape relationships between the Forestry Division and its own Wildlife Section, and between the central forestry administration in Port of Spain, and the outlying conservancies. The tensions and their sedimentation into institutional divisions interplay with debate over neo-liberal privatisation of state activities, such as timber production, and with the agendas of different international organisations. The World Bank, for example, is pushing for an autonomous authority to manage biodiversity and wildlife conservation, as well as for privatisation of timber plantations, seeing the future of conservation and production lying outside the Forestry Division. FAO, on the other hand, supports a broader-based notion of forestry professionalism which encompasses both natural forest management and conservation. International and regional organisations such as UNDP and the Caribbean Natural Resources Institute have supported training and practice in participatory and community-based natural resource management. These have been embraced by a number of foresters working in the conservancies and in the Wildlife Section, but less by senior staff in the central forestry administration.

During the 1970s responsibilities for the environment (as opposed to forests) switched back and forth between the Ministries of Agriculture and of Health (with their respective concerns for conservation and wildlife and pollution). In 1981, environment was added to the Ministry of Health. With a change of government in 1986, and as growing international environmental concern coincided with Trinidad's pervasive environmental problems following decades of strong economic, industrial and infrastructural growth, environmental issues acquired greater political prominence. Forestry became part of a new Ministry of Food Production, Marine Exploitation, Forestry and the Environment. The new Minister set up an inter-ministerial Standing Committee on the Environment, which recommended the establishment of a new National Environmental Office (NEO) reporting directly to the Prime Minister as a co-ordinating and monitoring body. In 1989 the government created a Ministry of Environment and National Service. This was disbanded when the ruling party (the NAR) lost national elections, and environment was again relocated, this time to the Ministry of Planning and Development. In 1999 it was once again established as a separate Ministry, and the Forestry Division portfolio moved to the Ministry of Environment after the 2000 elections.

Following the Rio conference in 1992, the government undertook to develop a legal and institutional framework to address environmental issues. World Bank funds helped to hire a consultant to co-ordinate the establishment of a specialised agency outside the ministerial structure. This, it was argued, would enable greater flexibility in staffing, 'insulation from political influence' and greater involvement of NGOs and the private sector. An Environmental Act was carried through in 1995 which established the Environmental Management Authority (EMA) within a legislative framework to co-ordinate sectors and institutions, and to make rules for specific areas of environmental management.

The EMA's first board of directors was dismissed for lack of progress and one of the most vocal critics, University of the West Indies (UWI) scientist John Agard, was made Chairman of the new Board. The EMA's self-image is of an autonomous, science-driven organisation: 'Usually politics and economics override all scientific considerations, hence one needs an independent agency, not under a Ministry'.[3] Agard drafted a new national environmental policy following both broader public consultation and inputs from UWI natural scientists. This was passed by Cabinet in 1999. The EMA has developed Environmental Action and Management Plans (funded by the Global Environmental Facility), and attempted to harmonise environmental laws and enforce ministerial alignment with national environmental policy. It has the function of 'policing' other ministries, via the EMA 'agent' in each ministry.[4] It has also created an actual Environmental Police Force within the police service but funded by and at the call of the EMA.

The EMA is also attempting to establish an environmental court in which technical experts would act as judicial officers to adjudicate swiftly over business developments with environmental consequences. It is envisaged that this would protect citizens and businesses, enabling them to contest environmental laws or applications impinging on their rights. The model signals a move towards a hybrid of United States-style legal contestation, and Latin American-style aggressive state intervention.[5] Plans for the court have provoked some ministerial opposition, not least because the EMA aims to limit politicans' capacity to authorise planning developments. All permissions will require an Environmental Impact Assessment. The EMA has also developed legislation concerning Environmentally Sensitive Areas, which overlap with state lands administered by the Forestry Division. This has generated turf battles detailed in Chapter 5, linked to different relationships with international donors, funding flows and particular projects.

During the oil boom (1973–83), Trinidad's national budget was able to fund forestry activities, with direct forest revenues covering only about a tenth of forestry expenditure. With oil bust, the incapacity or reluctance to lay-off public servants meant that operational budgets suffered disproportionately and became minimal. At this point, overseas development assistance became more significant. Loans from the World Bank and the Inter-American Development Bank in particular have supported semi-autonomous 'projects', such as the Eastern Northern Range Project and the project to develop a National Parks and Wildlife Authority. The Northern Range Reafforestation Project, funded by the government during the 1970s, continued in the 1980s with some UNDP and FAO funds. The UNDP office also administers a Global Environmental Facility programme offering small grants for community-based environmental initiatives such as tour guiding and wildlife protection.

Corporate sponsors now fund high-profile environmental activities, capitalising on the publicity that they offer and the green image that they iconise. Examples include the American Chamber of Commerce in support of turtle protection activities, beach beautification projects funded by oil companies, and Guardian Life's sponsorship of environmental education activities and a Wildlife Trust Fund whose community activities are monitored with UNDP assistance.

Since the late 1980s, environmental activities and debate in Trinidad have also been animated by an expanding number of NGOs. Some had roots in Trinidad's long tradition of interest in natural history.[6] While these organisations had long articulated conservation messages, they were joined, in the late 1980s, by organisations with conservation as their main *raison d'être*. Severe fires during an extended dry season in 1987 galvanised several researchers, ex-government staff and civil society organisations concerned with perceived destruction of Trinidad's forest cover to form the Caribbean Forest Conservation Association. This committed itself to the concept of community co-management of renewable natural resources, and multi-stakeholder involvement in planning and management. Environmental NGOs further unified to form COPE – the Council of Presidents on the Environment. NGO proliferation has been stimulated by the increased national and international respect and funding they can command.

Within Trinidad, NGOs have begun to be included on certain statutory and ad hoc Cabinet committees.

Community-based organisations and interest group associations have also proliferated. For example, hunters are represented by national and regional associations such as the South-East Hunter's Association. Community-based organisations have been established to promote community development through conservation linked to ecotourism and tour guiding. Examples include groups from several villages on the north-east coast involved in leatherback turtle conservation and tourism (e.g. Nature Seekers Incorporated, Grand Rivière Environmental Trust, the Brasso Seco Tourism Action Committee in the forests of the Northern Range, and the Toco Foundation which links environment to a wider range of community-based activities). The establishment and development of these organisations has been shaped by the constellation of funding and support possibilities from donors such as the Global Environmental Facility Small Grants Programme, and government, such as the Wildlife Section's support to Nature Seekers, and the Tourism Industry Development Corporation's support to the Brasso Seco Tourism Action Committee. Alliances have also been formed between NGOs and community groups. For example Grand Rivière Environmental Trust and the Caribbean Forest Conservation Association formed a joint venture of equal partners and submitted a joint proposal on community-based forest fire prevention for international funding in 1995.[7]

The boundaries between NGO and community-based organisation, and research and commercial activities, become unclear as different avenues are taken to attract funding, and as a flourishing private sector becomes increasingly involved in environmental activities through ecotourism. NGOs such as the Caribbean Forest Conservation Association increasingly see contracts for donor-funded projects and commercial organisations (e.g. in Environmental Impact Assessment) as necessary for survival – although this has at times generated strong resentment from members who feel this goes against the grain of a 'voluntary' ethos. NGOs can easily be perceived as a platform for the personal economic or political advancement of their leaders in an NGO-favoured policy world.[8]

Two main institutions are involved in research and professional training in forest and environmental matters, the Eastern Caribbean Institute for Agriculture and Forestry (ECIAF) and Trinidad's St Augustine campus of the University of the West Indies.[9] Trinidad offers no undergraduate or postgraduate programmes in forest issues, so staff wishing to enter the professional ranks of the Forestry Division for which such a degree is required must study abroad. In the early years, the forest school in Cyprus attracted many Trinidadians, but now most study in the US. ECIAF was established 1966 with FAO support as a regional training school for agricultural and forestry staff in the Caribbean. It attracted trainees from many islands, and thus established a network of acquainted and similarly trained foresters throughout the anglophone Caribbean. The first head was an Indian forestry professor, Kulkarni, who created the curricula before moving to run the FAO Northern Range Reafforestation Project. Initially they offered a two-year in-service training for forest officers. In the oil boom period the government actively sought and funded new recruits to train for subsequent jobs in the Forestry Division. In the oil bust, however, the school needed to become self-financing. The diploma was suspended. A wildlife and conservation course was run for game wardens and then a Forest Ranger certificate training programme. In 1990 ECIAF resumed the two-year diploma, but charged fees. Student numbers rose threefold in the 1990s, reflecting its relatively low costs and the growing opportunities its education provides for employment in environmental organisations, and not just in forestry.[10]

The ECIAF curriculum has evolved from a narrow focus on silviculture (1966–80) to encompass a broad spectrum of forest interests, including parks and recreation, research, wildlife, statistics and wood technologies. The Director – a Forestry Division employee – convenes the courses which are taught by professional foresters working in other capacities within the Forestry Division. Participatory and community-based approaches to forest management and conservation have entered the training through the experiences of younger staff who have studied abroad, participated in regional workshops such as those organised by the Caribbean Natural Resources Institute, and experienced participatory approaches in the Wildlife Section of the Division. The current ECIAF Forest Director plans to introduce such perspectives throughout the syllabus.[11] Lecturers are drawn in from other institutions, such as the Environmental Management Authority and University of the West Indies. In recent years, a visiting US professor of conservation biology has given lectures, as have several of his students. It has often been suggested that ECIAF link with the university to establish a forestry degree course, but despite agreement from both parties, this is on the back-burner, awaiting funding support from an international agency.

The University of the West Indies is a regional institution with campuses in Trinidad, Barbados and Jamaica. Trinidad's St Augustine campus is relatively well resourced, with good laboratories, information technology and library facilities, enabling academics and graduate students to pursue sophisticated research programmes. This research is not dependent on donor projects. Strong natural science traditions cover both plant science and zoology. Interests in the natural history of particular species is complemented by work ranging from cell genetics to marine and terrestrial ecosystem dynamics. There is one lecturer in Forestry, and a second with some forest research interests. Supported by graduate students, forestry research addresses tree population, seedling and canopy dynamics, and the impacts of silvicultural patterns on tree genetic diversity.[12] Many staff are involved in consultancies and commissioned studies for government and international agencies. Curricula and research are being re-organised in line with contemporary policy issues. For example, together with the National Herbarium on the UWI campus and strong Environmental Management Authority support, there are moves to establish a Biodiversity Centre. Environment is perceived as an area of demand by students who see strong potential for employment in Environmental Impact Assessments, monitoring and so on. In 1998 a new MSc on Science for Management of Tropical Environments was introduced. Most students are government or NGO employees.

Most research on environment is emerging from the natural sciences. Social issues are perceived as a gap, especially as natural science researchers come to confront them in the practical work and consultancies in which they are engaged.[13] The new MSc does not address social dimensions of conservation, with the exception of two lectures on participatory methods given ad hoc by a foreign trained researcher. Students based in the Faculty of Life Sciences seeking to transcend disciplines into the social sciences have a hard time. This is being addressed in part through the Sustainable Economic Development Unit (SEDU) established in 1996 within the Department of Economics in the Faculty of Social Sciences. Most of this unit's research has focused on economic indicators and policy instruments for sustainable development, and questions of sustainable tourism. Following campus-level discussions about interdisciplinary programmes, the SEDU director has drafted an environmental MSc programme from a social science viewpoint to complement that in natural sciences. Nevertheless, SEDU's focus is largely economic, notwithstanding some studies by associates.[14] Indeed, due to the split university, Trinidad's campus does not cover environmental sociology, anthropology or geography, although since the late 1990s its Centre for Gender and Development Studies has engaged with environmental issues, bringing to these its critical social science perspective and concern with questions of knowledge, power and difference.

Guinea

Rural environmental issues in Guinea have long been linked with the government department covering forests. This was established in 1931 as the national Service des Eaux et Forêts, part of the broader agriculture ministry. Since its inception, the service has focused on both timber production and environmental protection, each receiving greater importance in different areas at different times. As the service established government controlled forest reserves, and surveillance and prohibitions around fire-setting and timber felling, it came to be recognised by populations as a 'service of repression'. Expansion of staff and resources from the 1950s and especially after Independence meant that by the mid-1980s, the forestry administration – with its offices in each prefecture and agents in each sub-prefecture (the chef de cantonment forestier and his assistants) – was a major exactive force in rural areas. Between 1958 and 1986 the number of forest personnel increased from 138 to 3194, including many former soldiers. At times, however, the authority of what became the Direction National des Forêts et Faune (hereafter national Forestry Directorate) has been curbed by tensions with the wider agricultural interests of the Ministry of Agriculture, and by periods of austerity (Fairhead and Leach 1996, 2001).

The 1990s have seen a proliferation of governmental and non-governmental institutions dealing with rural environment and these have been linked with the increasing interests of international donors. These trends are also linked to the emergence of new approaches and engagements with publics, both within and outside the forest service. In particular, the Forestry Directorate claims explicitly to have altered its approach to emphasise partnership and participation with local populations.[15] These moves are linked to the more liberal government since 1984, the influence of international donors, specifically under German, European, World Bank and American programmes, and a charismatic national Director who embraced this change in the late 1980s, and presided over a major downsizing which retained professional staff but not soldiers.

External funding through donor development programmes and projects is vital to the operation of the Forestry Directorate whether in its Conakry offices or on the ground. Government budgets are contracting and revenues from timber concessions in the forest zone are controlled only in part by the Directorate. Yet although many donor-funded projects are under the authority of the Forestry Directorate, they have separate management and financial control structures, and there is considerable ambiguity about how far authority implies accountability. For example, United States Agency for International Development (USAID) projects (largely focused on watershed management in Fouta Djallon) and those of the German Development Bank (KFW) and Technical Cooperation Agency (GTZ) are managed from a separate office. The latter include the Projet Gestion des Ressources Rurales which has conducted forest reserve management (balancing production and conservation) in the forest region since 1996. A European Union programme co-ordinates an assortment of watershed protection and national parks projects from its own offices located in the compound of the Forestry Directorate. Many government advisors conceptualise these projects as separate players in environmental policy processes, emphasising how different donors protect their domains of influence.[16] Each of these projects employs both expatriates and government forestry staff, and many now contract NGOs to conduct their work. Tensions in control and co-ordination between expatriates and their national counterparts, and between projects and the national service, arise frequently. Donors also provide broader funding for policy development, national and prefectoral planning and training in participatory methods.

A major influence on this has been a German-funded technical advisor to the national Director.

Co-ordination between donors is a perennial problem.[17] Inter-organisational meetings were once tried, but not followed through. UNDP has an environmental 'focal advisor' who nominally co-ordinates donors, but is continually frustrated in this.[18] The Organisation for African Unity (OAU) has also been co-ordinating environment programmes, in particular the Upper Niger River Protection Programmes of USAID, UNDP and the EU. Drafting policy to co-ordinate activity also attracts donor competition. Since 1995, UNDP has also financed the preparation of an Agricultural Policy Statement (LPDA-2) which drew scientific expertise from FAO. The product was supportive of – and harmonised with – new forest and environment codes, and Guinea's growing orientation towards both market liberalisation and administrative decentralisation.[19] The World Bank had originally sought to finance LPDA-2, and remained involved through a separate 'capacity-building' project and negotiated a policy addendum to draw out the macro-economic liberalisation theme.

It was Guinea's National Environment Directorate, however, which represented Guinea at Rio in 1992, and which has responsibility for co-ordinating and enacting Guinea's participation in global conventions, such as those concerning biodiversity, desertification and climate change. With its genesis in the water and health sectors this directorate has been under several different ministries, most recently Natural Resources and Mining. It plays a co-ordinating role between ministries, and takes responsibility for national research and planning exercises such as the UNDP/World Bank supported National Environmental Action Plan (NEAP) of the early 1990s, and the Convention on Biodiversity supported National Biodiversity Strategy of the late 1990s. The environment code, which it prepared, has large sections concerning forests – even though forests and forest policy implementation are under Forestry Directorate control. The Environment Directorate controls no natural resources and has minimal budgets, running to a small national office and between two and four staff in each Prefecture. The latter admit that their practical work is confined to urban areas, with rural issues generally referred to the forestry administration.[20] The Environment Directorate nevertheless has certain donor-funded research and information projects.[21]

The European Union has actively promoted regional co-ordination, both through the information programme it supports (Programme Regional d'Assistance Technique à la Communication et à l'Information sur la Protection de l'Environnement, PACIPE) and through a growing number of trans-border national park projects. Regional perspectives have also driven the OAU co-ordinated Niger River Protection Projects, and the biodiversity priority-setting exercises led by Conservation International since 1999. In these, Guinea is regionalised in assorted ways: as part of the Upper Guinea forest region, as part of the major West African river watersheds, and – in some respects – as part of a geopolitical region shared with the francophone Sahelian countries to its north.

Other organisations which have acquired influence in rural environmental issues are broadly characterised as NGOs, but actually have a variety of relations with government. One of the largest and most influential is Guinée Ecologie, which acquired prominence when it helped co-ordinate the National Environmental Action Plan process. Founded by a nucleus of Environment Directorate staff, it has incorporated various researchers and government scientists, and now conducts consultancies both for government and donors, and represents Guinea at international NGO forums.[22] A second major national NGO is CENAFOD, which since the late 1980s has taken a lead in promoting and training for participatory approaches in environment and development, and which numbers former university employees among its staff. Longstanding links with international organisations promoting participation in development are attested by the large documentation centre. Both of these are specialist NGOs, entrepreneurial organisations well able to broker the international world with Guinean realities.

The burgeoning of specialist NGOs, often staffed by former (and current) public sector employees, is linked to the liberalisation and 'contractualisation' of donor project activities, as Chapter 6 will illustrate. Such organisations have rather eclipsed the low-budget, small conservation organisations of the early 1990s such as 'Friends of Nature' societies established by former teachers. They now sit alongside organisations promoting specifically local agendas, such as neighbourhood Development Associations within which residents and their urban and diasporic relatives interact to raise money and lobby for local interests. A rather different genre of 'civil society' organisation with environmental interests are the professional associations, such as the National Hunter's Association, and the Association of Traditional Medical Specialists. In several cases, donor organisations have been working with these. The President of the Republic presides over the National Hunter's Association, and has called upon them in civil defence.

Research and forestry/environment training in Guinea is carried out in three universities and a forestry training school. The former provide degree courses and the latter, technical training for lower-level extension staff. Only one university in Guinea provides undergraduate-level education in forestry. This is the Institut Superieur Agronomique et Vétérinaire Valéry Giscard D'Estaing (ISAV) of Faranah. Many of the students who pass through its five-year forestry diploma course have gone on to work in government or donor forestry and environment programmes. The Forestry Department sees itself as having transformed its approach since the early 1990s. As its head of department put it: 'Before, we saw that the forester came with his science and imposed it on the peasants. He came as a master. Now we emphasise the forester as a collaborator and partner'.[23] Students are now being trained in the approaches and practical techniques sought by modern environmental programmes emphasising 'participation'. New courses in information technology, sociology, communication, and the participatory natural resource management approach pioneered in French West Africa, 'gestion des ressources des terroirs villageois', have been added to the final year.

In rather sharp contrast with the generally lamented tendency in Guinea's higher education for producing students with training irrelevant to future employment (Boiro 1998; PADES 1998), training in ISAV's forestry department appears to be highly aligned with employment opportunities. Whilst this is partly a conscious strategy on the part of course convenors, there are also structural reasons why such alignment is hard to avoid. Library resources at ISAV are minimal. The forestry collection in the ISAV library occupies three of a total of eight dusty shelves of heaped documents. Social science texts are absent and ecology texts are old, predating important ecological research and publication in what has over the last twenty to thirty years been a fast-moving field. While more recent materials are to be found in the private collections of certain lecturers, these are largely the journals and newsletters distributed free by international development organisations.[24] Hence lecturers build their courses principally from reading project documents, participating in project meetings and workshops, and their own involvement as consultant researchers. The course on 'gestion des ressources des terroirs villageois', for example, was introduced alongside the practical application of this approach within the EU-funded Niger River Protection Programmes, also dating from 1991, which lecturers visited and worked on. Currently, the department is being reorganised to make space for a new Environment specialisation in response to job prospects linked to these issues. This will focus heavily on biodiversity and national park issues, linked to ISAV's collaboration with EU projects to develop new national parks.

Students' practical research assignments for their dissertations occupy the whole fifth year of the course. Even more than for course content, there are strong links between these 'memoirs' and donor-funded projects. Students generally conduct research for their memoirs as interns with donor-funded projects. As the head of department explained, 'It is not us who instigate the subjects. The projects have their preoccupations and suggest them to us; we identify the students to carry them out'.[25] Students like the employment potential of these arrangements: many interns have been retained as staff or subsequently contracted by projects. It is partly through these research requests and conduct that lecturers become aware of the emerging preoccupations of projects. Through the memoirs and supervision, they are able to reflect these in emerging coursework.

Several staff of the Faranah institute have research-based PhDs, but in their everyday work have little means or opportunity to initiate research programmes. While their promotion now depends on research publication, publication opportunities are highly limited. The most accessible 'publication' route is through projects and consultancy reports. Lack of finance also severely limits opportunities for independent research. ISAV operates its own central research budget but forestry department staff claim that this is invariably used up in 'more pressing needs'. A new university-based research funding envelope created linked to a World Bank financed programme (PADES) has recently become available, but is heavily oversubscribed, reportedly receiving 300 applications for its 5 million Guinean Francs (approximately $US 5000) in the first year. Hence ISAV staff research is heavily dominated by studies commissioned by development projects.

The University of Kankan, in Upper Guinea, does not have a forestry faculty, but environmental issues have become increasingly important to the work of its other departments, whether in teaching, research, consultancy or aspirations. In a round table of eighteen lecturers (out of about forty-five in total) to discuss environmental aspects of their work, lecturers emphasised the desire to establish a multi-disciplinary centre which could co-ordinate environmental research and (eventually) run its own teaching programme. Foreign academic support and funding is deemed essential for this.[26] In the meantime, disciplinary degrees incorporate various environment-related courses, from 'nature conservation' in biology to 'gestion des ressources des terroirs villageois' in geography. History and sociology do not have specific environmental courses, yet are anxious to emphasise the relevance of what is taught for environmental issues. In some contrast with ISAV, lecturers do not see project-linked fieldwork experiences as the central source of information for their courses. Rather, course materials tend to be drawn from international texts – although again this is hampered by limited library resources. As in Faranah, though, lecturers' research is strongly linked to donor projects. For example geographers and sociologists have carried out a socio-economic study for the EU Niger River Protection Programme, and others prepared a human impact study for the National Biodiversity Strategy.

Environment is central to the University Gamal Abdul Nasser in Conakry, the country's largest university. Indeed the pioneering and only PhD programme and Diplome d'Etudes Approfondi (DEA, roughly equivalent to MPhil) offered at this university, and in Guinea, is in Environmental Sciences. This owes its existence to the Canadian-supported Centre d'Etude et de Recherche en Environnement (CERE), the conception of the University of Quebec at Montreal. Formally created in 1994, CERE drew together lecturers in ecology, geography, chemistry, sociology, physics, botany, hydrology and soil science who received training in Canada and who still participate in exchange visits with Quebec lecturers. It has become a well-funded oasis within the financially strapped university, with information technology, laboratory materials and air-conditioned offices and seminar rooms. Introductory, compulsory courses cover environmental problems, ecosystems, research methods, modern mapping and interpretation of remotely sensed imagery, and information technology. Students then choose between ecology, hydroclimatology and biodiversity/sustainable resource management, before selecting from a broader range of options. Entrance to the course is competitive and follows a tough entrance exam; several of those inscribed are university lecturers at Conakry or Kankan.

Gradually, research activities at CERE are developing both in collaboration with visiting Canadian lecturers, and with an assortment of internationally-funded development programmes. CERE is also developing its own applied research interests through its student memoirs and in its contributions to the West African cluster of a United Nations University project on People, Land Management and Environmental Change (PLEC). Individual researchers in other departments have also forged their own contacts and reputations with development organisations, with several sociologists and geographers working regularly for the EU national parks and Niger River Protection Programmes, for example.

There are several routes, then, through which a grid of donor-funded projects, linked into internationalised perspectives on environment and development and in some cases into regional research networks, is shaping the ways in which research on environment is carried out in Guinea. These include commissioning university staff to carry out research and consultancy contracts; the practices of student dissertations, and the recycling of both of these back into teaching materials. These linkages are, in turn, shaping how understandings of environment develop among Guinea's future researchers, decision-makers and administrators.

Comparative issues

This sketch of policy and scientific settings in Trinidad and Guinea suggests important similarities and differences. Both Trinidad and Guinea have forest departments which originated within colonial regimes, where apparatus and debates concerning conservation of soil, water and climate were also those exerting social control over the rural world. In both countries forest departments have been joined by a proliferation of state and NGO institutions involved with environmental policy and research. In each country the different institutions find links and alignments with different international institutions. As will become clear, they also have different links with constituencies in wider society. Our cases will discern how scientific and policy processes, and their co-production, are configured within this differentiated field. This provides a very different picture from one generated by an analytic rooted simply in 'the local', 'the national' and 'the international'.

In both countries it is also striking how rural environmental issues have become important to tertiary sector education and research, and to student interest. There are major differences, however, in how research is configured in each country. Guinean universities are far more reliant on foreign donors and their specific programmes to enable (and hence frame the agendas of) research. Yet this dates only from the 1990s, following the relatively closed and strongly nationalist First Republic under Sekou Touré. European and American donor influence in Guinea has coincided with a period of intense global environmental concern, and these have shaped each other. Trinidad by contrast has a longer but lighter tradition of donor involvement, and far stronger, nationally-funded research institutions today. Despite these funding differences, however, both countries are now firmly linked into international networks of research and policy, and these clearly help shape the contemporary scientific community and the conduct of science itself.

In the cases that we now turn to – examining issues around biodiversity and sustainable forest management in Guinea and Trinidad – the importance of the political and economic histories and the institutional structures we have outlined in this chapter to the unfolding of scientific and policy processes will become apparent. Similar international processes and debates, as applied to broadly similar forest ecologies, have very different outcomes as they interlock with the specific research and policy practices which have developed in the particular political-economic and institutional settings of each country.

Notes

1. In particular he was concerned with whether vegetation associated with different soils, topography etc. represented particular edaphic climaxes (Tansley and Chipp 1926) or represented sub-climaxes (Clements 1936). Arguing (a) that moisture relations governed by the interplay of climate, topography and soil determined vegetation and (b) that landform and soil change on a geological timescale enabled vegetation to develop through juvenile, mature and senile forms, he concluded that climax had to be defined in relation to the development of soil and topography, and is the vegetation associated with mature phases (Beard 1946a: 142–151).
2. Although Driver also notes that this has been shifting since the mid-1990s, possibly reflecting a growing interest in Indian 'developmentalism' (Driver 2001).
3. Interview, Director of Environmental Management Authority, St Augustine, 7 May 1999.
4. Ibid.
5. Ibid.
6. For example, the Botanical Gardens and Herbarium established from 1811; the Field Naturalists Club established in 1893, the Orchid and Ornithological Societies of Trinidad and Tobago, and the Point-à-Pierre Wildfowl Trust founded in 1966, committed to wildlife protection and public education.

7. Eden Shand, *Trinidad Express*, 7 March 1996.

8. The Asa Wright Nature Centre in the forests of the Northern Range represents the reverse: a private estate which has grown as a tourist attraction for bird-watching but which has developed both research and educational programmes.

9. We do not discuss the Institute for Marine Affairs, nor the other UWI campuses in Jamaica and Barbados which have marine specialisms.

10. Interview, Director of Forestry, ECIAF, 3 July 1999.

11. Ibid.

12. Interview, Forest Ecologist, University of the West Indies, St Augustine, 7 May 1999.

13. Interview, Biologist, University of the West Indies, St Augustine, 7 May 1999.

14. These include the late John Cropper's UNDP-funded study on regreening the foothills of the northern range (Cropper 1997), critical sociological work on community institutions for resource management (Driver and Kravatsky 1998) and our own studies of science and policy.

15. Interview, Deputy Director, National Forestry Directorate, Conakry, 5 January 1999.

16. Interview, technical advisor, Ministry of Agriculture, Conakry, 7 January 1999.

17. Interview, European technical advisor, Ministry of Planning and Co-operation, Conakry, 12 January 1999.

18. Interview, UNDP focal advisor for Environment, Conakry, 7 January 1999.

19. Ibid.

20. Interview, Prefectoral Director of Environment, Kissidougou, 21 January 1999.

21. A notable example is the EU-funded PACIPE which conducts environmental communication and education throughout the West Africa forest zone from its coordinating office in Benin. PACIPE-Guinea's national director had been co-ordinator of the Environment Directorate's National Environmental Action Plan process. Interview, Director, PACIPE-Guinea, Conakry, 11 January 1999.

22. Interview, senior staff member, Guinée Ecologie, Conakry, 7 March 1999.

23. Interview, Head of Forestry Department, ISAV, Faranah, 23 February 1999.

24. For example, the French Arbres Tropicaux/Le Flamboyant; Forests, Trees and People Newsletters, PACIPE brochures, and information on participatory rural appraisal techniques from the UK-based International Institute for Environment and Development.

25. Interview, Head of Forestry Department, ISAV, Faranah, 23 February 1999.

26. Group discussion with departmental heads and lecturers, University of Kankan, 5 March 1999.

4   Biodiversity and conservation in Guinea

Introduction

This is the first of two chapters which focus, from different angles, on scientific and policy processes around biodiversity and conservation. Within the current cacophony of environmental voice in Guinea, biodiversity has become a key organising concept. Guinea was the second country in Africa to ratify the Convention on Biodiversity created in Rio in 1992. The concept of biodiversity is now central to strategising and daily work in the National Environment Directorate and the Forest and Wildlife Directorate, while many donor-funded programmes have reoriented their work towards biodiversity conservation objectives. How do those working in national organisations and their street and field level representatives understand and operationalise conservation of 'biodiversity'? How do Guineans relate to evolving international scientific and policy practice in its specific locales of application, and in the equally specific locales of national bureaucracies?

This chapter explores how, through specific practices, the evolving international vortex associated with biodiversity prioritisation and conservation is articulating with existing practices of science and policy in Guinea – including those rooted in earlier colonial and post-independence traditions. These articulations generate both reproductions and reworkings of international ideas, manifested in overlapping yet distinct, sets of practices characterising biodiversity conservation in modern Guinea.

Several kinds of scientific practices are now configured together (and funded) under a biodiversity label. These include: (1) the production of lists of plant and animal species which university scientists and projects carry out with donor support; (2) the exploration of ecosystem dynamics through 'cutting edge' sampling and computer modelling techniques; (3) the harnessing of traditional plant medicines by environmental NGOs and networks of healers to promote conservation, linked also with discussion and action concerning bio-piracy, multinational corporations and 'indigenous property rights'; (4) the promotion and commercialisation of semi-wild plants such as oil palms, which link conservation with land users' economic interests, and (5) the conservation of biodiversity with the assistance of 'traditional' hunters, linking protected area management with social scientific interpretations of their knowledge and status. We consider each of these sets of practices as played out in their national and local settings, with particular material implications. We then consider their influence in Guinea's engagement with international prioritisation for biodiversity conservation.

In Guinea, modern concern for biodiversity echoes older colonial environmental concerns. Contemporary science and policy draws on historically sedimented practices (science and policy traditions) shaped by the history of administrative succession: from colony, to independent African socialist state, to one party military dictatorship, to contemporary liberal democracy. The policy practices of each epoque have been shaped in relation to its predecessor. Thus, as will become clear, Guinea's radical pan-Africanist socialist state sought to promote African herbal medicine. This was in part a political act which gained its meaning in dialogical opposition to the alien colonial health regime which had earlier demeaned indigenous health practices. It also made sense in relation to economic realities then faced by Guineans in the isolated and bankrupt economy. Yet while the subject of the research was framed in opposition to colonial medical practice, the practice of research (what made it scientific) drew on colonially shaped scientific practice. Research sought to identify active plant chemicals, but not the social practices of medicine in which herbs were only a part. The policy thus trod a difficult line between Africanisation on the one hand (defined in opposition to colonial practice), and 'demystification' defined according to colonial traditions of 'scientific' practice. In doing so, it helped shape new meanings (for those involved) about what it is to be African and Guinean; what is natural and what is supernatural, what is cultural and what is 'mystification'. By tracking examples such as this, the chapter considers how ideas of nature and of society and culture are being reconfigured at the intersection of international and national scientific and policy processes.

An era of biodiversity

Guinea's Environment Directorate has been responsible for the negotiations and subsequent implementation of the biodiversity convention, and the production of a national biodiversity strategy and action plan. Whereas the Environment Directorate cannot implement, however, the Forest Directorate can, with its large staff managing state forests and forest law throughout its prefectoral and sub-prefectoral administrations. As we saw in Chapter 3, however, the Forest Directorate is heavily dependent on supplementary funding and infrastructure from donor funded projects, and this – along with the green conditionalities imposed on Guinea by international financial institutions – means that large parts of its activity are now inflected by donors' concerns, where biodiversity looms large. These and other ministries are represented in the newly-created Unité Nationale pour la Biodiversité (UNBIO), along with the University of Conakry, donors and certain civil associations.

That those working in forestry, conservation, agricultural and environmental jobs have been turning their attention to biodiversity issues is certainly linked to funding. But it is also stimulated by a developing interest in the subject. Through the national and international networks a mutually interested community (epistemic community) has developed which gives new meaning and application to the skills of many involved. For national university academics, biodiversity provides an opportunity for 'research', and for those in foreign universities, it provides funding and interest in 'cutting edge' research.

That the major European Union-funded Niger River Protection Programme, which was initially conceived as a watershed protection programme, has recently employed as its key ex-patriate a specialist ecologist skilled in ecosystem research (not hydrology), and that the refinancing of the program that he is responsible for flags 'biodiversity' as a major theme, clearly illustrates the shift (in donor interest) from concerns with watersheds to concerns with ecosystems and biodiversity.

National academics in universities and government research institutes have been incorporated into several of these developments. Many work simultaneously for non-governmental organisations which deal with environmental issues. International donors now often seek to work through NGOs rather than the state, and this enables talented government staff to work in a lucrative and better financed world in a freelance capacity. The more entrepreneurial NGOs have been quick to mobilise biodiversity and the funds it attracts. One, to give an example, is developing a biodiversity project with university staff to re-invigorate a national game reserve. It receives financing from the German national fund dedicated to international biodiversity conservation, helping spend the money which Germany is obliged to spend following its ratification of the biodiversity convention. The same NGO is developing a medicinal plant initiative.

Against this background, we now look at the spectrum of practices these state agencies, projects and NGOs engage in.

Scientific and policy practices around biodiversity

1   Listing diversity

Focused attention on biodiversity has heralded a resurgence of interest in the identification and listing of plant and animal species. Long before colonisation, European visitors to West Africa had begun to collect and name local flora. Early in the colonial period, botanical gardens and research centres collected, identified and classified plants, and as part of this effort established and managed plant herbaria such as that still housed at the Centre de Recherche Agronomique at Seredou in Forest Guinea (Bonneuil and Kleiche 1993).

Certain Guineans became indispensable to this process through their knowledge of the flora and their capacity to identify and distinguish plants. The Guineans involved became renowned for their botanical knowledge, and informally this contributed to their reputation as herbalists. While colonial taxonomic practice was largely about plant differentiation and naming, it also became closely associated with the personal qualities of the Guineans the colonialists worked with, as 'knower of the bush' and healer, to which knowledge of scientific names added an extra dimension. At Independence it was these few Guineans and their apprentices who took over the herbaria. Their skills were valued when the new state became interested in medicinal plants, as mentioned, and several were sent for botanical training in East Germany.

State funding interest in indigenous medical plants eventually waned following the death of President Sekou Touré in 1984, so the botanists had to continue with minimal resources and lack of recognition. They were kept busy 'tree spotting' (largely for forest inventories and forest exploitation), rather than for their herbaria and knowledge of diversity. Nevertheless the herbaria themselves, and people with a unique set of skills in managing them and a unique (almost mystical) knowledge of both botanical and indigenous plant lore, remained as an enduring legacy of early taxonomic priority.

Since the mid-1990s, however, the demands on these charismatic botanist-healers' time have rapidly increased as more attention is paid to making species lists; identifying endemic species and those 'in peril', and in totting up numbers of each. These lists are central to many university and ministry biodiversity studies. In 1999, for example, the charismatic botanist and manager of the Seredou herbarium was kept active in donor-funded programmes working for biodiversity. The national biodiversity monograph which was funded by the Global Environment Facility (UNBIO 1999) galvanised many institutions to make such lists, or at least to review older ones. Indeed in conformity with the stipulations of the Convention on Biodiversity an inventory of fauna and flora was compiled from secondary sources.

Species lists appear in justifications to prioritise particular locations for conservation (e.g. PROGERFOR 1995), yet their role in this is far from straightforward. First, species lists have generally been made in 'protected areas' such as forest reserves. Forest reserves have a long history in Guinea, being proposed in the 1900s and established from the 1930s onwards largely for their supposed influence on regional climate (Chevalier 1928; Adam 1968). The lists were drawn up in early ecological studies (e.g. Schnell 1952) within three logics: (a) the practices of the taxonomist-collector (locating new plants, interacting with metropolitan plant collections to establish their classification, coupled to the cult of naming in recognition of the finder); (b) the practices then used to

Figure 4.1 The Ziama forest reserve, Forest Guinea

define ecosystems (via plant communities – phytosociology); and (c) the practices of inventory for determining the 'economic value' of a forest. Significantly, there was little attention paid to diversity per se.

So reserves and parks which had their own logic of foundation proved to be the site of taxonomic practices – producing species lists for one set of reasons – which are now important to supporting the continued existence of such reserves for quite another, in an era of biodiversity conservation. The practice of compiling lists from secondary sources only reinforces this focus on existing protected areas, since these were often the sites of the past studies which are now cited and re-cited. The policy imperative to have protected areas, and the practices of taxonomic science, have thus mutually produced each other.

Virtually no comparable lists have been established for inhabited landscapes. The lists give the semblance of logical prioritisation to the parks and reserves which are long established, and by deduction, to the idea of biodiversity wealth and conservation in reserves, and biodiversity destruction in inhabited areas. In short, the presence of these reserves which were established for different reasons, has facilitated the co-production of science and policy around biodiversity in protected areas – in a similar way perhaps to how redundant leprosy hospitals were used to incarcerate and study people who in such settings came to be newly understood as 'mad' (Foucault 1973).

This has very real effects for the way conservation management is evolving in the region. In the Ziama forest reserve (Figure 4.1), for example, this logical association of biodiversity conservation with reservation has been reproduced both in the structure of its refinancing, and in everyday management practices. The Ziama forest massif was reserved in the 1930s as part of a so-called struggle against desiccation and savannisation. Since the mid-1980s, conservation efforts have been revalidated in a series of donor projects emphasising biodiversity, and in conformity with international ideas around conservation-with-development the reserve includes a zone of strict nature reserve/integral protection, surrounded by two buffer zones allowing different degrees of carefully-regulated land use by local populations (Baum and Weimer 1992; Bourque and Wilson 1990; Fairhead and Leach 1994). Studies by a German herpetologist became highly influential in the elaboration, planning and operation of a newly (German) funded programme. He carried out a series of transect studies and animal sampling exercises from which he compiled new lists of animal species, estimated the population numbers of certain 'endangered' species (such as elephants),[1] and identified several species as endemic to Ziama. He used the results of these investigations to argue for the importance of the Ziama animal populations in a global context, contending that as much of the reserve as possible should be designated a strict nature reserve. In the elaboration of a management plan, 35 per cent of the reserve was eventually demarcated as integrally protected, following negotiations with project personnel who supported competing uses of the reserve in timber production and farming, hunting and product collection by local populations.

The forest reserve received support from one funder, the German KfW, and the inhabited buffer zone outside from another, the German GTZ. The reserve project is responsible for ensuring 'biodiversity and habitat conservation', and the latter, for 'local participation and livelihood sustainability' (Schmidt Corsitto 1998; Kientz 1996). In this institutionally-divided setting, biodiversity and participation have come to be seen as trade-offs. As one ex-patriate project staff member put it: 'In village forests, biodiversity has no role. It does not interest villagers. In the forest reserve, the biodiversity aim must necessarily reduce the extent of participation; the more one has a goal of biodiversity conservation, the less one has participation'.[2] The reserve boundary thus came to be seen within the project as a dividing line between zones where important plants and animals might thrive, and those where farmers might be encouraged to intensify their agriculture and so reduce pressure on the reserve. As a Guinean critic observed, this structure precludes attention to the ways farmers have long used products from the forest reserve and integrated a huge diversity of 'wild' plants within their own landscapes.[3] Yet his critique is not practised.

Despite the list-making, those managing protected areas actually consider the lists to be of little use. This is exemplified in the newly-established Parc National de Haut Niger (PNHN) in Upper Guinea, funded by the European Union as part of a network of large new national parks in the region. The park centres on, but vastly extends, an existing dry forest reserve (of Mafou). A major goal of the park project is to encourage the reconstitution of the region's wildlife populations and faunal biodiversity by regulating the practices of commercial and subsistence hunting used by the Malinke populations who have long inhabited the area. To this end a series of buffer zones, with progressively more permissive hunting and land use regulations radiating out from a strictly-protected nucleus, has been established. Under the terms of a three-year contract with the park project, researchers in the biology department of the Technical Training Institute of Faranah are conducting a series of animal and plant species inventories. The researchers involved find this rather tedious and uninteresting from a scientific point of view. They claim they would prefer to be researching ecosystem dynamics, which they see as more important for advancing scientific knowledge of the region; 'there is not much treatment of systemic aspects of vegetation; this is a major lacuna'.[4] Yet given the social and funding relations of science in a Guinea where universities are chronically underfunded and foreign aid projects provide almost the sole context in which field research costs can be met and reports published, researchers have little choice but to work on the project's terms.

Paradoxically, however, those managing the park also see these qualitative inventories as of virtually no use in day-to-day management. As the Park's director put it: 'lists of species are fine for global biodiversity, but not for managers. We need to go deeper, to have quantitative information and information on ecosystem dynamics'.[5] From his perspective, data on species numbers and hunting kills is needed to assess how endangered species are relative to hunting.[6] It is actually quite unlikely that the scientific practices which might give such data could generate a precise estimate of the effects of hunting on particular species, given the more chaotic ecological dynamics affecting species numbers, and the difficulties of recording the outcomes of various, often secretive hunting practices. Yet aspiration to do this is used as a justification both for controlling hunting in a precautionary sense, and for creating the park as an arena for research to fill that data gap. In this case indeterminacy (unknowability) is constructed as uncertainty (knowable through further scientific research) (cf. Shackley and Wynne 1996).

2   Ecosystems and diversity

A second conception of 'biodiversity' elaborated through contemporary scientific practices highlights how diversity is embedded in ecosystemic relationships.

Attempts to categorise and identify the defining features of the varied ecosystems in Guinea have a long history, relating back to work by colonial botanists early in the twentieth century. Botanists such as Chevalier and Aubréville identified particular plant communities which they associated with the broad climatic zones extending from the humid coastal and forest zones, through transitional, Sudanian and Sahelian savannas in the north of the country, as well as more local variations linked to soil type (e.g. Aubréville 1949; Chevalier 1911). In keeping with ecological theories of the time, characteristic ecosystems were seen as stable formations, characterised by particular dominant trees – a 'climax vegetation' in relation to prevailing climate and soil conditions, unless 'disturbed' and 'impoverished' by human impact.

This analytical frame persists today in the sub-national biodiversity assessments, made by national university staff and commissioned by the Environment Directorate to inform the National Biodiversity Strategy and Action Plan. Four of the nine papers focus on 'human pressures on ecosystems' in each of Guinea's four major regions (e.g. Barry 1999; Diallo 1999). Natural and social scientists are working to assemble data from secondary sources in such a way as to present general arguments about 'loss of habitat integrity' under pressures from farming, burning, overfishing, overhunting, population increase and so on. The broad topics and orientation for these thematic papers arose in part from the requirements of the international convention, 'adapted to suit Guinean conditions'.[7] Such adaptation nevertheless neatly slotted into a long tradition of both botanical and social science work in Guinea, framed by equilibrium assumptions from colonial times onwards (e.g. Adam 1948; Paulme 1954). Notably, this work also supports the reserve strategy for biodiversity conservation.

Simultaneously, however, another research programme is being conducted by expatriate researchers as part of the Niger River Protection Programme. This is using a highly detailed quadrat survey method and computer modelling technique to generate patterns of species association in relation to soil, climate, land use, and the culture of it. Proclaiming that the modelling enables the research practice to be entirely inductive, 'without a-priori', the expatriate project leader, and force behind this research, sees the method as an ultimate tool in objective ecosystem analysis.[8]

This fresh approach provides a radical departure from both species-listing and climax ecosystem classification. First, it examines species diversity in inhabited landscapes, treating these not just as impoverished ecosystems which would be better represented in reserves. Second, it focuses on the forest-savanna transition zone as a species rich tension zone (a site of speciation), rather than a species-poor zone (a site of degradation).

There are clear ways in which this research is shaped in its co-production with policy. Not only is it being conducted by an environmental programme, but it has already become the policy of this programme to work to promote biodiversity in the lived-in landscapes where it works. And for regional political reasons the project must now work in the forest-savanna transition zone. Both these dimensions are crucial to the refinancing of the programme, which has been uncertain. The expatriate hired had the skills and impetus to conduct this research.

Nevertheless these scientific practices are perhaps more significant for the way they speak to an international scientific community, enrolling certain Guinean and expatriate researchers working in Guinea into a global actor-network developing hi-tech ecosystemic research. Indeed the field methods and analytical practices were first established in the key researcher's earlier work in Central Africa as a university-based ecologist, and have been refined amongst an international network of scientists with whom he keeps in close contact, seeing research in Guinea as feeding into an international scientific and methodological endeavour. To date, Guinean university biologists who conduct national biodiversity research have been 'confined' to carrying out taxonomic studies for donor projects. Most do not even know of the existence of this research.

It is perhaps ironic that Guinean natural and social scientists, academics and project staff remain locked into colonial scientific paradigms, the view of nature they embody, and the reservation policy it has endorsed. The new, expatriate driven, science presents a radical departure from this. Yet it does not just depart merely in 'academic' ways. The new science is in dialogical relation to the old not just in method, but in its policy practice. It may counter deductive methods about climax vegetation with generative ones, but it simultaneously counters the social exclusionary biodiversity conservation of reserves with an apparently socially incorporative policy of 'participation'. Yet, as in the case of the dialogical reversal in medical research and practice under Sekou Touré that we have described, this apparent reversal depends ever more on the 'practice of science', and its capacity to differentiate the 'good' aspects of African practice (in this case land management for biodiversity) from the problematic. Indigenous framing of biological issues, and the debates that villagers have do not enter the picture. The adjudication of good and bad practices concerning African social life are again scientified, and in social relations of science as – or even more – alien than in colonial times.

3   Medicinal plants and diversity

A third set of practices considered within the rubric of biodiversity concerns medicinal plants. Numerous donor-funded projects are attempting to compile knowledge of the availability and uses of plant medicines in Guinean village territories as part of their new biodiversity focus. Related initiatives include projects (e.g. Guinée Ecologie 1998), workshops and meetings to encourage environmental and health NGOs and 'traditional healers' to pool information and discuss strategies for biodiversity conservation, such as the major

German-funded workshop in Mamou in 1999 organised by the NGO Guinée Ecologie.[9] Such practices suit the current generation of development donors concerned to link biodiversity conservation with participation and to carry out development by working through 'traditional' forms of organisation and authority.

This dimension of biodiversity also generates interest among many Guineans. The taxonomist-herbalists discussed earlier now find themselves in great demand as brokers between healers, professional botanists, donors and government staff. They are popular not least because they can speak – and help integrate – the various languages. Numerous younger university-educated people have aspirations to 'join the circuit'. One in Kissidougou spends his spare time collecting and collating village information about plant medicines, and plans to produce a book which he hopes will attract the attention of ministerial and donor personnel interested in this aspect of biodiversity.[10] Many Guineans who share this perspective are already in positions of authority in the national bureaucracy, and they have not found it hard to enrol others to their perspective.

Modern biodiversity concern is giving new force and credibility to Guinea's national association of traditional healers, which now has representation on the national biodiversity alliance UNBIO. It is also giving such healers new authority as local 'opinion leaders' in the context of environment, development and education programmes, such as the European Union-funded PACIPE which works in part through prominent local healers in attempting to communicate its particular brand of environmental conservation message. Such processes clearly do not involve all 'healers', given that the use of plant medicines is an everyday practice for most Guinean villagers and knowledge and skills concerning them are very widely distributed amongst village communities. Indeed, the networks and opportunities afforded by biodiversity concerns are shaping new forms of social and authority division amongst local medical practitioners.

Biodiversity interest has thus given renewed impetus to practices which promote local plant medicines. As mentioned earlier, during the First Republic under Sekou Touré, scientific and policy practices around plant medicines were most strongly promoted. Indeed all pharmacy students were required to conduct a study of the medical uses of a particular plant. These studies followed a general protocol which included: (a) botanical examination, (b) determination of chemical constituents, and (c) documenting pharmaceutic and therapeutic importance (e.g. Doumbouya 1974; Soumah 1976; Sylla 1975). The majority of such studies were conducted between 1972 and 1978 by students from Institut Polytechnique Gamar Abdul Nasser, Conakry for their Memoires de Diplome de Fin d'Etudes Superieures. They were rendered possible in part through funding from East Germany, which was highly supportive of President Sekou Touré at this time. The studies also drew on considerable support from ex-colonial botanist-healers. Botanical and chemical analysis was largely conducted at the

Institute de Recherche Agronomique at Seredou, where the old memoirs are still to be found.

The studies formed part of a broader set of practices associated with the political philosophy of this phase in the First Republic, heavily influenced by the writings of Sekou Touré and his ideologues. The key motives, as clarified in the students' introductions to their dissertations, include first, national self sufficiency, which is easily understood given Guinea's self-imposed economic and political isolation during this period; second, a valuing of national patrimony, and third, a revaluation of elements of African popular culture – albeit in the terms of modern science. For example:

> The strategy of Ahmed Sekou Touré teaches us that we will never have sufficient foreign exchange if we must continually import the medicines we must have to satisfy our needs; but if we valorise our flora, our fauna and our diverse natural resources to find this or that medicine, it is certain that we will thus be able to satisfy all our needs because our cultural patrimony and our natural resources are inexhaustible (Kourouma 1987: 2).

> Speaking of African values, the Secretary General of the PDG Sekou Touré has always taught us that 'Africa has values which Imperialism ignores and will always ignore; Imperialism does not know Africa and it will never know it' (Barry 1974: 1)

> Our popular medicine is a rich mine and is marked with the impressive character of our historical legacy. The revalorization of this popular medicine through a painstaking exploration of our flora, and its restitution to all the people of Guinea remains a pressing and 'exultant' duty of every militant of our country (Barry 1974: 1)

The pharmaceutical research practices of the era were thus shaped by, and contributed to, discourses which simultaneously promoted modernist science and 'authentic' African culture. The practices of cataloguing medicinal plant knowledge and repackaging it in the terms of (medical/pharmacological) science, and of valorising vegetation, are very similar to those performed in the context of international biodiversity concern today. In both cases, medicinal plant knowledge is extracted from the social relations of its day-to-day practice in village settings (cf. Agrawal 1995). But whereas under Sekou Touré this interest derived from a focus on human health, the interest of international discourse focuses on vegetation health, and whereas it was earlier locked into a nationalist discourse, international interest in biodiversity conservation is locked into an internationalist one.

Nevertheless, Guinean historical experience continues to shape its engagement with international discourse. In particular, Guineans are particularly sensitive to bio-piracy (the exploitation of local biodiversity resources by other nations or corporations). This has been important to most 'southern' perspectives on international conservation discourse, but it carries added weight in Guinea for at least three reasons. First, because there is a long history of the exploitation of local plant resources by foreign powers, both colonial and from the soviet bloc. Second, the plundering of Guinea's other mineral and timber resources by foreign companies is today of great significance, and there have been numerous popular insurgencies against them. 'David and Goliath' stories of these struggles are on the lips of rural and urban publics alike. Third, bio-piracy presupposes 'bio-wealth', affirming the idea that Guinea is tremendously rich in biodiversity resources, giving weight to the economic importance of conservation (past and future). Thus the concern is less with 'international wealth' and 'plants for plants sake' than with national wealth, and the economic benefits of conservation.

When actively contributing to international debates concerning this issue, Guinean national spokespeople also bring a second distinctive perspective. Generally in international discourse, concern with biopiracy is juxtaposed with 'indigenous intellectual property rights'. The Convention on Biodiversity and related discussions have constructed indigenous people not only as a social category, but also as a legal entity in international law. Indeed internationally, those self-defining as 'indigenous' have been pursuing their causes through international law – and their self definitions as 'indigenous' are not unrelated to this (see for example Kingsbury 1998). But Guinean spokespeople reject the 'indigenous' polarity of this debate, continuing to see the practice of valorisation of biota as a 'nationalist' enterprise, and understanding 'indigenisation' of rights as a threat to state authority and stability.[11] This category, they feel, is socially divisive where national politics has such a tendency to become ethnicised. In effect, the language of indigeneity promotes ethnogenesis; the antithesis of African nationalist discourse which those working in ministries had learnt at school. With the conflicts in Sierra Leone and Liberia on the border, this is also a very modern concern.

Once again, the particular way biodiversity is being mobilised in the country has been shaped by national history; by a sedimentation of practices from colonial times, transformed dialogically during independence, and transformed again in contemporary debate.

4   Economic plants and diversity

Extending out of interest in medicinal plants, the practice of 'biodiversity' in Guinea also draws on a fourth set of existing practices which concern economically-useful wild plants. Projects are keen to 'show villagers how valuable are products such as tree nut oils, palm oil, honey and dental sticks'. In project rhetoric, such an approach is linked to 'participation', especially among certain groups such as women's groups. It also conveniently links economic incentives to biodiversity protection. Focusing on the latter, one project worker noted:

Biodiversity is one of our strategies for the protection of natural resources which enables us to fuse economy and protection. We were oriented only towards protection, and it didn't work very well. Now with an economic emphasis, peasants are more interested. For instance, honey is a product of biodiversity, so is palm oil and palm nut oil.[12]

Many institutions have carried out village-level surveys of potentially economically-useful products. One local NGO worker who was involved in this way emphasised the benefits which this approach could, as he saw it, bring to local livelihoods: 'The people in the villages think the bush has nothing, but there is much – honey, medicinal plants – we need to show villagers that what is around them is valuable'.[13] With a similar aim of 'showing people the value of what they use', the Kankan project of the Niger River Protection Programme has commissioned a local NGO to carry out studies of the role in household economies; market potential and transformation technologies for six key useful plant species.[14] A number of botany students in Faranah also carried out studies of local plant use for their final year dissertations during the 1990s (e.g. Dopavogui and Kourouma 1993).

These practices of survey and documentation, and the project practices of 'facilitating local involvement in conservation' that staff imagine will flow from them, are focusing on a highly select number of useful plants. All of these are already widely used and semi-domesticated. Villages actively preserve wildlings, and sometimes transplant them for accessibility and convenience. In this respect the plants could be considered as more 'agricultural' than 'wild'; a point overlooked by those discussions which make a general equation between biodiversity and 'wild plants' and associate the latter with undisturbed 'nature'.

Projects have thus found fit to teach villagers the value of their own environment. In doing so they simultaneously construct an 'ignorant peasant' who does not know the value of the resources around them, and an 'intelligent project' which does. When explicitly challenged with the idea that villagers might already use and value palm oil, honey and so on, personnel promoting this perspective tend to respond with the notion that this is specialised, not generalised knowledge, thereby allocating development projects a role in the 'diffusion of information'. They also suggest that villagers may use these products, but are ignorant of their market value, thereby allocating projects a role in promoting commercialisation.

It is not difficult to trace these practices back to the colonial botanical gardens and their role in the commodification of wild plants. Botanists in the first decades of the twentieth century also sought out useful 'indigenous species' – of rubber, coffee, and so on – and so on, and sought to propagate and improve these products with a view to commercialisation.[15] This was with resources that were to be extracted from the local ecology and economy to serve the needs of a colonial administration, rather than developed locally in building synergies between local livelihoods and conservation as today's projects would emphasise.

But then, the plants concerned were generally recognised to be semi-domesticated by local populations, and indeed an aim of colonial policy was to domesticate and improve these plants further in order to enhance their economic value. Modern biodiversity concern, in contrast, seems to dictate a definition of these as 'wild' plants, not least because this confirms the relevance of developing them in a 'biodiversity' project. Other possible interpretations of biodiversity which would guide practices around these plants differently – for instance emphasising agro-biodiversity and the ways local plant use practices conserve and enhance genetic diversity among domesticated species – are hardly evident in Guinea. The difference is telling. Those practising this aspect of biodiversity policy in Guinea consider biodiversity to be something of nature, something wild; the antithesis of farming and land use.

5   Conserving biodiversity through traditional hunters

In a fifth set of practices, emerging since the late 1990s, 'traditional hunters' are being promoted as the key agents for securing biodiversity conservation objectives. In what several donor and government institutions hail as a radical new approach at the cutting-edge of 'participatory' management of national parks and protected areas, conservation policy is being co-produced with social science studies of hunter's knowledge and social roles.

The historical connections between hunting and conservation in Guinea are long and largely oppositional. In particular, early forest conservation efforts followed closely on the heels of the protracted armed struggles with local populations through which the French had taken power; wars which pitted the French against Mande armies and the hunter-warriors who led them. As oral histories emphasise, hunting skills and experience were strongly linked to those of war and defence. Key war leaders such as Samory Touré also had strong reputations as hunters, recalling similar traditions among their earlier ancestors in the foundation of the medieval Mali Empire (e.g. Niane 1965). Once forest reserves had been established, in many cases on lands emptied of their people by war-related death and flight, a system of French-militarily trained forest guards was put in place to protect their boundaries. This was a structure of control separate from, and indeed in opposition to, hunters who as defeated warriors, representatives of local populations and land and resource users themselves, remained – often bitterly – excluded.

Hunter's 'brotherhoods', as those associated through initiation, apprentice-ship networks, and shared ceremonies are frequently termed, continued to act as a forum for mobilisation against the French throughout most of the colonial period. Administrators saw them as a dangerous threat to their precarious authority and made sustained efforts to suppress their activities. Hence it is not surprising that post-independence, hunters took the opportunity to reconstitute themselves as an organised administrative force. The first prefectoral hunter's associations, such as Kankan, date to this new climate of the early 1960s and were respected by the First Republic's regime, although only in an overtly 'demystified' form.

The new generation of biodiversity-focused parks and reserves of the 1990s is developing, it would appear, an inverse relationship with hunters from its colonial predecessors. European donors and the forestry agents they support are dispensing with guards around several national parks and forest reserves, adopting a policy to work instead through hunter's brotherhoods, now newly respected for their knowledge and authority as custodians of the bush. Working through a 'traditional organisation' supports the self-representation of donors and government departments as part of contemporary, internationalised 'best practice' in conservation, which is both 'participatory' and respectful of 'culture'.

The respect accorded to hunters and their knowledge in these approaches contrasts strongly with the widespread disrespect for (or ignoring of) farmers and their knowledge in other current biodiversity practices in Guinea. 'Traditional hunters' are also conceptualised rather differently from the way 'traditional healers' are treated when biodiversity is equated with medicinal plants: whereas healers and their knowledge are desocialised and (re)packaged in western scientific terms, the traditional hunter is imaged as thoroughly social, with knowledge embedded in forms of esoteric power, and central to the forms of local social organisation which can ensure conservation. This imagery draws on, and serves to promote further exemplars of, a certain genre of social scientific study of people-environment relations and hunter's place within them.

Such studies, among both foreign and national analysts, embed hunters in images of past, harmonious community natural resource management, as a central pillar of Mande society and its once apparently successful management of lands, vegetation and fire. The breakdown of hunter's brotherhoods is imaged as a casualty of colonisation and modernity, bringing about environmental destruction (e.g. Fofana 1990; Zeroki 1990; Steiglitz 1990). In this way, the new imagery of the hunting persona simultaneously constructs a particular image of past society and environmental history (Fairhead and Leach 1996). PACIPE has been particularly active in promoting this new image of hunter's societies. As one study it commissioned argues:

Hunting is the activity of people gifted in sorcery, friendship with supernatural beings and deep knowledge of plants and animals. In short, of people with superior powers. It is useful to recall the key role played by the hunter in traditional society. He is the founder of $\frac{3}{4}$ of all villages; the selector of good farmland; the prospector of watercourses and forests; the finder of hideouts and sites rich in animals. His social role covers all aspects of existence and life: as protector of the community against all forces of evil; as courageous defender/warrior; as skilled healer; as supplier of fish and animal protein; as volunteer for sensitive missions in the interests of the community, and as organiser of cult ceremonies such as funerals (PACIPE n.d.)

The study interprets writings from the Sundiata period 760 years ago to suggest that Mande communities have a coherent set of rules regulating natural resource use – a *wa ton* ('bush law') – associated with mythologies linking people with the bush (*wa*) and telling of dangers if these laws are transgressed. Hunters, key in ensuring that these laws are kept, are thus central to a moral and rule-bound 'good community' living in harmony with nature.

Several environmental programmes have been engaged in practices to reinforce – or perhaps transform – hunters' brotherhoods. PACIPE has been supporting the formation of district, sub-prefecture, prefecture and national hunting associations, in a federated structure which mirrors the present national administration. Senior members of the prefectoral administration attended the election of the prefectoral hunting offices, while the national association has the President of the Republic as its figurehead. The National Association is represented on UNBIO. At a prefecture level the new hunter's societies have had to sign 'nature charters' aligning them with national forestry and environment codes and the objectives of the administrations that write them. In particular these give hunter's brotherhoods responsibility to respect the hunting calendar, protect endangered animal species, fight bush fire, and reinforce all environmental education and natural resource management programmes in the prefecture. While PACIPE suggests that charters are drawn up with the hunters concerned, it is notable that all prefectoral charters to date are identical. In the buffer zone of the Parc National du Haut Niger, the chief hunter of each village has been appointed head of a village *wa ton* committee, empowered to allocate a limited number of hunting and fishing permits, and to regulate who hunts where, when and what, and who sets fire when, where and how. And Toma-speaking hunters are now employed as forest reserve guards by donor-supported conservation programmes around the forest reserves of Ziama and Diecke in southern Guinea (GFA 1998).

However, other ethnographic representations from the region (e.g. Leach 1994; Fairhead and Leach 1996; Jackson 1988; McNaughton 1988), suggest aspects of the hunters' positioning in rural social relations which are overlooked or obscured in modern conservation-related representations. These include the ambiguity of the hunter's 'social' position: in their fraternising with bush spirits, their long sojourns alone in the bush, their reputation for possessing powerful and esoteric 'fetish' medicines with the capacity to harm and disrupt the social fabric. Viewed thus, hunters operate more on the fringes of 'normal' social relations, with unpredictable and dangerous agency, than as pillars of local socio-political life. Equally, regional ethnographies suggest the ambiguous relationship with other central pillars of modern Mande sociality, most notably Islam. The central Mande city in Guinea, Kankan, is also the heart of Islamic scholarship and teaching. Yet what hunters play up, by way of land spirits and esoteric sources of power, Islam frequently plays down. Imams and hunters' society leaders are both patrons who compete for clients, albeit mobilising very different resources. These tensions are played out in every village in the region, albeit textured by their particular political histories (see Ferme 1992).

The imaging of hunters' brotherhoods in environment and development discourse also – conveniently – sidesteps distinctions between 'real' hunters and other hunters; what senior hunters sometimes call 'small boys with guns who just go out and shoot'. The derogatory 'small boy' in these constructions of masculinity connotes less age, and more lack of experience, knowledge and medicines, or – where practiced – formal initiation. Yet there are many hunting practices in which younger men, particularly, do engage, from trapping, to hunting cane rats with fire and dogs, to shooting monkeys for money. Their distinction from 'real' hunting is fragile: increasingly so as commercial hunting brings money-power, at the same time as declining animal numbers diminish opportunities to demonstrate other-worldly powers through impressive kills.

The desire of hunters' brotherhoods to enforce their control over all gun hunters in this context is strongly supported, if not stimulated, both by conservation organisations and by the Guinean state. Studies conducted under conservation auspices describe 'free' hunters as anarchic in their practices, unguided by sound resource management principles, and the major cause of environmental degradation through fire and over exploitation of bushmeat. In the region of the Parc National du Haut Niger the authorities now stipulate that only card-carrying members of the hunters' brotherhood may be armed, and that the brotherhood should police this and report infractions to government officials. In this process, new distinctions are being constructed between these associated, globally and ecologically aligned hunters and 'other hunters'. A Guinean project director within the European Union programme spoke of 'setting hunters against hunters' – in this case the project supported *wa ton* leaders against those who came from outside the park buffer zone to hunt for commercial sale.

For the Guinean state, the hunter's association is now its 'second army'. Enforcing those with guns to join hunters' brotherhoods is part of a policy to control arms in the countryside, a real state security issue given current regional instability. Indeed the head of the national hunters' association stated publicly in a rural radio interview that 'our government has two armies of which we are the second'. And a senior hunter of Kankan's association made an even more explicit radio call to arms: 'We are the same as soldiers. The latter are in the town and we are in the bush. But we have the same work.

So our friends who are outside, we invite you to unite, strengthen yourselves and to do hunting as it should be done'.[16] The president has further drawn Mande hunters into the military side of the state and reinforced their links with national political interests by deploying them as fighters alongside the Guinean forces defending the borders from Sierra Leone's rebel war. And linking these environment and security concerns, both hunters and the state are now using the discourse of environmental protection to argue for the protection of 'their lands and themselves' against 'foreign infiltrators', with the hunters authorised to provide such surveillance.

The hunter leadership is actively exploiting this new co-operation with the state to strengthen its hand in rural social and political relations. As Moussa Konde, a senior hunter from the prefecture of Mandiana, stated in a radio interview: 'We hunters have seen that hunting has abandoned its customs a little. Today, anyone who puts a gun to his shoulder declares himself a hunter. It is this that we want to discourage. No-one who hasn't been initiated at the hunter's altar (*dankun*) can be in our association, today or tomorrow'.[17]

But while some spokespeople imagine hunters' brotherhoods as close to the state through these associations, it is also the case that hunters have simultaneously used long-proven strategies to distance themselves from too close an alignment, maintaining their autonomy. Thus tellingly, in one radio programme, a senior hunter described the new structure of state-aligned hunters' associations as 'the project's brotherhood', referring to the European PACIPE, and conflating its personnel and motives with the state as villagers frequently do. In the prefecture of Mandiana, hunters have placed powerless junior hunting apprentices (*donso den*) at the helm of village, district and prefectoral offices, confident that they can easily be called upon to administer policies acceptable to the elders, but that they can be just as easily stalled in enforcing unpopular measures. Where senior hunters are placed in such official positions, they are – as the Kankan PACIPE leader admitted – not the senior 'traditional' hunters, but 'those who are canny, and can negotiate well with the administration'.[18] This simultaneous proximity and distance from the state is also underlain by ambiguity in Mande hunters' relationship to party politics. As the 'second army', hunters are seen to be supportive not only of the state administration but also of the party in power, Lansana Conte's PUP, with President Conte as the hunters' figurehead. This party is highly unpopular in the Mande region, which largely supports the oppositional RPG. Throughout the Mande region, it can be assumed that hunters' integration with state services, state-supported projects and the state-sponsored national hunters' association is in delicate balance with vehement political opposition to the party in power. It could be further argued that hunters' new-found status within development and national security provides a basis from which to build what could become an armed oppositional political force. When project staff complain that hunters in Kankan have become 'politicised' and difficult to work with, it is this set of tensions which is at stake.

The potential reach, and regional significance, of the new relationships and tensions forged in the hunter-parks nexus should not be underestimated. The European Union has identified hunters' societies as the new force for conservation across West Africa, and regional conservation programmes in which these newly-shaped hunters' associations might operate are developing apace. PACIPE alone covers six West African countries, while many other donors are jumping on the bandwagon to 'work through hunters' societies'. Meanwhile, trans-border national parks are being developed along Guinea's frontiers with Mali, Guinea Bissau, Côte d'Ivoire and Senegal. These trans-frontier parks are interesting not just for their scale and reach, but also for the links between environment and national security now used to justify them. Both governments and international donors are well aware of the potential for insurgency to develop in the 'boundary wildernesses' which straddle many African borders; a legacy of the placing of colonial boundaries in areas depopulated by warfare and now sparsely inhabited by semi-itinerant people of ambiguous nationality, engaged in semi-legal trade and mining activities (cf. Richards 1996). As European Union programmes suggest, border parks they fund will bring 'a controlling presence' to these areas, in the form of patrols, management and park.[19] Notably, this perspective on the meaning and function of African parks appears to contrast sharply with the earlier European attempts documented so well by Beinart (1989), Anderson and Grove (1986) and others, which sought to preserve perceived wildernesses as empty, 'pristine' places without people. Yet this latter perspective has not disappeared from the visions of donor and government officials, and the two remain very much in tension. Hunters' brotherhoods are located within this tension as the envisaged 'controlling presence' who will simultaneously keep unwanted people out of lands designated for wildlife.

Through these new environmental initiatives, then, hunters are being asked to play roles in defence which re-invoke older forms of hunter-warriordom, now hitched to modern state interests. But reinforcing hunters' associations does not necessarily ensure their allegiance to the party in power. And while development agencies are drawing on anthropological texts and idealised versions of traditional society in reinvigorating hunters' societies in Guinea, many Guineans are noting the success of the hunter-based 'Kamajor' civil defence forces across the border in Sierra Leone in organising against the RUF and indeed elements of the state. What development agencies might see as a peaceful participatory approach, ceding control over environmental affairs from paramilitary forest guards to 'traditional organisations', is paradoxically transferring control to Guinea's 'second army'; a second army which is becoming the primary army in regional warfare. Thus as international ideas around conservation approach

articulate with national scientific and policy practices in Guinea, new and unexpected dynamics are being unleashed, concerning both ethnicised political
processes, and hunters' own re-negotiations with each other and with organs of
the state.

Setting priorities for biodiversity conservation

These five sets of biodiversity-related practices illustrate how concepts emanating from an international scientific and policy field are operationalised
in national and local settings. Yet today there are also many occasions on
which Guinean nationals are called to take part in internationally-orchestrated
forums and discussions related to aspects of biodiversity. In these, concepts
and practices generated nationally and locally, at the intersection of international and local scientific and policy traditions, may be fed back up to
be presented internationally. To exemplify how this happens, we take the
case of the international biodiversity priority-setting workshop for the forest
region of West Africa convened by Conservation International in December
1999. We examine the conceptions of biodiversity demonstrated by Guinean
delegates, and how they were deployed.[20] Yet the case also illustrates how
the very practices in such international forums can lead discussion simply
to confirm prior framings of the issues concerned. Amidst these practices,
more localised perspectives have little power to challenge or alter the terms of
debate.

Nine Guinean participants from government departments and national NGOs
attended this huge regional meeting to set biodiversity priorities within the
Upper Guinean forest zone, itself already identified as a large-scale biodiversity 'hotspot' by Conservation International. The workshop, with funding from the Global Environment Facility and several business corporations,
brought nearly 200 scientists – conservation biologists, botanists, zoologists,
and some sociologists and anthropologists – policy-makers and government
and NGO representatives from six countries to a coastal resort in Ghana for five
days.

'Hotspot' itself is an emotive concept drawn from conflict prediction, con-
juring a sense of urgency. Technically, biodiversity hotspots describe areas of
high species richness, high concentrations of endemics and high endangered-
ness (Mittermeier *et al.* 1997). The director of Conservation International's
centre for Applied Biodiversity Science set out the workshop aims in the opening plenary session: to draw together scientific knowledge about biodiversity
and pressures on it in the region; to mobilise new international resources; to attract the attention of national politicians to conservation/biodiversity issues, and
to stimulate new networks and collaboration. Scientific premises include that
(a) published data is scarce, suspect or non-existent; (b) that data gaps can be

filled by bringing together the best local and regional experts; (c) that common resources and ecosystems are currently managed with little co-ordination between countries, and that (d) there are needs for a quick assessment of priorities to feed into national planning.

As the workshop unfolded, it became obvious that it was framed so as to deliver dramatic messages about the urgent need for biodiversity conservation and funding for it. This was evident in its structuring: four days of priority-setting, first in thematic and then in regional groups, followed by the preparation of glossy maps using Geographical Information Systems technology to expose priorities formally to media, donors and politicians on the final afternoon. The mass of scientific expertise and the authority and fundability of the conclusions were seen as inextricably linked: as one of the Conservation International organisers put it, we have 'brought together the best in the world . . . we will come up with the best information that no-one can question'. The linkages between regional integration, attracting world attention and arresting degradation were also emphasised: as the head of Conservation International's West Africa programme argued, the degradation of the Guinean forest block into fragments in different countries has reduced global recognition of it as a single regional ecosystem. Yet optimism, he suggested, lies in the fact that there are, globally, more technologies and resources available for conservation than ever before: the task ahead is to bring these into Upper Guinea so as to 'rescue this hotspot'. Nevertheless, nationalistic concerns came into tension with the promotion of a 'regional hotspot' image. In the opening plenary session, a Guinean representative of the United Nations Development Programme, but also of the NGO Guinée Ecologie, for example, critiqued the dominant discourse of regional integration in arguing that Conservation International should link with the cultural priorities of each country, but this suggestion was given no further attention by the organisers.

The first two days involved discussion in thematic groups, either biological (plants, mammals, insects, reptiles, aquatics and biogeography) or socio-economic (land use, population, conflict, protected areas). The Guinean delegates met together and agreed to distribute themselves throughout these scientific working groups to ensure that national priorities (largely for protected areas which already received donor funding) were not overridden by 'expert' scientific criteria.

The biological-social distinction, with the requirement that experts identify with one or the other, followed the workshop's conceptualisation of biodiversity as associated with 'original' forest vegetation on which human 'impacts' constitute 'threats' and 'pressures'. 'Opportunities' exist only in what can be done by policy-makers and conservation initiatives. Both this conceptualisation, and the requirement that groups generate consensus (and 'fix' it on a map), led to certain aspects being framed out of discussion. Uncertainty or differences of opinion amongst scientists were to be dealt with by rating 'level of expert confidence' (on a 1–5 scale) on working group forms, but nowhere in the process was there scope to record more fundamental debate or questioning of framing assumptions. In this context, mismatches were evident between the consensual outcomes mapped and recorded, the personalised data origins and often heated arguments that took place within the groups, and – even more striking – the different perspectives which many scientists expressed in their published research or discussion of it outside the workshop sessions.

The mammal group, for example, began by mapping areas that were important for 'endangered species'. The Guinean representative in this group took the opportunity to emphasise the numbers of endangered elephants which species lists had revealed in the Ziama forest reserve. Then several European group members decided that given paucity of data, they would use three types of animal as the focus for their mapping: antelopes, primates and carnivores, and ranked areas according to presence of species listed in IUCN's 1996 book of threatened species. Discussion ranged largely around individuals' knowledge and opinions, frequently of a place and species-specific kind. Yet the lines drawn on the map from this gave the impression of general agreement by a group. The ideas of a specialist on small mammals and bats, concerning how farming dynamics in rocky landscapes of the Guinea highlands created high diversity of small mammals, were raised in the group, but dropped from the map.

The plants group was led by a Dutch forest ecologist who had been involved with the large European forest research project ECOSYN. He, and a Swiss botanist, used its analytical framework and findings to orchestrate the discussion. A working document had been prepared especially for the workshop, assembling data from four sources: (a) a rare species list; 279 woody and herbaceous species confined to one or two Upper Guinean countries; (b) ECOSYN maps of species distribution, mainly as single dots, compiled from herbaria, forest inventories and floristic surveys, for twenty-eight species; (c) published maps for forty-one species confined to one or two countries; (4) forest areas in Cote d'Ivoire, Ghana and Liberia, from the ECOSYN database, marking forest condition from 1 (hardly any left) to 7 (excellent). The results of this process indicated almost the whole of the Ghanaian forest zone as top conservation priority, with important areas also in Cote d'Ivoire and Liberia, ranking key forest areas in Sierra Leone and Guinea as much less important. The Guinean and Sierra Leonean group members had been much less vocal in discussion. But their colleagues critiqued this apparent 'consensus' when the map was presented in plenary, arguing that plant inventories in their countries were far from complete, and suggesting that the ECOSYN research project's priority countries had biased the outcome.

The socio-economic working groups were asked to identify threats and determine impacts, and to depict these geographically – ranking areas according to a 'pressure index' for the given threat. Thus people and social issues were defined only as threats to 'natural' biodiversity, whether through their population growth, land use or conflict. Indeed the forms to be filled out for each threat left no space for any other process: instances where perhaps people might be living with or enhancing biodiversity. As the completed forms testified, these practices of form construction fit supportively with conceptualisations of biodiversity in terms of human pressure on natural ecosystems. As for the biological groups, several participants voiced rather different perspectives outside the sessions. But in the plenary presentation of socio-economic groups' findings, the maps and pressures appeared with consensual clarity: agriculture, logging, firewood, timber, non-timber forest product collection, urbanisation and refugees.

The priority areas resulting from each group were compiled in a set of large, coloured maps prepared overnight by CI's Geographical Information Systems (GIS) team. Participants were then re-grouped to reflect geographical areas, and asked to consider the maps together, and in the light of them, address where and what sort of conservation action was needed. Regional integration was seen as key: both in attracting donors and because so many priority areas crossed national borders. Indeed one of several cross-cutting thematic groups was to consider 'landscape connections', covering such issues as cross-border parks and corridors. To promote such a 'spirit of cross-border integration' in the face of potentially nationalistic interests, the geographical groups were not by country, but consisted of five zones which crossed national borders; Guinea being part of two of these. As the regional integrative groups started to work, the African national representatives tended to take over the process – and many international participants became drifters or opted out. National representatives were very keen that 'their' priority projects and protected areas be included, and were somewhat disgruntled when there proved insufficient overlap between the maps of the different scientific groups to justify this.

The plenary discussion, interestingly, raised several comments from national participants concerning the need to be sensitive to and incorporative of 'local perspectives'. For example a Guinean delegate argued that 'we have spoken of many problems linked to people, but we are ignoring the importance of local interests in resources and sustainable use'. He gave the examples of medicinal plants (on which he has been working in Guinea), and of nere and karite (shea butter), thus voicing conceptualisations of biodiversity linked both with medicinal and economically-useful plants. Such comments from the floor, which were starting to raise questions publicly outside the main framing of the debate (questions discussed in the bar, but not so far in the workshop plenaries or recommendations), nevertheless found no traction as the workshop deliberations were now drawing to a close. The Conservation International West Africa programme director summarised recommendations that would be given to donors that afternoon: to pursue regional conservation strategies uniting governments; that donors use the maps etc. for prioritisng actions; that messages are used in the global media to generate awareness of the region; that countries engage in national follow-up; to publish, share and repatriate data, and to promote capacity-building and partnerships. Another CI staff member stressed the need for short-term solutions too. 'Some of these won't have time to involve full community participation, or even to be sustainable, but they are needed before it is too late'. The programme director used this point to conclude on, recalling a 'timebomb' icon: if 'nature for its own sake' – the recurring phrase of the workshop – is to be saved, the task is too urgent for the niceties of local involvement. Within the following year, the workshop maps and recommendations were distributed on CDRom to a large range of donors, and 'fed back' – once again – to national governments through presentations in the six countries concerned.

At one level, then, the workshop with its slick, upbeat style and sophisticated use of technology appeared to garner consensus and support. But undercurrents of dissent – from the framing of biodiversity and people-biodiversity relations, and from the regional emphasis – were also evident in discussions which found no exposure: in plenary remarks not picked up, and particularly, outside the sessions themselves. Such dissent was certainly voiced by Guinean delegates whose work, alliances and contextual interest focused on biodiversity as used by people as medicines or semi-wild plants, or who deemed local people – as 'traditional' hunters or healers – as possible partners in conserving biodiversity, rather than simply as threats to it.

Furthermore, certain donors – ostensibly the audience for the workshop outcomes – also 'saw through' the process. As a West Africa-based World Bank staff member responsible for disbursing Global Environment Facility funds commented, this is just the latest of the ongoing set of biodiversity prioritisations he had attended. 'IUCN did their Africa priorities, WWF their ecoregions . . . given all these, I could justify a project absolutely anywhere in relation to one or the other'. Yet he also noted, on the ways donors respond to the results of priority-setting exercises: 'It may be nice to know that there is X or Y bird there, but in the end, conservation – and where one chooses to do it – just depends on institutions and politics'. In this, he suggested that the 'expert science' of the priority-setting may be less important for its content than for the weight of authority it lends when justifying conservation projects motivated on other grounds.

Conclusions

'Biodiversity' as an explicit organising concept for conservation is new to policy in Guinea. Here we have tried to explore the ways in which Guineans and expatriates working in the country have interpreted and operationalised it. The different sets of biodiversity practices that we have explored in this chapter are not associated exclusively with particular people. Rather, people and institutions, and the alliances they form, are engaging simultaneously with practices that we have considered separately.

To understand the emergence of these practices in Guinea today, it has been necessary not just to consider how the international vortex articulates with national and local scientific and policy traditions, but to do so in relation to the specific history of the country, and to contemporary social and political circumstances. Taking a practice perspective to do this allows attention both to the sedimentation of history into 'structure', and the capacity for people to be the creative agents, or bricoleurs.

Those mobilising the biodiversity concept are grappling with its relevance to their work and its applicability to policy, latching on to existing sets of practices. The impetus from biodiversity has not left scientific and policy practice unscathed, as enduring phenomena. Rather these have been subtly changed in form and in meaning for those conducting them. Yet this has occurred in a dialogical relationship with practice-as-was.

This case also illustrates how scientific and policy processes produce and reproduce social and natural categories. For all their variation, the perspectives we have discussed here all, in their different ways, present biodiversity as a 'nature' which people might act on or exploit, but from which their lives are ontologically distinct. Species lists drawn up for reserves iconise their superior diversity, but remain uncompared with inhabited landscapes. 'Semi-domesticated' plants (for want of a better phrase) are recast as 'semi-wild' ones, detached from the social processes of their establishment. In affirming such categories, these perspectives exclude both key alternative local framings, and a range of other ecological, historical and social analyses which would point to a dynamic landscape perspective on forests – seeing vegetation patterns throughout the region as shaped through the interaction of social and ecological processes over time. Paradoxically, it seems that even foci with the potential for building such a landscape perspective – such as oil palms, long managed, used and spread by people – become detached from the social processes of their establishment in their reconfiguration into the 'wild plants' of international biodiversity debates.

Despite avowed attempts to 'include people' in biodiversity conservation, then – to move from colonial exclusionary approaches to modern 'conservation with development' and 'participation' – the framing and institutional/funding imperatives linked to international biodiversity debates have pushed those working within their ambit further towards practices which reproduce western, colonial distinctions between nature and culture. Where villagers' perspectives have been incorporated, this has been only partially, with 'good' and 'bad' practices in African social life being adjudicated by scientific enquiry based on alien values. Nevertheless, it is partly through engagement with local social and political processes that this reshaping has occurred. To the extent that certain hunters, 'traditional' healers and village authorities, for instance, engage with these emergent possibilities for their own ends, they are active, not passive in these social and moral transformations, and in the range of material effects which might ensue.

Notes

1. Listing practice (what is listed, and what is significant to the list) is also shaped by culture. Certain species have, for instance, come to iconise (or embody) the idea of 'endangerment'. Elephants are one example; chimpanzees, are another, having come to stand for their own endangerment and habitat loss without, seemingly, a need for research into their changing status and whether they (or their habitat) are in fact in danger. How chimpanzees (and other icons) have acquired this status would require a full genealogy of iconography, but European debates about their export from West Africa for scientific experimentation in the 1960s would come into it. Yet chimpanzees (which are not in the least endangered according to villagers in many parts of Guinea) carry very different significance in local debates.
2. Interview, aid official, forestry project, Nzerekore, 15 February 1999.
3. Interview, Director, Institut de Recherche Agronomique, Seredou, 18 February 1999.
4. Interview, Head of Departement Eaux et Fôrets, Institute of Faranah, 23 February 1999.
5. Interview, Park Manager, Parc National du Haut Niger, Sidakoro, 26 February 1999.
6. Ibid.
7. Interview, Head of Biodiversity Section, National Environment Directorate, Conakry, March 1999.
8. Interview, European consultant, EU Niger River Protection Programme, Conakry, 15 March 1999.
9. Interview, senior researcher, Guinée Ecologie, March 1999.
10. Interview, NGO leader, Kissidougou, 2 February 1999.
11. Interview, Head of Biodiversity Section, Direction Nationale de L'Environnement, Conakry, March 1999.
12. Interview, second NGO leader, Kissidougou, 1 February 1999.
13. Interview, NGO leader, Kissidougou, 2 February 1999.
14. These are *Carapa procera*, *Xylopia aethiopica*, the shea butter tree, *Parkia biglobosa*, the oil palm *Elaeis guineensis*, and *Lophira alata* which furnishes chewing sticks. Interview, Project Manager, Kankan, 9 February 1999.
15. For example, Rapport d'ensemble sur les produits du pays, 1896, National Archives, Conakry, 2D173; Chevalier, A., Rapport sur les nouvelles recherches sur les plantes à caoutchouc de la Guinée française, 1909, Senegalese National Archives, 1G276.
16. Interview, Kankan Rural Radio, 29 August 1998.

17. Ibid.
18. Interview, Project Manager, Kankan, 9 February 1999.
19. Interview, European consultant, European Union programme, Conakry, January 1999.
20. Data and participants' statements given in this section were recorded during participant-observation of the Conservation International meeting 'From the Forest to the Sea: Biodiversity Connections from Guinea to Ghana', December 1999.

5   Biodiversity and conservation in Trinidad

Introduction

Science and policy around 'biodiversity' in Trinidad have become deeply embroiled with ongoing controversy over the establishment of national parks. This chapter focuses on the unfolding national parks deliberation, exploring the ways that biodiversity concepts and practices have become incorporated within and shaped by it. The focus is thus less on the transformation of scientific and policy practices in articulation with globalised biodiversity discussion (as in the last chapter), and more on how competing practices and visions of science play into a particular and highly politicised policy process. This reveals how science plays into politics and resource control; into competition and turf battles between government departments, and into public contestation of policy objectives. The case can thus discern how political processes mediate the moral and social implications and effects of science and policy.

Since the 1960s there have been various moves to create a system of national parks in Trinidad. The rationale, location and extent of the proposed parks have repeatedly been elaborated at a nexus between conservation activists and their NGOs, the Wildlife Section of the state Forestry Division, conservation biologists at the University of the West Indies, and government and private sector interests in promoting ecotourism. These institutions are variously supported by international scientists and funders, keen to establish protected areas to blend international conservation goals with national development.

Despite many plans, legislation and implementation have been blocked. Although this has been attributed variously to lack of political will in a government of Trinidad and Tobago more committed to industrial development issues, and to inefficiency and infighting amongst the people and organisations promoting protected areas policy, in this chapter we explore further reasons, rooted in the relationships between science and policy, and the social relations through which scientific and policy practices have evolved.

In short, and as the chapter will argue, the proposed national parks system, in its varied permutations, continues to be focused on the preservation, not use of lands that are in part privately owned, farmed, forested, hunted, squatted or otherwise illegally used. There is a tension between 'participation' as practised within this scientific and policy nexus (principally involving community-based conservation organisations promoting a 'win-win' ecotourism agenda), and 'participation' in the policy process by others, especially through wider political systems. Land users whose rights and interests would be curtailed express critique via the press, the law, administrative politics and party politics, not via project-managed participatory or deliberative processes. To date, resolution has been in favour of land users who have succeeded in blocking the national parks legislation politically. Their success in this is assisted by opposition both from other bureaucracies (principally Forestry), which would lose control of resources should an autonomous national parks authority (advocated by donors) be established, and from legislators and politicians concerned by the costs and wisdom of taking large loans, and who are sceptical of the internationally-influenced science shaping the proposals.

Historical context

These scientific and policy processes around biodiversity and protected areas must be understood in a broader historical context. Trinidad's history has left the state in control over 50 per cent of the island's land, with environmental debates hinging on the proper management of state land, shaped by the social make-up of the state. Linked to this, national debate concerning environmental problems in Trinidad turns on the question of 'squatters on state land' and 'abuse of state land by its custodians'. Environmental debates have thus been shaped as the flip side of the politics of land allocation by the state. At the same time, there is a strong tradition in natural history among a Trinidad elite, fuelled in the nineteenth century by its botanical gardens. In 1893, for example, the Field Naturalists Club was started by a group of scientists and professionals as a group for the study of natural history, and by 1894 its regular publications were advocating conservation messages (Mootoosingh 1979). This local expertise has long left national environmental debates in tension with international debates. There is a tradition of strong national capability, linked to a sense of national administrative autonomy. On whose terms, this tradition would ask, is one to be 'part of the wider world'? Debates internal to the country often become politicised and polarised in this way, questioning whether they are driven by actors in the international field (who 'do not know the country') or by Trinidad's people and issues.

After Trinidad's pre-Colombian population collapse, the island became all but deserted by the 1770s. The Spanish and then British authorities encouraged colonisation by granting land, yet by 1838, only 5 per cent of the island was cultivated. Crown land was not granted to freed slaves, so that they would be forced to become wage labourers on plantations. Many former slaves preferred, however, to squat illegally on state land, provoking administrative attempts at control over squatting (Pemberton 1996; Brereton 1981).

Despite most state land being covered by forest or cocoa forest, the late nineteenth century saw recurrent administrative concern with forest clearance and its impact on climate (Hart 1891). The environmental debate was linked to control over squatting which was recognised as a principle cause of forest decline:

> The wanton felling and burning of forests . . by a roving set of semi-civilized African Squatters, principally 'Congos' and 'Cangas,' who, after reaping one or two crops of rice or corn, abandoned the place and wandered to some other convenient locality, generally fertile virgin lands, to do likewise. Whole tracts of rich forests have been thus ruthlessly destroyed (Devenish 1875, in Hart 1891:7).

From the 1880s, certain administrators suggested that forests be reserved. As Pemberton (1996) shows, this was functional to the elite in restricting sales of crown land to small farmers, thus promoting their availability as a labour force. Others felt it irrelevant and limiting to cocoa-driven economic growth. When an Indian forester was sent to report on forests (and on reservation), reservation sceptics felt undermined by external expertise:

> the opinions expressed from this Colony were to the effect that his services were not required in Trinidad, and that my predecessor, Mr. Prestoe, reported in strong terms that he saw no cause for a report from such an officer, and was of opinion that local experience was quite sufficient to guide Government in its Forest policy (Hart 1891: 1).

Others, more in favour of reservation, sought justification for it in international 'good practice', but linked to national capability. Thus Hart himself drew positive comparison with European and American conservation, yet sensitive to accusations of being driven by external colonial interest, was careful to draw also on Trinidad's history of environmental concern and its wardens' ideas in reserving riversides and river heads.

The expression of internally-contentious issues in terms of arguments for and against 'outside' influence has become a recurring theme in the evolution of conservation in Trinidad. This can be seen, in turn, as linked to Trinidad's status as an island with its very particular social and economic history, at once needing engagement with the wider world but on its own terms, not as a 'colony' or – in modern times – as an 'aid dependent' poor country.

Early conservation under the Forest Department

Following Hart's report of 1891, a second Indian forester's report foreshadowed the establishment of a forestry branch of the Crown Lands Department in 1901. In 1918 this became a fully-fledged Forest Department.[1] The administration soon began to designate areas of crown land as forest reserves, created and managed for their indirect environmental benefits (their maintenance of climatic conditions for agricultural crops, preservation of water supply and prevention of erosion and flooding). While the Forest Ordinance of 1913 regulated timber production in forest reserves on state lands, it was not until the late 1920s that timber production became an important Forest Department concern (Marshall 1925).

Increasing forest exploitation in the 1940s brought about an interest in preserving small areas of 'relict' natural forests, supposed to represent the country's major natural forest types, as 'nature reserves'. The Forest Department began to set these aside in the 1940s using existing 'prohibited area' legislation which provided for strict control, making entry an offence (Shand 1993: 239).

Concerns with wildlife protection also emerged early in the twentieth century, with Trinidad's first game sanctuary established in 1928 (Thelen and Faizool 1980: 5). Legislation concerning the conservation of wildlife enabled the creation of wildlife sanctuaries in 1933, with thirteen established between 1934 and 1968 (Bacon and Ffrench 1972). These were generally in forest reserves, but some extended into state lands (Shand 1993: 239). A dedicated Wildlife Section was established within the Forest Department in 1950, while the Conservation of Wildlife Ordinance No. 16 of 1958 (becoming law in 1963) made further provision for the establishment of wildlife sanctuaries, where hunting was prohibited.

These early reservation efforts shaped subsequent scientific and policy practices in several significant ways. First, they created reserves and sanctuaries which existed in the landscape, and which would continue to influence subsequent decisions about the siting and management of protected areas. Second, they created a sense of experience, status and authority in the Forest Department as the state agency with the capacity to control and manage lands reserved for environmental purposes.

The recreation issue and early discussion of national parks

During the 1960s, several trends made these environmental provisions – now of the post-independence Forestry Division – appear insufficient to activists within the country. First, pressures from human use – especially squatting, illegal timber felling, and quarrying – were seen to be growing. These were particularly apparent to urban-based observers who could find evidence for these supposed trends in the highly-visible Northern Range (Figure 5.1). Second, protection was deemed piecemeal, partial and ineffective. For example, in wildlife sanctuaries hunting was prohibited, but other activities affecting wildlife habitat such as tree plantation and quarrying were not; and in forest reserves, the 1913 ordinance allowed squatters to be charged for timber removal but not to be evicted

Figure 5.1 Trinidad's Northern Range near Port of Spain, with forest cleared for agriculture

(Thelen and Faizool, 1980). In short, the existing legislation did not prohibit activities seen to destroy 'natural heritage'. Third, the Forestry Division itself felt that wildlife conservation efforts took a hit and miss approach.[2] High degrees of scientific uncertainty about wildlife populations, requirements and habitats were hindering management, suggesting that effective management needed better data.

It was concerns with recreation, however, that prompted the first concerted government reflection on national parks. A shorter working week and increased urbanisation and industrialisation contributed to the growing demand of Trinidadian citizens (or at least those vocal in the press) for a variety of outdoor recreational activities (Thelen and Faizool 1980). Nature-based recreation would, it was argued, improve national health and living standards by providing the population with 'meaningful' ways to spend leisure time.[3] At the same time, internal tourism would distribute the benefits of urban economic growth to Trinidad's more rural regions. Such discourses were promoted especially by those visiting nature parks on holidays abroad, who felt that Trinidad's impressive flora and fauna, scenery and waterfalls could be similarly deployed. Hence arguments were made for the creation of national parks oriented mainly towards recreational, aesthetic and educational values.

Evident in several earlier documents,[4] recreational emphasis figured strongly in the deliberations of the first dedicated government committee on national parks issues. Its recommendation for a statutory authority with responsibility for national parks and wildlife conservation led to the formation in 1972 of the multi-ministerial National Environment and Conservation Council (NECC), to advise on proposed national parks. When, in 1973, the government selected four areas for national parks development (Caroni Swamp, Navet Dam, Valencia Dam and Chaguaramas) the guiding features were notably recreational ones (NECC 1973).[5] Then, in 1974, the National Environment and Conservation Council proposed a National Parks Service within the Forestry Division to develop and manage a wider parks system including Forest Parks, Local Parks, Wildlife Sanctuaries, Nature Reserves, Historical Sites, View Points and Private Parks.[6]

While national concerns guided these deliberations, they were also inter-animated and shaped by emerging international conservation agendas: in particular, through negotiations for a project supported by the Organisation of American States (OAS).

The OAS National Parks Systems Plan

Discussions for this OAS project, 'The Regional Development of the Northern Range with special emphasis on Re-afforestation and Rehabilitation and to the Establishment of a National Parks System', were to frame much of the debate around national parks in Trinidad during subsequent decades. They were initiated during two OAS missions to Trinidad in 1973 and 1976. In 1977 the government established an Inter-Ministerial Committee to make proposals for the creation and management of national parks,[7] assigning the Forestry Division responsibility. It is unclear whether the Division's success in gaining such control was because it had a broader vision for national parks, because it already controlled land, or because it had the promise of OAS project backing. The OAS project began in 1978, with the remit to establish a plan for a system of national parks and protected areas and to prepare a policy from which legislation could be enacted (Thelen and Faizool 1980).[8] It was co-ordinated by the Forestry Division, with OAS technical assistance under a Mr. K. Thelen, who had recently planned national parks in Chile and had links with both the Food and Agriculture Organisation and IUCN.

The vision and strategy for national parks had to meet multiple agendas, linking emerging international perspectives with both national recreational concerns and the environmental protection ideas by then developing within the Forestry Division under its Chief Conservator Bal.S. Ramdial. Ramdial had studied for a PhD in the USA and drew on the US approach to national parks as a wilderness carefully managed for recreational use, applying this in his study of the Caroni swamp (Ramdial 1975).

A first and fundamental objective of the National Parks System which was proposed was the 'preservation of vegetative communities and species' (Thelen and Faizool 1980). Vegetation was classified according to Beard's 1946 study of the natural vegetation types of Trinidad and Tobago, which provided a basis on which to select and preserve representative examples of natural vegetation assumed otherwise to be at risk of destruction. The eventual systems plan stated that: 'Of the 26 faciations [Beard's vegetation classificatory unit], 21 will be provided with what is considered to be sufficient quantity of representation'. Second, conservation strategies followed the growing international emphasis on 'endemics', influenced by an IUCN study identifying 100 threatened endemic plant species (in Thelen and Faizool 1980:42). A third objective was to protect critical wildlife habitat areas, although greater emphasis came to be placed on protecting key game species from hunting than on protecting habitats from destruction (Thelen and Faizool 1980). The protection of numerous representative habitat areas was seen as an appropriate precautionary strategy to overcome uncertainties in scientific information about different mammals' habitat requirements.

The major emphasis, then, was on how land use had destroyed natural vegetation, and the need to protect representative areas. The balance was tipped decisively towards preservation: 'Choices involving trade-offs between preservation and some aspect of use that will significantly consume or alter the resource must *always* favour preservation' (Thelen and Faizool 1980). Other priorities, such as recreation and tourism were accommodated within other types of park: thus the clash between different visions of national parks was resolved within a multi-purpose system. The plan included sixty-one protected areas in six categories (thirteen scientific reserves; eight national parks; eight natural landmarks; thirteen nature conservation reserves; six scenic landscapes; thirteen recreational parks; see Map 5.1 for major examples).

From 1978, the OAS-financed project was assigned to a nascent National Parks Section in the Forestry Division, comprising a half time national counterpart, two and then four foresters. This 'informal' Section, which had to compete for allotment of personnel with at least eight other sections within the Forestry Division,[9] drew up management plans for a number of areas. A draft policy was prepared in early 1979 and distributed to the government and NGOs for review. Meetings and discussions were then held with other interested agencies and groups,[10] representing government, industry and the scientific community, but notably not farmers, hunters, or other citizens. The executive director of the IUCN Commission on National Parks visited Trinidad and Tobago to give his input on the document's second draft. Not surprisingly, then, the final version of 1980 was wholly in line with the international 'best practice' in protected area strategy of the time: 'To protect in perpetuity those areas of the country which represent significant examples of the country's natural heritage and to encourage

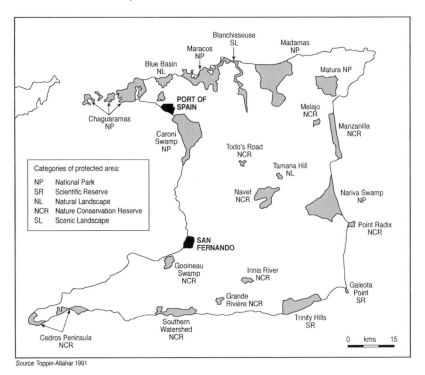

Map 5.1 Proposed system of National Parks and other protected areas in Trinidad

public understanding, appreciation and enjoyment of the heritage in ways which leave it unimpaired for future generations' (Thelen and Faizool 1980: 1).

The National Parks Policy was approved in principle by Cabinet in 1981.[11] Although it had been anticipated that implementation could begin under existing legislation, new more comprehensive and focused legislation was simultaneously prepared (Wade and Bickram 1981). However, this was given very low priority and ultimately dropped. Several factors could account for this legislative failure and lack of government follow up. The first factor relates to competition between government departments for control over national parks: what one might label as 'bureaucratic bickering', but which also concerns contested access to the significant resource flows and status accruing to the institutions managing such internationally high-profile areas. Departing from the systems plan, the draft legislation provided not for management from within the Forestry Division, but for the establishment of an autonomous 'National Parks Authority'. This, it was argued, would fit with international best practice: 'a way recognised by competent authorities world-wide as the *right* way' (Wade and

Table 5.1 *Land status within the OAS 1980 National Parks System, Trinidad*

Land status	Per cent of area of National Parks and Protected Areas System
Forest reserves	31
Wildlife sanctuaries	12
State land	33
Private (17,000ha)	24

Bickram 1981: 4). It was also argued that the Forestry Division's previous experiences disqualified it from competence: a perspective which played up the Division's work in production forestry but overlooked its work in environmental protection.

> To place this responsibility within an existing organisational structure would be to encumber it with precedents, traditions and practices that could be detrimental; and perhaps to subject it to conflicts and competing influences in decision-making, financing and most importantly choices in protecting the resource. It would be a definite mistake to place the administration of parks within the same organisational unit as Forestry because of the diametrically opposed . . . philosophies of management of resources (Wade and Bickram 1981: 4).

It was proposed that the Authority's supporting council would be empowered to circumvent normal public service hiring procedures, on the grounds that 'It will be important for the authority to be able to respond quickly and effectively to specialized research needs, problems etc.' (Wade and Bickram 1981).

In its opposition to the Forestry Division, the legislation thus went against the grain of national deliberation. It thus played into Trinidadian sensitivities to outsiders calling the tune.

A second factor in legislative failure relates to land acquisition, questioning more fundamentally the political feasibility of the overall approach. Twenty-four per cent of the land in the sixty-one proposed areas was private, so the systems plan was also a major state land acquisition plan (Tables 5.1 and 5.2). The policy stated that the private land would be obtained under the Land Acquisition Ordinance, which enables state-mandated agencies to acquire land for 'public purposes'. Adjacent to parks, Town and Country Planning Legislation (1960 Ordinance) was to be used, covering the preservation and protection of forests, woods, trees, shrubs, plants and flowers on private lands. It was envisaged that the acquisition process would begin with negotiation, possibly proceeding to land exchange, the acceptance of donations, and compensation for keeping to specified 'acceptable uses'. If these proved unsuccessful, compulsory purchase would be enacted. The policy and legislation did not, however,

Table 5.2 *Tenurial status of selected parks as proposed in 1980, Trinidad*

	Land area (ha)		
	Maracas	Matura	Eastern Tobago
Forest reserves	200	3200	1700
Wildlife sanctuaries	900		100
State land	1500	100	500
Private	2200	200	3400

problematise either the extent to which the state could afford this, nor the legality of forced acquisition. According to an influential political senator this would require a change in the national constitution and therefore a (highly unlikely) 3/5 majority in parliament.[12] Indeed a decade later, the problems posed by land acquisition on such a scale were noted by the national parks consultant to Trinidad's National Forestry Action Plan as a major factor hindering development of the system (Toppin-Allahar 1991).

A third set of reasons relates to potential conflicts between national parks and other state development objectives, questioning the government's commitment at this point in Trinidad's political and economic history. A senior forester interpreted the legislation as dropped because national parks were seen as anti-development, clashing with demands – and state land acquisition – for oil development, sand and gravel, extraction and construction at this peak oil boom time.[13] Furthermore as Shand *et al.* suggest, the national parks policy 'was never incorporated in any national plans because the government of the day, distracted by an embarrassment of riches in petro-dollars, had abandoned the discipline of central planning' (1993: 212).

The Systems Plan and government policies in the 1980s

Despite failed legislation, and perhaps in anticipation of its eventual enactment, the Systems Plan continued to guide Forestry Division activities concerning protected areas. The OAS lightly financed the National Parks Section during the 1980s to implement the plan incrementally through existing prohibited areas legislation, with eight of the then existing wildlife sanctuaries and forest reserves declared as prohibited areas between 1987 and 1990. The idea of prohibition as the basis for management 'pending other legislation' cemented the idea of prohibition, not just of particular activities, but of entry in general. The legacy of legislative practice thus reinforced exclusionary protectionism as the management style for Trinidad's national parks.

The Forestry Division linked a growing emphasis on public education and recreation with its environmental protection concerns. A key feature of a new Forest Resources Policy (Forestry Division 1981)[14] as compared with the 1942 policy which had been in place previously was the encouragement of 'public understanding, appreciation and enjoyment of the country's natural heritage' (Ramnarine 1997). In 1982, The Forestry Division completed five and ten-year Development Plans for the National Parks Section in conformity with both new forest policy and the National Parks Systems Plan, but budget cuts following a shortfall in revenues from the petroleum sector meant that their objectives were not met.[15] With a change of government in 1986, environmental issues were treated more favourably, with forestry within the same ministry as environment. The Standing Committee on Environment that was set up to review and co-ordinate policy continued to recommend that the national parks function remain with the Forestry Division. The Forestry Division drafted a National Forest Resources Plan appearing in 1989, which again considered the Parks Systems Plan as official government policy, and prioritised three new areas for national park development: Madamas and Matura in the Northern Range and the Nariva swamp. Again, implementation was impeded due to post oil-boom cuts and legislative difficulties.

The OAS project ended in 1988 with only five of the sixty-one areas in the 1980 Plan managed in accordance with its recommendations.[16] In 1989 four historical sites and landmarks previously managed by the Tourism Board came under the National Parks Section. But otherwise, the Section simply maintained areas that it already managed, undertaking minor improvements such as upgrading interpretative programmes for visitors (Lackhan and Ramnarine 1996b).

By 1989, emergent international discussions around biodiversity had entered Trinidad's policy arena. In March that year, a workshop on biodiversity and genetic resources was held, attended by international experts from IUCN and the Commonwealth Science Council (CSC) who sought to identify critical species for biodiversity conservation. A biodiversity advisory committee was established within the Ministry of the Environment and National Service, incorporating academics from the University of the West Indies and several NGOs.[17] A proposal for the development of a biodiversity-focused National Conservation Strategy was prepared in 1989 with the assistance of IUCN as part of its global strategy. But with a change of government, and the arrival on the scene of another major donor-supported initiative, the Tropical Forestry Action Plan (TFAP), this project was also put on hold (CARICOM/FAO/ODA 1993: 23).

A Draft Forest Resource and National Park Conservation Act (1990) had been prepared by the Forestry Division in an attempt to address the need for national parks legislation. It made reference to only two of the six categories in the 1980 Plan and made no provision for dealing with the private lands issue (Toppin-Allahar 1991; CARICOM/FAO/ODA 1993: 11). The Act did not fare well with the change of government. On submission of the draft act the chief Parliamentary Council decided to remove the national parks component for consideration under separate National Trust legislation, against the strong objections of senior forestry staff.

The Tropical Forestry Action Plan was a major international planning exercise, backed by the FAO, the World Bank, UN Development Programme, World Resources Institute, Rockefeller Foundation and major bilateral donors. In the Caribbean region it was initiated in 1988, linking CARICOM and the FAO, and financed by the UK. A Country Mission Team arrived in June 1991 to extensive media coverage. The National Co-ordinator chosen for Trinidad's National Forestry Action Plan (NFAP) was Mr. Faizool who had been the Trinidadian counterpart for the OAS National Parks project a decade earlier. When it reported in 1992, the country mission team accepted much of the 1980 Systems Plan, and formulated projects for the phased development of thirty-two of the sixty-one areas during 1992–96 to put before an international round-table of prospective donors (Shand *et al.* 1993:242).

The Tropical Forestry Action Plan's consultant reporting on national parks (Toppin-Allahar 1991) felt there to be conflicts between such nature conservation and other projects being advocated under the Plan (e.g. for upgrading forest roads and the sawmill industry). These conflicts were of the same type that had caused Wade and Bickram a decade earlier to divide production forestry from national parks. The team nevertheless recommended that the national parks function remain with the Forestry Division, although also advocated removal of the Forestry Division from the public service to create an independent Forestry and National Parks Commission (Chalmers and Faizool 1992). These arguments responded to some of the critiques that were constantly levelled at the Division, concerning its inflexibility, slowness in decision-taking, and weak implementation capacities.

Once again, these proposals came to nothing. The National Forestry Action Plan failed to secure any funding. Certain Trinidadian environmentalists blame the plan's emphasis on forest-based industrial development, rather than biodiversity conservation which following the 1992 Rio conference had become the international funding priority.[18] Others highlight the downturn in international interest in the Caribbean following the end of the cold war.[19]

The Wildlife Section and participatory approaches to conservation

The Forestry Division's insistence that its National Parks Section be the institutional locus for further national parks development was not uncontroversial.

During the 1980s, a sustained critique of the Forestry Division was gaining force, both from within, and from outside it, via environmental NGOs, the public and media reportage.

These critiques focused on several issues. First, they highlighted the Division's incapacity – indeed ill-will, it was claimed – for participatory and co-management approaches. Second, they emphasised the environmental problems caused by the Division's own focus and expertise on plantations and natural forest management for timber. Third, they pointed to the Division's incapacity to deal with forest loss on both private and state forest land, accusing the service of negligence – or complicity – in illegal timber felling.

Much dissent originated from within the Forestry Division's own Wildlife Section. In the 1980s, this radically transformed its approaches to conservation, to embrace 'community participation' and co-management in a manner which contrasted strongly with the rest of the Forestry Division, but which was more aligned with emerging international 'best practice'. In this respect, the particular way that co-management entered scientific and policy practices were shaped by Trinidad's particular administrative configuration, and its cultural and political embeddedness, in turn playing into it.

Wildlife management had earlier focused partly on protection and prevention of species loss, but had also broadened to encompass heritage values, recreation, tourism, education and environmental diversity.[20] In 1982, the Wildlife Section took over management of Caroni Swamp National Park from the National Parks Section.[21] It was also assisted by the FAO and UN Development programme in a project to provide basic wildlife information, filling gaps exposed during deliberations for the National Parks Systems Plan.[22]

A certain zoologist who had trained at the University of the West Indies was a key figure in this project. Concerned about the 'disconnect between "us" and "them"' which she saw as pervading the Forestry Division's work,[23] she viewed it as logical to pursue the involvement of communities in conservation. She argued that attempting to police those whose livelihoods depend on resource exploitation, and who frequently know much more than the so-called professionals, was futile. Her pioneering work in this project drew members of the National Hunters' Association and many other stakeholders into wildlife management, exploring and valuing their knowledge alongside the practices of zoology and conservation biology (e.g. James 1983).

In 1984, this zoologist became head of the Wildlife Section. During the next few years, the leatherback turtles of the north-east coast beaches provided her and dedicated Section members with an arena for developing pilot approaches to community-based conservation. One project at Matura beach (see Figure 5.2) became the Section's flagship: a group of youth in a settlement with a turtle-hunting history formed the NGO 'Nature Seekers Incorporated' in 1990, becoming conservation managers and tour-guides (James and Fournillier

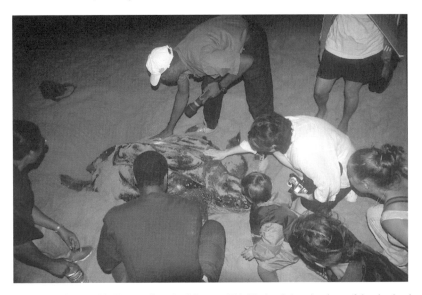

Figure 5.2 Ecotourism in Matura, Trinidad: night viewing of leatherback turtles

1992). The Wildlife Section also introduced an honorary game warden system, empowering those working with wildlife with some responsibility for enforcing legislation to maintain it. In this, they forged links with a number of civil associations – hunters among them – throughout the country.

The Section Head and her colleagues sensed resistance from the Forestry Division. One interpretation, which she herself emphasises,[24] was the Division's continuing focus on production forestry and little else, least of all community-based approaches. The Forestry Division, however, continued to claim a longstanding broader, conservationist vision.[25] In their view, the divisiveness emerged from the Wildlife Section. What is certain is that strong tensions emerged between the two, fuelled by different interpretations of the conflict.

First, from the vantage point of many working in Wildlife, professional staff in the Forestry Division had become 'office foresters' under the conservatorship of Bal Ramdial, out of touch with field-based realities despite the impressive image in Ramdial's public education programme. From the vantage point of those in Forestry, however, the 'co-management' approach was not so new (having been pioneered, albeit in a different way, with woodworkers, as discussed in Chapter 6), and nor was it proper co-management, as members of the NGO Nature Seekers were actually on the Forestry Division's payroll.

Representations of the projects in Wildlife Section and NGO literature, foresters argue, deliberately mislead on this point.

A second line of tension concerned management style. Participatory and co-management approaches necessitated and engendered a management style very different from the bureaucratic, regulatory approach of the Forestry Division. This contrast, accentuated by the Wildlife Section head's own charisma, generated a cohort of staff which came to see itself as distinctive,[26] having a culture of innovation, initiative-taking and direct communication between field officers and Section heads.

A third line of tension concerned orientation to national or international agendas. Deprived of national funds, and promoting a strategy embraced by international organisations, the Wildlife Section was relatively successful in attracting international attention and funds for its work. Senior Forestry Division staff saw this as inappropriately bending Trinidadian 'realities' to international faddism, and increasingly resented international consultants arriving 'every month to tell us we should be doing participation'.[27] Indeed their attitudes towards participation seem to have become more extreme and entrenched within this dynamic, exemplified in statements by those in the Division's upper echelons such as: 'local people are thieves engaged in timber stealing who could certainly not be trusted in the management of the valuable timber resources currently controlled by the state'.[28] Within the Wildlife Section, however, international support only served to underscore their contempt for the 'office foresters' whom they saw as 'backward' and 'top down'.

These tensions were further accentuated as differences over participation fed into wider social tensions within the Forestry Division, and became personalised. This turned on feelings that the Forestry Division was institutionally (and personally) racist and sexist towards the Wildlife Section head – who was of 'African' origin – and her predominantly female staff, manifested in limited opportunities for their further study and promotion. Those in Wildlife defined themselves as working for a modern, anti-sexist, anti-racist organisation (in contradistinction to Forestry), while Forestry Division staff tended to decry the Wildlife Section's interpretations as promoted unprofessionally by a sisterhood lacking 'proper' forestry qualifications. The particular structuring and staff composition of the Forestry Division thus allowed differences in approach to be compounded by insider/outsider, racial, and gender-based ascription, no matter what their veracity, exposing key fractures in Trinidad's social politics.

Accusations of corruption played further into this division. The Chief Conservator of Forests, Ramdial, was considered by many as corrupt: a charismatic figure whose impressive rhetoric was not borne out in action, and whose conspicuous wealth fuelled rumour of personal enrichment 'on the side'. His many supporters claim this was malicious gossip. People still have clear views as to whether Ramdial was a hero or a fraud; views which still map onto institutional differences within the Forestry Division. Certainly none of this ever came to the courts. This personalisation exemplifies the Trinidadian tendency to emphasise 'scandal and excess' in personal relations: Trinidad's celebrated bacchanal (Wilson 1973; Miller 1994; Mason 1998).

The term 'bacchanal', which captures the individualistic values and licentious behaviour epitomised at carnival, is a recurrent theme in Trinidadian popular and academic commentary, and a motif through which wider social behaviour, from politics to everyday life, is discussed. Bacchanal has become synonymous with scandal, but carries a variety of connotations, including spontaneity, getting away with it, gossip, disorder and confusion; values which can be evaluated positively or negatively in different circumstances. It keeps alive the sense that personalised interests infuse public institutions, and celebrates the moral value in exposure of scandalous behaviour. The effect is to focus analytical attention on personalised, charismatic action – on agency – rather than underlying institutional and social structuring. Yet as will become apparent, such a focus, and the way in which attention to the bacchanal appears to account for the failed implementation of a national park system seemingly desired by all, may perhaps occlude from vision more deeply-rooted reasons why policies fail. In this sense, a focus on the bacchanal can be understood as a narrative style, in which an elite came to play up and blame policy failures on interpersonal issues between themselves (competition, power play), without acknowledging the structural reasons for such failure (relating to their relationship with the wider population, and their relative powerlessness to have their way).

The change of government in 1986 brought the Wildlife Section approaches into favour. The personalised discourse came to the fore, where it was used by the new Parliamentary Secretary to remove Ramdial from the Forestry Division to a non-functional position as conservator within the ministry. His replacement was titled 'Director' of Forestry and was more supportive of the Wildlife Section. Tensions cooled somewhat. Nevertheless, the rift in management styles and approaches was wide by then, and the Wildlife Section largely carried on in its own way, using the emerging importance of community-based organisations to lever money out of the Forestry Division with threats of popular uprising, and attracting international funding for globally-popular community-based approaches. Strains continued, periodically prompting administrative actions. In 1997, for example, when the Forestry Division and Wildlife Section were both under new leadership, the Division enacted a new personnel policy requiring forest officers to circulate between jobs and specialisations. One use (intended or otherwise, but interpreted as intended by those bearing its brunt) was to rotate the dozen officers with experience in participatory wildlife management gained with the Section's earlier, charismatic leader, and 'put them out to the conservancies', with their very different bureaucratic hierarchies. Interpreted within the Wildlife Section as an attempt to disempower it, this was notably also a policy which re-emphasised the forester as an all-rounder, able to integrate wildlife, production forestry, watershed management and conservation concerns: precisely the image the Division was stressing in its battle to retain the 'turf' of national park management.

In the late 1980s, a new Eastern Northern Range Project also adopted and developed participatory approaches with OAS support. Its eventual fate – many plans but little action – can be traced largely to the tensions between the Forestry Division and Wildlife Section which hindered necessary collaboration. The particular need to conserve the extensive forests (old forest and regrowth over abandoned cocoa) of Trinidad's northern range mountains had been under discussion within the Forestry Division since the early 1970s, given perceptions of threat from timber 'theft', from agricultural squatting on state land, and from new use of private land. The inter-ministerial project drew its national coordinator from Forestry, and aimed to develop a management plan and propose fundable projects to protect the forests, diversify production and increase living standards. A major part of the plan was the development of Matura National Park, whose important Mora forests had been highlighted in the 1980 Systems Plan. But unlike the 1980 plan, the Eastern Northern Range Project attempted to use participatory planning procedures to discuss developments with people from communities and local government. It also planned numerous income-generating activities – from wildlife farming to jam preparation from forest and orchard fruits – to help secure local support and fulfil income generation aims. However the project suffered both from lack of funds for implementation and from severe problems of co-ordination. Largely shunned by the Forestry Division, whose jurisdiction it competed with, whose approach it contradicted, and for whom it symbolised external intervention, it was also largely shunned by the Wildlife Section, already doing community-based conservation in the Matura area, and sceptical of yet another well-funded planning exercise. Amidst these tensions the Eastern Northern Range Project's key vision of integrated management of all resources dissipated.[29]

The expanding roles of non-governmental and community organisations

Increasing numbers of environmental NGOs, highly vocal in the press, levelled further critical voice against the Forestry Division in the 1990s. The increased national and international respect and funding which NGOs could command enabled members to participate in national and international policy processes. Within Trinidad, NGOs had begun to be included on certain statutory committees[30] as well as in foreign projects and contracts which increasingly stipulated NGO involvement. Larger NGOs started to link up with small NGOs and community-based organisations such as Nature Seekers Incorporated and the Toco Foundation in the north-east. Such community-based organisations could now access international funds through mechanisms such as the Global Environment Facility small grants programme. In Trinidad this was overseen by the former head of the Wildlife Section who had pioneered participatory approaches and was now in a senior role at the UN Development Programme. Community organisations also became vocal in the media and in environmental campaigning, with Nature Seekers, for example, protesting against the establishment of a 750-acre ecotourism resort in the Matura area.

Discursive coalitions also began to emerge between concerns with community-based approaches and tourism. It was recognised that carefully planned and controlled ecotourism would greatly enhance the tourism drive being promoted as part of post oil-boom attempts to diversify the economy. The Tourism Master Plan of Trinidad's Tourism Industry Development Corporation described eco-tourism's promise to generate employment, attract capital to remote parts of the country, and provide for profitable and sustainable use of forest areas.[31] The Tourism Management Plan (TIDCO 1996), developed by Canadian consultants, placed an emphasis on the development of parks as major tourist attractions, proposing sites in Chaguaramas, Caroni, Nariva and the Northern Range. The ecotourism industry was fast-growing, at a rate of about 18 per cent per year, offering revenue flows predictable enough to bring new lending agencies (such as the Inter-American Development Bank and World Bank) into nature conservation. Ecotourism was increasingly seen as a 'win-win' option which united the goals of conservation, community involvement and economic development, since communities could help manage and share in ecotourism profits. Nevertheless debates between conservationists and tourism officials also ensued over type and scale of ecotourism development, given the possibilities for visitors and resort development to alter ecosystems and have negative impacts on sensitive habitats.

This emphasis on possible win-win opportunities between national parks and community-based organisations, in particular those focusing on tour guiding and turtle protection, marginalised other longstanding interests. In practice, in such initiatives only certain sections of the community gained profile (in most cases some youth, and some families managing guest houses). Others – in particular, those land owners, farmers, squatters and hunters whose use of lands earmarked for the park or its buffer zones might challenge the win-win scenario – became excluded. But while marginalised within environmental policy processes, such groups in fact made up an effective majority (spanning the economically powerful and powerless) capable of orchestrating major political opposition to the eventual product of those processes. This opposition is grounded in very different experiences of the relationship between land use and biodiversity.

Ecotourism approaches generally embrace 'participation', yet see land use as largely incompatible with biodiversity conservation. In short, 'nature' can be protected while 'communities' are compensated with tour guiding employment and revenues. Interviews with farmers living around the proposed Matura national park, however, suggest many more compatibilities between existing land use and wildlife protection than scientific and policy debates have acknowledged. For example, the park plans iconise the destructive effects of farming in the retreat of the rare Pawi bird further and further up the hills of the Northern Range. Yet many farmers accuse 'short-term, profit-seeking chemical farming' of giving them a bad name. They claim that their own practices of mixed cropping and intercropping, of planting fruit and timber trees amidst cocoa, of encouraging useful wild plants whether for food, fibre or medicine, and of using little or no fire produce a diverse landscape which is 'attractive to Pawi'.[32] The opportunities which such complementary land uses present to biodiversity conservation and national parks development have been obscured by the ways the co-production of science and policy have excluded such farmer perspectives from serious debate.

International conservation and Trinidadian national parks

In 1992, the Rio conference gave immense international profile and funding legitimacy to conservation agendas. In this context, the Forestry Division immediately rewrote its National Forestry Action Plan proposals – published just three months earlier – to reflect the major concerns aired there, particularly biodiversity and community participation, in the hope of securing more donor funding for them.

The biodiversity emphases of the Rio conference had also been underscored by the preparatory Fourth World Congress on National Parks and protected areas in 1992 (Barzetti 1993). Latin American and Caribbean participation in the Congress, supported by the Inter-American Development Bank, focused specifically on protected areas in the region.[33] At this time, the Bank funded a study in Trinidad and Tobago to generate a Protected Areas project within a larger Land Rationalisation Action Plan that it was considering funding. This project, designed to kick-start the original OAS Systems Plan, was the 'green' component (and conditionality) of an otherwise production-focused programme.

Consultants based with the non-governmental Caribbean Forest Conservation Association and others worked alongside the National Forestry Action Plan team in this study (Shand et al. 1993). Baulking at the negotiations and costs involved in dealing with the private land question head on, the proposals emphasised co-management between local communities and the National Parks Section of the Forestry Division. This was in line with approaches that the consultants had already advocated in other contexts, and with the best practices of the Inter-American Development Bank and IUCN best practice. Co-management was intended to overcome the prevailing problems of encroachment by land users into national parks, and apparent lack of public awareness of and enthusiasm for them. It was also necessary given the Division's inadequate staffing. Park boundaries were to be redefined and demarcated incorporating local consultation, and ecotourism was to be promoted as a principle means of securing local involvement and revenues.

The project drew on the prioritisation of areas in the Forest Resources Policy, finding these largely adequate to fit biodiversity concerns, although it dropped the proposed Madamas park (which encompassed 1600ha of private land), focusing (in Trinidad) on just Matura and Nariva. It was to develop pilot models which could be replicated. Matura was considered particularly suitable because the Nature Seekers' successful 'community' management of leatherback turtles could, it was thought, translate directly into a key role for this community-based organisation in national park management.

The proposed project aimed to strengthen the Forestry Division's National Parks Section through technical assistance and staffing. It referred back to the 1980 Systems Plan (though notably not to its contrasting 1981 legislation) in seeing this as the appropriate way forward, noting that the National Parks Section had specifically been 'formed to be the recipient agency for technical assistance from the OAS in the area of parks and protected areas' (MALMAR/LTC 1992: 4–23).

The broader Inter-American Development Bank Land Rationalization and Development Programme was accepted by Cabinet in late 1992. It provided a series of fundable projects, including the five-year protected area development project. Many of these projects eventually proceeded under the Inter-American Development Bank-funded Investment Sector Reform Programme and Agricultural Sector Investment Programme. However, from 1993 the World Bank took over development of the protected areas project – apparently because the Inter-American Bank could not fund a project to meet its own conditionality. The World Bank was at this time already developing a 'Natural Resources and Environmental Management Project'. The National Parks project became a component of this, linked with what then became a Watershed Management Project.

Predictably, the first World Bank Mission of 1994 identified national parks and watershed management as priorities for funding. With Japanese government funding, preparatory studies commenced towards a project proposal for the World Bank. C. Hollis Murray, a doyen of Trinidad forestry, having headed the Division before moving to the global FAO Forestry Division, was appointed Studies Co-ordinator. The contract for these preparation studies – the first to select priority areas for national parks development, and the second to prepare management plans – stipulated NGO involvement and was won by the

Caribbean Forest Conservation Association. The study team comprised this NGO's head along with a conservation biology professor from the University of Wisconsin as international consultant, and an MPhil student at the University of the West Indies who had studied in the Matura area. The World Bank stipulated a participatory planning approach, so a multi-stakeholder consultation was held in preparation for the studies.

This team was concerned about the System Plan's model of many, rather small protected areas to represent Trinidad's variety of vegetation communities. The Wisconsin professor articulated a different view, emanating from animal ecology and conservation biology, that only much larger conservation areas would be effective. This echoed emerging arguments in international debates, where, as we saw in Chapter 2, by this time a strong coalition of scientific and NGO interest was starting to advocate large-scale eco-regional approaches instead of isolated national parks. It also echoed the calls of Trinidadian NGOs to conserve the entire Northern Range. Moreover, given the strengthening view that the private lands issue could be resolved through co-management, rather than land acquisition and eviction, there was no reason why park areas could not be significantly larger. Hence a coalition emerged between the perspectives of co-management and of conservation biology, and linking certain Trinidadian and international perspectives.

This Wisconsin professor had first visited Trinidad in the early 1990s with a Fulbright grant, subsequently becoming an occasional visiting lecturer in Conservation Biology at the University of the West Indies and the Eastern Caribbean Institute of Agriculture and Forestry. It was through a 1995 university course that he and his students developed their scientific arguments for larger conservation areas. These drew in particular on the 'umbrella species' concept, which holds that the organism with the largest transboundary range, if adequately accommodated, will provide an umbrella of protection for the rest of the biological community. On an estimation of the space demands of twenty forest-dwelling mammals they concluded that a single or clustered set of protected natural areas would need to encompass at least 31,250 ha to protect Trinidad's forest-dwelling mammals fully.[34]

More broadly, this professor had long been advocating a holistic and eco-centric approach which shunned resource and disciplinary distinctions (e.g. between wildlife and forestry) in favour of preserving biological diversity through maintaining ecosystem health. Accordingly, his scientific perspective on national parks departed from the Systems Plan in how to classify and prioritise ecosystems. He and his students argued that Beard's established classification (Beard 1946), which guided the Systems Plan, was strongly biased towards the timber production concerns which had then dominated the Forestry Division, as it focused on dominant associations of large trees and generally commercially-valuable timber trees as indicator species. The professor and one of his PhD students mounted a challenge to Beard's work, aiming to reclassify Trinidad's ecosystems according to current conservation criteria (such as biodiversity). They mounted a major study to carry out inventories in sample plots of plant, animal, bird and some key indicator insect species (bees in particular), and to use advances in landscape ecology computing to see how these variables cluster.[35] This study was extremely well-disseminated even prior to its conduct. Notably, though, the questions that farmers raise about the impacts of land use on biodiversity seem not to figure in these reclassification attempts, which are premised, again, on the study of natural, unused landscapes – seen as separate from the landscapes people are living in and using.

The team member from the Caribbean Forest Conservation Association supported the argument for a larger-scale co-management approach. During a study visit to the UK he had been exposed to the British and European approach to national parks, not as wildernesses but as 'protected landscapes' including economically-active residents. Another of the professor's students, who was also a member of the Caribbean Forest Conservation Association, publicised the new vision of national parks in several newspaper articles during the mid-1990s, in one case defining national parks to include 'the co-ordination of various human-related activities within a carefully managed area that usually incorporates valuable natural systems'.[36]

The scope to incorporate this emerging landscape perspective into the prioritisation and management plans prepared for the World Bank proved to be limited. These eventually followed the Systems Plan and Inter-American Development Bank study in choosing only slightly-enlarged Matura and Maracas areas in Trinidad, while the proposed chapter setting these parks within a broader strategy for a Northern Range Conservation Area was neither written up, nor carried through into the draft legislation.[37] Whether this was because of broken writing commitments within the project, anticipated political impossibility, or pressure from within the Bank or Ministry to conform to the Systems Plan remains unclear.

Although the World Bank project appeared to be a direct follow-on from the Inter-American Development Bank protected areas project, it nevertheless had one fundamental difference. It stipulated that an independent National Parks and Wildlife Authority – not a section of the Forestry Division – should be the implementing agency. Furthermore, it went the step further of giving the new Authority responsibility for wildlife management. As in the 1981 draft legislation for an autonomous National Parks Authority, the justifications turned on separating conservation from production forestry, and side-stepping the drawn-out bureaucratic procedures of the public service. It was now fuelled by several other factors. There was a perceived need for innovation and flexibility to implement community-based approaches.[38] An autonomous agency was in line with the World Bank's neo-liberal policies. The suggestion was also appealing to those formulating the World Bank plan, who could more easily find a personal role in a park operation under an independent agency, and to those in the Wildlife Section still frustrated by their administrative subordination to the Forestry Division, and keen for independent access to international funds.[39]

In 1994 Cabinet approved, in principle, the development of a new National Parks and Wildlife Act which would lead to the establishment of an autonomous authority. Approving a Bill is one thing, however, and seeing it through to enactment quite another. Two New Zealand legal consultants were commissioned to draft the bill, with a number of its technical Schedules to be developed by a national expert committee comprising ministerial, NGO and university representatives.

Increasingly, the promise of a win-win between tourism and national parks shaped park planning. Instead of a broader landscape approach, the World Bank focused on potential tourism revenue flows, while Cabinet similarly highlighted the importance of links with the tourism industry. In playing up co-management with tourist organisations (such as hotel entrepreneurs and community tour-guiding associations), the plans played down participation and co-management with other land users, such as hunters and farmers. Thus policy began to be shaped more by the financial strictures of the loan (emphasising tourism) and the policy agenda of the loaning bank (autonomous management), rather than by local politics (pressure from land users and so on), and local administrative politics (tensions between the Forestry Division and its Wildlife Section, and the reluctance of the Forestry Division to cede control). While several tourism-focused community-groups began to prepare for national park status, others in the same communities began to organise opposition, and while the National Parks and Wildlife Sections prepared for autonomy, the Forestry Division prepared to resist. The active support of high profile community-based organisations such as Nature Seekers Incorporated was sufficient to give the appearance of broad community support, but this occluded from vision what came to be a powerful opposition uniting certain publics with certain state agencies.

Public comment on any proposed legislation was, by the mid-1990s, required as part of Trinidad's policy process. Individuals and groups are invited – through the press and other channels – to make inputs before a Bill is passed and enacted. In the first half of 1997, the joint National Parks and Wildlife Bill was circulated for public comment. It received heavy criticism from three angles.

First, strong opposition came from hunters. The President of the national Hunters' Association of Trinidad and Tobago (HATT) brought public attention to two sections of the Bill: Section 109 which empowers officers to enter premises and seize any articles without the occupier's consent, and Section 95 which allows someone to be charged for an offence up to three years after it was committed. The Hunters' Association objected in letters to the Prime Minister,

Attorney General's office, Ministry of Legal Affairs and in national newspapers that the draft Bill was a threat to democracy and citizen's rights and should be withdrawn.[40] A stream of letters to the press echoed these convictions, accusing the Bill's authors, associated politicians and conservation authorities variously of sinister intentions, Hitler-like brutality, infringement of civil liberties and vastly over-extended authority.[41] By this time, the PNM government whose Cabinet had approved the establishment of an autonomous authority in 1994, had been defeated by a coalition between the UNC and NAR. Fearing loss of political support, the minority NAR, particularly, distanced itself from the Bill, claiming that it was irresponsibly drafted, violated citizens' constitutional rights and over-empowered certain groups.[42]

A second set of criticisms turned on the proposed autonomous authority. Public media commentary claimed the Bill gave the proposed National Parks and Wildlife Authority too much power, overlapping with both the Forestry Division and Trinidad's recently-established Environmental Management Authority, and their respective legislation.[43] This echoed the Forestry Division's own critiques: current national policy documents located National Parks within the Forestry Division, why was this Bill so out of line? The Division argued strongly that it had been and remained the most suitable agency for dealing with national parks, on the grounds of its experiences in developing the Systems Plan and a variety of conservation tools (e.g. slope limits to cultivation, new legislation to control felling on private lands). Indeed a new 1997 Forestry Bill which set out these provisions for private land was already being debated in Parliament. The Acting Director of Forestry argued, fundamentally, that Trinidad and Tobago were too small to apply the national park models developed in countries such as USA, New Zealand and Canada (apt comparators, as the countries of origin of the World Bank, Wisconsin professor and legal consultants). Other senior foresters raised strong concerns that the 'grassroot' users had not been factored in: an implementable, sustainable policy required their needs, expectations and fears to drive the legislative drafting/evaluation process. It is not surprising that such grassroots issues were raised by foresters, who for all their bureaucratic problems had a tradition of working with, regulating and thus hearing the concerns of local users.

Third, commentators raised problems over the private land issue. Rather than take the co-management route with land owners, the draft bill sought to acquire all lands within parks. A key senator argued – reflecting many landowners' opinions – that the State should not simply be allowed to declare areas of private property as national parks. If the State wanted to protect an ecologically important area on private property, then it should make arrangements to negotiate over conservation. Finally, as a fourth issue, the Schedules which the draft Bill contained – such as those concerning rare species – were pointed out to be full of errors.[44]

Under such criticism, the deadline for comment on the Bill was extended and a new draft went into preparation, in which the concerns of hunters were to be represented.[45] The unpopular 1997 draft Bill was eventually withdrawn in early 1998, with a view to reformulating its components in two separate Bills, one for National Parks and Protected Areas, and one for Wildlife. This time the drafting committees for each included representatives from several Ministries, environmental NGOs and civil associations such as the national and South-East Hunters' Associations,[46] with wider consultation as needed – although notably still heavily slanted towards environmental organisations, rather than grassroots forest users.

Yet again, the new drafts proposed (a) that legislation be administered by an autonomous National Parks and Wildlife Authority,[47] and (b) that the Maracas and Matura parks include large areas of private lands. Local landowners again organised opposition. Critics again suggested that the proposed legislation contradicted constitutional rights concerning 'enjoyment of property' and 'rights of way', and had not been harmonised with other environmental legislation. Moreover, these Bills were drafted with many straightforward errors, ranging from inconsistency of definitions and measurement units to flawed lists of scheduled species. Rumours abound concerning how such a flawed draft was submitted: Was it carelessness, a transmission of the wrong draft to printers or an act of sabotage? In any case the Bills had to be shelved before they could reach parliamentary debate. In the eyes of the senator who is the most knowledgeable politician on this subject, they were 'legislative rubbish' and 'almost certainly drafted to meet conditionalities of the international funding agencies, reflecting the thinking of bureaucrats who can only see uniformity of approach'.[48] Deliberations continue, as yet unresolved, concerning the administrative home for national parks, their financing and their legal framework.

Hunters and challenges to the conservation biology perspective

Hunter's challenges to the science and policy surrounding national parks reflect not just their concerns over civil liberties and resource use rights, but also a fundamentally different set of visions concerning nature, society and what national parks should be. Government staff and international conservation biologists generally see hunting as a prime threat to wildlife and biodiversity. However, recreational hunters strongly deny such accusations. Emphasis on the effects of hunting overlooks, they argue, the effects of the Forestry Division's own timber production practices on wildlife populations and habitats, as well as the impact of oil pollution; processes linked to 'the expansion and the development of the country'[49] against which the hunters lobby.

The South-East Hunter's Association, based in the Rio Claro area in the south of the country, goes further to argue that there has not been a general reduction in the populations of hunted species. Their (or at least their president's) argument is based on tracking wildlife populations through a set of scientific practices and theories that they have developed through experience. These contrast with – indeed contradict the findings of – conventional conservation biology. The hunters argue that the diameter of the circle in which an animal runs when chased by hunting dogs can be used as a gauge of its territory and hence population levels, with a smaller circle suggesting smaller territory and higher population. They observe how the correlation between running area and population varies not only by species but also by terrain and other factors. The president and members of the Association are using numerous observations to build this up into a reliable methodology. Notably, this is a method which depends on the *use* of animals and protected areas for its application.

In this way, hunters have inferred population increases of certain animals in areas where the Wildlife Section had considered them to be in decline. Moreover, the South-East Hunters' Association critiques the monitoring methods used by the Section and by certain conservation biologists (e.g. Nelson 1996). These are based on the mandatory data sheets which all licensed hunters must complete to record their kills. Hunters, Association members claim, frequently fill these out not at the time of the hunt but at the end of the hunting season, making them inaccurate.[50] Furthermore they frequently do so 'strategically': If the reported number of kills is too high, they will be blamed for over-hunting, but if too low, the authorities will think animal numbers are in decline; both may presage restrictions on hunting, so the sheet is filled out at a 'happy medium' level.[51]

This illustrates an instance of 'citizen science', where a citizen's organisation has explicitly contested the methods and findings of expert science by conducting its own investigations. The contestation extends beyond the content and methods of science, however, for these different analyses of wildlife and hunting are linked to the production of different (competing) social categories, and through them, to social dimensions of conservation.

The practices of the Wildlife Section and the perspectives of conservation biology place the problem of mammal decline with 'hunters' in general, imaging them as irresponsible resource users, and supporting anecdotal perceptions of hunters as disobeying state laws by hunting out of season and at night. They support moves both to tighten hunting regulations and to exclude hunters from an expanded system of protected areas. In contrast, the Hunter's Association science is embedded in images of hunters as noble, knowledgeable and law-abiding. The Association's leaders take pains to distinguish their members from illegal 'poachers', farmers and marijuana growers, whom 'proper' hunters would be able to control should they be given access to wildlife sanctuaries and national parks. They argue that it is in precisely the areas from which these 'real' hunters are excluded – Trinidad's current wildlife sanctuaries – that poachers and forest-clearing marijuana farmers have free-est rein, and where mammal populations have suffered most.[52] Thus, just as effective measurement depends on using wildlife and their habitats, so does effective management. Citizen science arguments create conceptual space for hunters to be conservation partners with the state, in helping to control the wayward.

The citizen science in this instance was pioneered by the Association's president who holds a science degree and a public sector job. His educational engagement with scientific and government institutions, together with his social standing in Trinidad, has given him a basis from which to deconstruct and critique university and government studies, as well as to hold his own in discussions with academics and senior government staff. Such discussions have taken place both when researchers have been invited to the Association's own monthly meetings, and in the various consultative committees now formed around policy developments. However, the Association's membership is highly diverse, including smallholder farmers who must join hunting associations in order to hold legal permits for their firearms, and find there a platform expressing their interests. Their social backgrounds (largely rural and 'Indian') are notably shared with many staff of the production-focused Forestry Division, but are different from the urban, more 'African' and European origins of the Wildlife Section and others taking a more internationally-aligned, 'reverential' perspective to wildlife and conservation. The South-East Hunters Association members have also acquired confidence as citizens since the first 'Indian' government came to power in 1996, and from the successful national Hunters' Association-orchestrated public protest through the media against the 1996 National Parks Bill. Hunters thus feel themselves in a position to critique government science and policy. Trinidadian citizens are also well aware of the growing internationalism of the environmental movement and its leverage on research and policy development in the country, around national parks as well as other issues. Contesting the scientific and policy practices of the University of the West Indies and the Wildlife Section is in this context also a contestation of this internationalism, and the ambiguous control of agendas that it represents.

Nevertheless, hunters' engagement also reflects emergent concerns over threats to their status. The decline of oil revenues and ensuing unemployment have led people to return to rural subsistence occupations, illegal or otherwise, and in this context the social identity of these 'hunters' (vs. poachers. . . .) is fragile.

The Environmental Management Authority

Interplaying with these struggles and turf battles between citizens and government authorities, by the late 1990s, was Trinidad's Environmental Management Authority (EMA) and its own proposals for protected area management.[53] While many of the EMA's advocates had seen its key roles in the neglected and unco-ordinated areas of industrial waste and pollution, from an early stage it focused on issues such as turtle protection which overlapped with existing national parks debates. This reflected both a desire to garner public support around established and emotive environmental issues, and the expertise of the first professionals re-cruited. Within the 1995 Environmental Management Act the EMA emphasised creating rules for the designation of 'Environmentally Sensitive Species' and 'Environmentally Sensitive Areas', the latter being large conservation areas in which environmental clearance certificates would be required for a wide range of developments on public or private land. Political and media commentators noted the potential for these rules to overlap and cause conflict with the work of both the Forestry Division and the proposed National Parks and Wildlife Authority.

As the key agency enacting Trinidad and Tobago's commitments to inter-national conventions, the EMA was also given responsibility for developing the country's National Biodiversity Strategy and Action Plan. This provides yet another forum for scientific and policy discussion around protected ar-eas. On the one hand, the process is strongly influenced by conservation bi-ology concerns, particularly via the Wisconsin professor who is an interna-tional consultant to the EMA team, and his PhD student who is a member. On the other hand, the EMA claims an innovative participatory process for the Strategy's development, under a team leader who has experience with par-ticipatory management within the Wildlife Section.[54] The participatory pro-cess has involved the discussion of five sectoral reports at meetings with key stakeholders from ministries and industry, followed by a series of thirteen con-sultations around the country. However, consultation at these public meetings, advertised through the press, has not generally been wide, with attendance in most cases quite low and dominated by vocal community leaders. The con-sultations have also been orchestrated and framed within the EMA's general support for a national parks and protected areas approach to conservation. In this context there is little evidence that fundamentally different perspectives – such as those of the farmers and hunters who emphasise biodiversity in lived-in-landscapes – have come to be recorded within these meetings. While the implications of the biodiversity plan process for the protected areas de-bate are not yet clear, then, it seems unlikely that they will bring radical transformation.

Conclusions

As international scientific and policy processes around biodiversity have inter-played with policy debate over national parks in Trinidad, they have contributed to the emergence of distinct sets of institutional alliances. In the scientific inquiry and policy debates around how national parks should be established, managed, controlled and funded, and by whom, opposing discourse coalitions have emerged. The Forestry Division has, over time, sedimented practices that integrate wildlife management with other forest functions such as timber production and watershed protection. These have been developed within historical control of land, and assumptions of national stewardship. In contrast, the Wildlife Section has sedimented practices of managing and researching wildlife populations with local communities, within a linked ideology and practicality of community control. Each of these sets of practices has linked with those of other institutions – perhaps conducted for rather different reasons, but which nevertheless find common ground with them. The Wildlife Section's research, pilot programmes and management practices around local wildlife status, management, and control, has thus become associated with the research of international conservation biologists, their linked consultancy activities with members of conservation NGOs, the creation of community-based organisations and the promotion of ecotourism. As international institutions promoting and funding biodiversity conservation and national parks have influenced Trinidad, they have played into tensions between these coalitions (or traditions) of scientific and policy practice, and in doing so, amplified the distinctions between them. International imperatives have thus interlocked with national and more localised scientific and policy processes to shape inter-departmental and inter-ministerial schisms and 'turf battles'.

At the same time, globalised science and policy surrounding parks and participation have played uneasily into Trinidad's particular scientific and administrative practices and political history. Localised struggles to participate in the parks debate have sometimes been at odds with the orchestrated approaches to participation – and the vehicles for it, such as community-based ecotourism projects – which dominate international best practices. To date, resolution has been in favour of those who, although marginalised from the participation invited by donors and 'projects', have succeeded in blocking the national parks legislation which has regularly overlooked their interests (helped, it must be said, by significant opposition within quarters of the government such as Forestry, and the poor quality of legal drafting).

The same is not true of the science driving the problematic which the policy process is addressing. The chapter has indicated how policy debate has shaped scientific inquiry, and how it itself has been shaped by it. Yet the co-produced science/policy held within the University, Wildlife Section, EMA and NGOs has not incorporated the perspectives of land users; indeed it reproduces and adds new impetus to forms of social and moral objectification rooted in Trinidad's political and economic history, which contribute to further stigmatisation and exclusion. In seeking to have their perspectives taken seriously, those voicing alternatives frequently distance themselves from such objectification by labelling others. Thus hunters, in their citizen science, represent themselves as socially and morally distinct from 'poachers', and organic-farming small-holders on questionable forms of tenure distance themselves from commercial, profiteering squatters.

Just as the citizen science of the Hunter's Association took against dividing parks off from other land categories, finding that such divisions leave non-parks dangerously exposed to development and parks dangerously exposed to illegal use, so the citizen science of farmers points in similar directions. It tends to support the contention of the Hunters' Association that Trinidad and Tobago are too small to have sixty-one parks: instead, 'all of Trinidad and Tobago is a park'. These perspectives point to a more integrated approach to biodiversity conservation, where there are lived-in landscapes. This is more in keeping with the approaches to multi-functional landscapes now being considered by certain international conservation agencies, but as yet not fully operationalised in particular countries, and in Trinidad, failing to find a foothold. Such citizen science is certainly not impartial, linked as it is to local users' interests in continuing to control resources. But it is no more partial, on this count at least, than the perspectives of those in the Wildlife Section or of the conservation biologists undertaking studies for parks. While there may be cynicism from scientists concerning the validity of such citizen science, the inverse is equally true, as public disrespect grows for conservation science.

We have noted the way in which internally contentious issues in Trinidad can easily become expressed in terms of arguments for and against 'outside' influence, and how this has become a recurring theme in the evolution of Trinidad's environmental policy. Put another way, external influences have played into internal tensions (frequently exacerbating them) as certain protagonists garner international support and funding, whilst others shun it, regretting the expensive, 'ill-informed', 'meddling' international consultants it brings. In a similar vein, personal differences have played into inter-departmental tensions, and exacerbated them. We have explored this in relation to personal differences within the Wildlife Section and Forestry Division. Those involved in Trinidad's environmental policy process could certainly verify that differences of professional opinion seem to hinge on personal animosities and vested interests. Clearly such personal issues, and individuals' magnetism and charisma, influence everyday practice. Yet charisma owes a lot to the way leaders play out their roles amidst more historically-sedimented clusters of practices and forms of alliance. Trinidad's high profile affair with things 'bacchanal' often gives the impression that it is personalised scandal which produces administrative paralysis. Yet in as much as it detracts attention from the more enduring aspects of these tensions, a focus on the personal can be seen to overlook – and indeed widen – disjunctures between those within powerful scientific and policy institutions, and broader society.

Notes

1. The colonial Forest Department eventually became the Forestry Division after national independence.
2. Forestry Division, Progress Report Wildlife Section (in Lackhan and Ramnarine 1996a), 1976–79: 25.
3. Project brief to Permanent Secretary, Ministry of Agriculture, Lands and Fisheries, 'Assistance to Regional Development of the Northern Range with special emphasis on Re-afforestation and Rehabilitation, and to the Establishment of a National Parks System', OAS Technical Cooperation Programme 1974/76, 1976/78).
4. Carlozzi, 1964; Forestry Division, Progress Reports 1968–70, in Lackhan and Ramnarine 1996b; Forestry Division, Annual Report 1971, Section 11, pp. 68, 70.
5. The government sought assistance to develop the first three, whereas Chaguaramas was designated a National Park in 1974 within the separate Chaguaramas Development Plan. Chaguaramas was a special case; it had been a US base during the Second World War and its closure was a highly politicised issue in Trinidad, leading to subsequent questions concerning the status of the land. With the nationalist sentiment which led to the closure contradicting the principle of returning the land to elite owners who had been dispossessed, creating a national park was an alternative.
6. Appendix E, Review of the National Environment and Conservation Council 1972–74.
7. Forestry Division, Progress Reports (in Lackhan and Ramnarine 1996b) 1976–79: 23.
8. Only after four years of consultation did the OAS reveal that they were not able to provide the technical orientation required by the Trinidadian government for the Northern Range aspect of the programme. They agreed, however, to supply technical assistance for the establishment of a system of National Parks.
9. The Establishment of a System of National Parks and Protected Areas. Final Report (Phase 1) Number 02-45A-405-TD1 Prepared by E. Thelen, OAS Project Director. Page 7.
10. 1979 Forestry Divison, Annual Reports, Section 13.4, pg. 50.
11. Forestry Division, Progress Reports 1980–82: 25 (in Lackhan and Ramnarine 1996b).
12. Interview, Senator and zoologist, Port of Spain, 16 June 1999.
13. Interview, Head of FRIM, Forestry Division, Port of Spain, 21 May 1999.
14. This was prepared for the Eleventh Forestry Conference held in Trinidad in September 1980, but never formally adopted; nevertheless it guided Forestry Division practice during the next couple of decades. Interview, Head of FRIM, Forestry Division, Port of Spain, 21 May 1999.
15. Forestry Division, Progress Reports (in Lackhan and Ramnarine 1996b) 1980–84: 8.
16. Caroni, Aripo Savannahs Scientific Reserve, Cleaver Woods, San Fernando Hill Natural Landmark and Quinam Bay Recreational Site.
17. It included the presidents of the following organisations: Asa Wright Nature Centre, Archaeological Society, CFCA, Citizens for Conservation, Crusoe Reef Society, Point-à-Pierre Wildfowl Trust, Trinidad and Tobago Biological Society, University of the West Indies Biological Society.
18. Eden Shand, 'The Geopolitics of Forest Conservation', *Trinidad Express* 21/9/95.

19. Interview, Senior Forester, FAO, Bridgetown, Barbados, 20 June 1999.
20. Forestry Division, Progress Reports 1980–82: 23 (in Lackhan and Ramnarine 1996b).
21. Ibid: 7.
22. Forestry Division, Progress Reports 1980–82: 23 (in Lackhan and Ramnarine 1996b).
23. Interview, senior zoologist with UNDP, Port of Spain, 2 June 1999.
24. Ibid.
25. For example, interview, Head of FRIM, Port of Spain, 5 June 1999.
26. Interview, Forester I, Rio Claro, 25 July 1999.
27. Interview, Chief Conservator of Forests, Forestry Division, Port of Spain, 5 June 1999.
28. Ibid.
29. Interview, Head of Forestry at ECIAF and ex-national director of ENRP, Port of Spain, 8 July 1999.
30. Such as the Wildlife Conservation Committee, as well as ad hoc Cabinet committees such as the 1987 Standing Committee on the Environment.
31. Nicole Leotaud, 'Tourism the eco-friendly way', *Daily Express*, 1 January 1998.
32. Interview, organic farmer, Matura, 30 June 1999; interview, part-time farmer, Matura, 30 June 1999.
33. 'Parks for life: enhancing the role of conservation in sustaining society', Report of the Fourth World Congress on National Parks and Protected Areas, 10–21 February 1992.
34. Eden Shand, *Daily Express*, 3 July 1996.
35. Interview, conservation biology researcher, Port of Spain, June 1999.
36. Nicole Leotaud, *Daily Express*, 7 July 1996.
37. Interview, Head of CFCA, Port of Spain, 1 June 1999.
38. Interview, national co-ordinator of World Bank National Parks Project, Port of Spain, 15 June 1999.
39. Lisa Sankar, *Sunday Express,* 30 June 1996.
40. 'Wildlife Bill a Threat to Democracy', *Trinidad Guardian*, 22 May 1997.
41. For example: Etienne Mendez, 'Letter to the Editor' *Trinidad Guardian* 9 June 1997; 'Parks' Bill Needs Serious Work' Kris Rampersad *Sunday Guardian* 25/5/97; S. Gomes of San Fernando, 'Letter to the Editor', *Sunday Guardian*, 1 June 1997; Lystra Lythe of Sangre Grande 'Scrap this wildlife bill', *Trinidad Guardian*.
42. 'NAR: Wildlife Bill Negative,' *Trinidad Guardian* 23 May 1997.
43. Kris Rampersad, 'Parks' Bill needs serious work', *Sunday Guardian* 25 May 1997.
44. Ibid.
45. The Minister of Agriculture responded by meeting with HATT, and planned to set up a joint committee between officers of the Ministry and HATT representatives to discuss changes to the proposed legislation ('Deadline for comment on Bill will be extended', *Trinidad Guardian*, 23 May 1997).
46. Nadra Gyan and Christopher Starr, *Sunday Guardian*, 31 May 1998.
47. Nicole Leotaud, CFCA column, *Daily Express*, 27 May 1998.
48. Interview, Senator and zoologist, 16 June 1999.
49. Interview, President of the South East Hunters' Association, Rio Claro, 6 July 1999.
50. Winsie M. of Mayaro, 'Letter to the Editor', 24/8/96, *Trinidad Guardian*.

51. Interview, MPhil student working with north-eastern hunters, St Augustine, 15 May 1999.
52. Interview, President of the South East Hunters' Association, Rio Claro, 6 July 1999; 'South hunters: Ganja crops destroying wildlife' by Richard Charan, *Newsday*, 8 May 1999.
53. Interview, Head of EMA, St Augustine, 6 May 1999.
54. Interview, Co-ordinator of Biodiversity, EMA, 28 May 1999.

6   Sustainable timber production and forest management in Guinea

Introduction

This is the first of two chapters which consider science and policy processes around sustainable timber production. We begin with Guinea where a radically new policy approach to forest management has been attempted (at least for forest resources outside state reserves), based on principles of decentralisation and co-management. As we indicated in Chapter 2 these issues are at the core of the international policy vortex concerning sustainable forest management, and criteria and indicators for it. Thus it is possible to represent co-management in Guinea as an instance of local alignment to the international configuration of science and policy in 'Tropical Forest International'. However, there are alternative perspectives on the origins and motivations for this policy change, which see it as generated locally. In this chapter, we consider this apparent contradiction as part of an exploration of how this policy change has come about, and the practices and institutional relationships that it involves.

We begin by exploring the different ways that those involved in developing the new policy approach explain what it is addressing, and why – issues which are revealed in narratives of policy origin. While the policy means many things to many people, with different state agencies, NGOs, and donors narrating its institutional origins in different ways, it will become apparent that it is the convergence of these disparate motivations that enabled it to emerge. Thus, rather than look to different institutions for its origins, one can look to this convergence, and to the generation of the specific practices (of registration, surveillance, monitoring, forest mapping, inventory-making, plan creation, committee establishment, training, meetings and so on) which constitute the approach. While we shall consider how the meanings of particular practices relate (at times dialogically) to earlier uses, and how 'new' practices relate to wider (including internationalised) scientific and policy communities, we shall also explore how they are part of a particular economy that is driving the policy process.

No coherent 'official' perspective sees this new policy approach as a logical outcome of villagers' interactions with their landscapes, past or present. For example, villagers' testimonies presented in our earlier work, which suggest the

Figure 6.1 A village in Kissidougou prefecture, Guinea, in its peri-village forest island

anthropogenic origins of many peri-village forests (see figure 6.1), and the landscape and forest-enriching effects of many everyday practices (e.g. Fairhead and Leach 1996), are not seen to question the need for complex project and state procedures to organise, monitor and educate villagers to manage forests. In this context, many villagers (unconcerned at the adequacy of their own forest management) have become anxious about the motives for the new policy approach and its implications for future forest control. Many fear it as a step in resource alienation to the state. Whether the approach is imaged as devolution of, or extension of, state control over forest resources – highly contrasting representations among those working to develop and implement the policy – is, thus, in some senses, to miss the point. Rather, it implies a growing external imposition of management which is experienced by villagers as a loss in autonomy and an economic threat.

We begin with a summary of the practical and legal changes which have taken place, and then explore a range of explanations given by those involved in the policy process to explain what has happened and why.

Forestry Groups in Guinea

Granting rights over forest trees back to villagers heralds a major change in forest policy direction in Guinea. Until now, and since the mid-colonial period, the state forestry service has claimed rights to decide which trees may be felled, and by whom. Villagers could not be certain of gaining revenue from timber felling apart from compensation for collateral damage. While *de facto* villagers might exploit their own trees, the Ministry of Agriculture and the Presidency could sell logging concessions covering village territories. That the timber from one tree would meet the cost of bridewealth in marriage might suggest the importance of forestry revenues to villager and minister alike.

The new approach allows villagers to constitute 'Groupements Forestiers' (Forestry Groups) to which the state hands over forest management and revenue rights. The approach currently has high profile in the national Forest Directorate and has been embraced by many donor-funded programmes in the country. It has involved new laws, major training initiatives, and new social and political structures at the village, district and prefecture level.

The approach has arisen in the broader context of the Forest Directorate's attempt, since the early 1990s, to transform itself from a 'service of repression' to a service which works in collaboration with local populations.[1] Militarily-trained forest guards have been dismissed and many forest agents have been trained in participatory methods. The new Forestry Code made provision for de-volution of forest control to Guinea's elected Rural Councils, with each elected committee supported by a state forestry service representative. In 1996 the Ministry took a step further to permit the legal establishment of village and private forests,[2] although this has yet to be passed by the country's National Assembly.

The Forest Directorate now permits the establishment of 'village forests'. Administratively, the national Director of Forestry must sign a dossier of re-quest from the Group concerned. To assemble the dossier requires that those with tenurial rights over parts of the forest are identified, give their consent and that their territories are documented. The forest must be mapped and sub-jected to a forest inventory and management plan which shows a zonation to be agreed in conjunction with the sub-prefectoral forest administrator, the Chef de Cantonnement Forestière. Typically, such zonation would include priority areas for tree crops (coffee, oil palm), for enrichment planting, for water source protection and for timber exploitation. Completing the dossier also requires the Group to constitute a management committee (seven to eight people), and (in the case of village Groups) a village development plan and fund that forest revenues can feed into. Before the request is submitted to the National Direc-tor, it needs to be approved and signed by prefectoral representatives of the many ministries. Formally, trees become the property of the Group, and deci-sions to fell can subsequently be made by the Group management committee, although only after requesting a permit from the local forestry service. In prin-ciple this is supposed to be refused only if the proposed felling contravened the previously approved forest management plan. Once a Group has a permit, it can negotiate with a timber contractor to carry out the felling, and can use contractors who are not 'approved' and registered as such by the prefecture administration.

The legal framework and the enaction of the approach are nationwide. In Guinea's Fouta Djallon region, the rationale was largely to enable those who wanted to constitute a business group to invest in forestry on their land. In contrast, in Forest Guinea the approach is largely focused at a village level, covering existing 'village forests'. In Kissidougou prefecture, for instance, most of the 800 or so villages already have a peripheral ring of forest of 10–400 ha, established by today's residents or their ancestors, and the idea of creating a Forestry Group is to put these forests under the control of a Group representing the village population. Where villages do not have forests, it is hoped that they will constitute Forestry Groups to develop them. The creation of Forestry Groups is accelerating: in Kissidougou, five were ratified in 1997, eleven in 1998 and today there are more than fifty. As more are created, pressure has mounted from the projects managing them for their federation, first at the sub-prefecture level, and then prefectorally.

Numerous donors and their projects support the creation of Forestry Groups. Indeed to date the only Forestry Groups created have been those supported by such projects. In particular, several projects within the huge Niger River Protection Programme funded by assorted donors (European Union, US Agency for International Development, etc.) have promoted the approach within their areas of operation, in conjunction with support to the state forestry service. The German GTZ supports the establishment of Forestry Groups elsewhere in Forest Guinea. The European Union funded project has been of particular importance in Kissidougou. In line with broader internationally-driven moves towards administrative decentralisation and market liberalisation, many donor-funded programmes have contractualised their operations. Thus many former forestry service or project employees have now formed 'NGOs' and must tender for contracts as independents. There are three such NGOs in Kissidougou. Alongside such contractualisation, the European Union programme has also slimmed down its staffing structure and interlocked itself with the local forestry administration which it had once almost duplicated (or swamped). Those few who still work for the project now formally also work for the prefectoral forestry service, as sub-prefecture representatives.

Narratives of origin of the Forestry Groups approach

People involved in developing and implementing the Forestry Groups approach narrate its origins, the problems it seeks to address and the events which brought it into being in contrasting ways. Examining several of these narratives, we make no attempt to adjudicate between them and their alternative truth claims, but explore each as an integral part and product of the political field in which different people and institutions are involved in Forestry Group practice.

1   NGO I – links with French consultancy

Staff of one of the new NGOs in Kissidougou narrate the Forestry Groups approach as the innovation of two French expatriates and the Guinean personnel they worked with.[3] As they explain, one of these expatriates was under contract to a French consultancy organisation, and had been working in Kissidougou prefecture since 1991 as a technical advisor to the Niger River Protection Programme. The other worked for the same consultancy firm but visited Guinea irregularly as a senior advisor. In a key meeting in 1995 these Frenchmen argued that if Guinea already had 'groupements' (Groups) for pastoralism and vegetable gardening, as promoted in development projects throughout the country, then why should they not have forestry Groups. The senior consultant drafted the guide for procedures (Projets Bassins Versants 1997), and the more junior consultant lobbied successfully for the addendum to the Forestry Code that eventually permitted their creation.

The policy was proposed to the Forest Directorate which took it on willingly, both as a way to meet its new goal of incorporating local people into resource management, and as a showcase in innovation. As one of the NGO members put it: 'This is the first time in Guinea and in the world'. The NGO staff respected the junior expatriate for his dedication and persistence in pushing this innovation through, while the influence of the senior expatriate was boosted by his charisma as an international mover: as they put it, he 'has travelled to more than forty countries, never spending more than four months in each; he is a really senior expert'. Unusually for expatriates, they say, he was 'with the people', 'bearded, a heavy drinker of palm wine who ate local rice'.[4]

The influence that the NGO staff attribute to the consultants is linked to personal loyalty. The French expatriates had particularly supported the establishment of this NGO. Most of the founder-members had been student interns with the project that the expatriate managed, and had gained contracts from the project after their studies. The NGO still imaged its loyalty to the French team as mutual, stating that the French team encouraged the NGO to price itself out of the market when solicited to collaborate with other international consulting firms which might compete with theirs. The NGO attempted to create as many Forestry Groups in Kissidougou as possible to assist the junior Frenchman's reputation before his final departure from Guinea at the end of 1998.[5]

This account highlights the experience of interdependency between development workers and expatriate staff. International dimensions of community forestry are personified and localised in the agency of key expatriates, and in particular events which instantiate this, in a way which also upholds the NGO's own agency and status – supporting their future competitiveness in a contractualised development world. Thus the interplay between international consultancy organisations and national NGO networks is locked not just into general interdependency between African and European organisations, but also into competing, personalised patronage networks and practices in the acquisition of aid contracts.

2   NGO II – student intellectuals

A second NGO also describes the Forestry Groups approach as an innovation originating in Kissidougou, but locates the original ideas and innovative practices in a highly contrasting way: in a set of student studies carried out by final-year forestry students of Guinea's agricultural university, the Faranah-based ISAV.[6] As its leader narrates, the European Union Niger River Protection Programme supported several students to conduct studies relating to participation and the reservation of forests in the interests of village communities during the early 1990s (e.g. Kamano and Kpoghomou 1995; Millimouno and Telliano 1997; Kolie and Mara 1993). It was these studies, the NGO leader claims, that provided most of the ideas and practical procedures which subsequently came to comprise the Forestry Groups approach. While the Programme had, in effect, commissioned the studies, it was students' own work and vibrant discussion between them about the Programme which generated important new ideas and made it practicable; Ideas such as the participatory form of forest inventory created to replace cumbersome conventional inventory procedures. Thus 'the Niger River programme decided to take these brilliant studies and work with them'.[7]

In this version of events, the senior French consultant only elaborated a guide on the basis of ideas and practices emergent within the students' studies and their dynamics within the project. And the 1995 meeting highlighted in the earlier NGO narrative was not a significant turning point; rather, it was simply to inform and train certain sub-prefecture forestry agents and to launch the guide. It was an event for dissemination, not innovation. Indeed members of this NGO are somewhat aggrieved that the French consultants have gained so much personal credit for the approach.

These two accounts both locate the origin of Forestry Groups within donor-funded project practice in Kissidougou. Both NGOs – with their founding involvement of university students and ex-project interns and contract workers – have emerged along with the Forestry Group approach, which is central to their claims to expertise, sense of identity and funding. The different weight that the two NGOs attribute to the students and to the expatriates of the project may reflect each member's different experiences with the expatriates concerned – as well as, perhaps, assumptions being made during our interviews. Both accounts certainly present Kissidougou as an important experimental field in which formal research and learning-by-doing in project practice have generated a novel approach, ripe for replication around the country by the NGOs which have helped spawn it.

This sense of innovation enables the NGOs to represent themselves as uniquely capable of replicating and training others in the approach: important in a competitive world of NGO tendering. Indeed the ongoing creation of Forestry Groups is crucial to NGO survival, since most of their project contracts consist in lengthy surveying, village meetings and paperwork, all of which are involved in the preparation of Group dossiers – an issue we shall explore further later.

3   NGO III – Solidarity against loggers

The third NGO in Kissidougou differs in that ten of its twelve members used to be employed as extension staff either by the Niger River Protection Programme or by the state forestry service. They remain better equipped – having retained their project motorcycles – and the staff are slightly older. As former (or continuing) state employees, they remain more securely linked to the state administration despite their NGO status.

These NGO staff narrate the origins of the Forestry Group policy within the practices of their earlier extension work.[8] A key problem they had identified was the virtual 'theft' of timber resources by chainsaw operators who would fell trees in peri-village forests, giving villagers only one plank in ten – and then offer to buy the latter at very low prices to 'save villagers the difficulty of transporting them'. Encouraged by the project, extension staff carried out demonstration fellings 'to show villagers the value of their wood, and that their resources were being stolen from them'.[9] Together, extension staff and project administrators struggled to introduce Forestry Groups as a means to get timber revenues into the hands of villagers, alongside re-vitalising 'traditional' technologies such as pit-sawing which would reduce village dependence on external chainsawyers.

In this account the Forestry Groups approach is still of local origin, but arose through a struggle against local political-economic conditions which the villagers and the project were facing. The approach is portrayed as enabling villagers to negotiate better with loggers. A major role of the village management committee is in conducting such negotiations to the benefit of the village, so that wood can be used locally, and villagers get a better price. The potential value of federations of Forestry Groups lies in strengthening this negotiating power.

Figure 6.2 Pit-sawing timber for local use in a Guinean village

4   *Expatriate advisors – state forestry service as predator*

A different perspective again is prevalent among many expatriate forestry advisors, reflecting a cynicism towards the intent of many nationals of the Guinean forestry service. They see overt messages about 'sustainable forest management' on the part of national, prefectoral and sub-prefectoral forestry agents either as a mask for their pursuit of personal and political interests in timber exploitation, or merely as a means to access the personal financial advantages that donor-funded projects bring. They treat overt messages about participation with distrust, as rhetorical statements detracting attention from 'real' interests in maintaining state control over forest resources for financial and other reasons.

These perspectives are linked to expatriates' claimed personal experiences in their own projects, of the staff they work with, and of the central Forest Directorate's attempts to appropriate their budgets. Continually defensive of the budget lines they control, they also draw on experiences of practices of corruption, and on stories which circulate of forestry administrators using their positions to extract personal profits from timber resources.

Emerging from these views, several expatriate advisors narrate the Forestry Groups policy as originating in a struggle against the state forestry service. As the senior manager of a 'participatory' forestry project put it: 'There is a need to protect villagers and their forests from the state'.[10] Through such claims, aid officials position themselves as part of a worldwide movement towards community forestry and co-management: a geography in which the nation state is seen largely as an obstacle.

The successful enaction of legislation permitting Forestry Groups in Guinea is presented as the result of the pressure applied by a group of donors to the national Forest Directorate as a condition of continued funding, especially at a key donor 'roundtable' in March 1997. Moreover, several expatriate advisors express the view that the Directorate is still resistant to the approach, and has stalled on signing the dossiers for new Forestry Groups. From their perspective, only the forthcoming appointment of an expatriate forestry consultant within the ministry, with special responsibility for the Forestry Group issue, promises to 'unblock' the situation.[11] Expatriates also view the support of the prefectoral forestry service to the movement with suspicion. Will the prefectoral authorities attempt to exert control over village forest resources once the maps and inventories have demonstrated their value? And does the local forestry service's involvement with each Group through signatures and monitoring represent a route for individual agents to exert leverage over timber for personal profit? Some projects are taking steps to circumvent this. One, for example, is treating one particular village as a 'social laboratory' in which a Forestry Group is being established and will be monitored in relation to these questions, alongside other aspects of local forest use and management (Ravesloot 1999).[12]

Donor-funded projects, despite nominally working under forestry service authority (*tutelle*), thus image themselves as allied with villagers, initiating and promoting Forestry Groups in an uphill struggle against the real (private) interests of state forestry agents.

5   *State forestry service – management where there was none before*

Members of the prefectoral forestry service narrate the origin of the approach differently again. Those in Kissidougou prefecture, at least, suggest that it arose from within the state forestry service itself, and its own conscious efforts to improve the efficiency, coverage and sustainability of forest management.

Through Forestry Groups, their maps and inventories, management plans and state monitoring of these, there is a sense of management of village forests where there was 'no management' before.[13] Sub-prefecture foresters monitor village forest management, while it is envisaged that the improved capacity to monitor tree stocks will improve tax collection from felling, and stifle illegal operators. Moreover, participation means that 'villagers do the work of forest management themselves. It is no longer necessary to send so many foresters'.[14] By giving villagers responsibility for carrying out these tasks, monitored by state forestry agents, there is a much greater chance that they are actually done, than where a small number of forestry agents attempt to do it themselves. 'Participation' is thus defined as an efficient means towards a state-defined forest management end.

In addition to this efficiency argument, there is a coverage argument. More land is 'classified' and brought under state influenced management, albeit to the benefit of the village and not the state. The forestry code can be applied with rigour in more locations than would be possible through the capacity of the under-staffed forest service itself, or associated projects. There is also a sustainability argument. Villagers will become 'fully conscious of the need to preserve forests around their villages' through the education, 'sensibilisation' and technical advice associated with the constitution of Forestry Groups, and so be in a position to conserve forests in a durable way – at least for the 99-year lease that they are given.[15]

In this narrative, the Forestry Groups approach is located within the broader shift towards 'participation' as an orientation for the Guinean forestry service since the early 1990s. Its origins are thus traced back to the instigators of this orientation in Guinea: to the late Forestry Director Mamadou Oury Bah, German consultants who supported him, and the training they initiated (e.g. De Leener 1995). In imaging Forestry Groups as an extension of state activity, prefectoral forestry administrators consider the formation and monitoring of Forestry Groups as their role, and one which they can and will assume in the future. Donor projects are not indispensable. In short, this perspective narrates Forestry Groups as a transformation towards greater effectiveness and scope of state forestry activity, not a diminution.

Noticeably absent from all these administrative accounts concerning the origin of Forestry Groups is agitation for the approach from villagers. This we explore once we have examined some further reasons for its administrative momentum.

The economy of a policy

To understand more fully the institutional and narrative positionings discussed above requires attention to the financial flows associated with the approach.

These help account for the enthusiasm and rapid development of Forestry Groups by all institutions and administrators involved, whatever their particular narration.

The creation of Forestry Groups entails a great deal of money changing hands. Currently, much of this originates from donor project funds which are channelled in a variety of ways through the practices of Group constitution and monitoring, creating an economy surrounding forests that is independent of the value of timber.[16]

The NGOs which establish Forestry Groups are major recipients of these funds, received through contracts for their work in (a) training local forestry service staff, (b) *per diems* for attending project meetings, and crucially (c) creating the dossiers for Forestry Groups, with contracts specifying a given number to be completed and signed in a specified period. There is considerable financial pressure for NGOs to get the work done and meet the terms and conditions of their contract. For a time, NGOs carrying out contracts for the Niger River Protection Programme could assist villages in accessing major infrastructure (schools, bridges, wells) from a different project funding envelope. Their capacity to provide this *quid pro quo* for the establishment of a Forestry Group was very effective in generating village interest. As this possibility has been curtailed with reduced infrastructural budgets, strong tensions have become apparent between the desires of the NGOs to establish Forestry Groups, and villagers' concerns, as we explore below.

Many people have financial incentives in the Forestry Groups approach. The sub-prefecture forest service staff who monitor the work of the NGOs are paid for this and for training others. They receive *per diems* and transport costs for attending meetings. Ministerial representatives at the Prefecture level who sign their approval of the request for a Group are paid for their work and signatures. The need for many administrative signatures is explained, at least by Kissidougou's NGOs, as an important way 'to involve' a wide range of state institutions in the phenomenon and in the decisions about it, so that they cannot object later. Villagers receive *per diems* and transport costs for attending training sessions and other meetings called by the project. Half of the receipts go to the Group's village development fund.

The National Forestry Director (or his head, the Minister of Agriculture) can request money for signing off on Forestry Group dossiers. According to some sources, one donor project had to pay so much for signing off on eight community forests that in January 1999, a further twenty-eight awaited signatures as the project's next round of financing had not yet come through. Senior expatriates on a different project claim to have been asked for 'several million' Guinean Francs to sign off on each of five dossiers.[17]

In this economy, the creation of a thick dossier, with many forms compiled and procedures conducted, generates both more paid work for NGOs in administering them, and more payments for officials to sign off at each stage.

Moreover, the more paperwork and the more complex the procedure, the more training is required – and the more training contracts around the country NGOs need to conduct. These are paid for both by donor projects and the administration. As one donor succinctly put it: You have to 'buy Forestry Groups in travel expenses, *per diems*, and *moyens logistiques*'.[18]

Cynically, but realistically, one could argue that NGOs have a financial interest in creating more and more paperwork and ever more complex procedures, surveys and so on, since these expand their work. This also inflates the importance of their 'know how' in the creation of Forestry Groups, rendering their expertise more unique and in demand. Paradoxically, then, while NGO staff may claim to support devolution of forest control, their economic interests in the work actually encourage greater state bureaucratic involvement in the creation of Forestry Groups.

National attempts to limit the size of any given Forestry Group have played into this multiplication of labour. The Forest Code now stipulates that no Group may control a forest of more than 100ha, unless a signature of approval by the Minister is given (a lengthy, potentially expensive affair, which by 1999 had not yet been achieved). This ruling has many interpretations. For the 'management where there was none before' narrative it is justified because a village could not be expected to manage a forest larger than this. Within the 'state as predator' narrative, 100ha is construed as the maximum forest area negotiable from a state which wants to retain control of forest resources. A third interpretation, with an eye for the Forestry Group economy, is that there are payments for every Group, at every level. It thus makes financial sense to create more, smaller Forestry Groups rather than a few larger ones. One village sought to establish a single Group to manage their 400ha forest but was encouraged by the NGO involved to divide it into four, each with its own dossier and management committee. There were no losers in this exercise, except perhaps villagers now encumbered by four separate committees.

The Forestry Groups policy has thus created a whole new set of revenues from forests, giving momentum to the approach, and shaping its form. The only financial losers might appear to be the donors, but it is they who need to spend the money and it is attractive for them to do so in what they can sell internationally and to their home constituencies as a 'cutting edge' and 'participatory' development approach, and that boosts their status within the co-management-appreciating epistemic communities of 'Tropical Forest International'.

Administrative visions of locality

In discussions about the Forestry Group approach, several donor, state and NGO staff made mention of villager's own forest use practices in positive terms. Some referred to the soundness of 'traditional' forest management techniques, and to villagers' dissatisfaction with state and project forestry approaches, as evidenced, for example, by the burning of tree nurseries (see also Fairhead and Leach 1996). Indeed many administrators express awareness of the anthropogenic origins of forest patches in Forest Guinea. This awareness derives either from their own experiences in their home villages, or perhaps from exposure to those anthropological and historical studies such as our own in Kissidougou, which suggest that peri-village forests are generally the legacy of historical and recent vegetation-enriching practices in settlement, farming and everyday life (Fairhead and Leach 1996).[19] Nevertheless, while arguments about sound local vegetation management are sometimes used by administrators to support the 'responsibilisation' of villagers, they do not undermine the perceived need for elaborate project and state procedures to create Groups, educate villagers and monitor their activities. In short, there is no narrative seeing Forestry Groups as a logical outcome of villagers' past and present management of their dynamic forest landscapes.

Furthermore while accepting villagers' capacity to sustain and enrich their environment can be supportive of the policy shift towards Forestry Groups, it can also undermine it by suggesting that villagers are already managing forests effectively, rendering Forestry Groups (and much of the action of the forestry service, NGOs and projects) irrelevant. Administrators evade this contradiction in several ways. First, it is sometimes simply ignored, with local vegetation management drawn into debate when deemed appropriate, and excluded when not. Second, it is resolved in a 'breakdown of tradition' argument. Traditional techniques used to work, so the argument goes, but no longer do. In this way, the myth of a romantic past threatened by modernity is created and reproduced through the structural tensions inherent in administration. Third, the modern is described as being grafted onto the old. This can be imaged technically, in arguments about integrating science and tradition, or economically, in arguments about showing people the new value of their old products.

Both these latter aspects of narration construct the technician as 'modern'. Simultaneously, an image is constructed of what it is to be 'a villager', living in 'broken tradition', not being modern. Such images are reproduced frequently in Guinea's administrative circles, and can be seen to emerge from the day-to-day practices of local foresters and development staff, or field-level bureaucrats. In short, endlessly reproduced images of a lost arcadia and an incapacity of 'peasants' to cope with modernity without external support are not merely truths in the culture of intelligentsia. Rather they are a necessary corollary of the positions that administrators work in.

Perspectives from the village

The Forestry Group approach does not appear to have emerged from villagers' agitation despite the fact that it is an approach which supposedly works 'in their interests'. At first sight this is surprising, given that 'grassroots action' and agitation from below have been noted as important influences in accounts of the emergence of community forestry elsewhere (e.g. Joshi 1997).

Yet villagers are hardly concerned about their forests or problems in the ways they are using and living with them; forests which as their own historical accounts and everyday experiences confirm, they have generally established and adapted to meet different requirements over many generations. They are far more concerned about the dangers of forest reservation (*classification*) and the exactions (formal and informal) of the forest service if they break forest codes.[20]

With boundaries, inventories, management plans, state signatures and increased state surveillance, Forestry Groups are easily taken for forest 'classification'. Many villagers understand it as such, done as it is 'by the state' and 'for the project', even if is also 'for the village'. For those distrustful of the future intent of the forestry service, then, formalising a Group is a step towards formal alienation. In law, a Forestry Group forest is considered a reserve, 'for the villagers'. Yet there is, indeed, a clause in the legislation that if villagers are deemed by the forest service not to have fulfilled their part in the management contract, the state has the right to take over management. The extent to which villagers are informed of this is unclear, but their fears seem well-grounded.

The reticence of one village in Kissidougou to be involved begins to reveal some of the anxieties that this new policy momentum raises. In discussions, members of the management committee of the Forestry Group said that when the village was first approached by the sub-prefecture forestry representative to discuss the possibility of creating a Group, villagers were afraid and stalled.[21] They feared that their own forest, created by themselves, would be reserved for the state. They feared losing further control over resources which they knew to be valuable. The forestry officer went to the village five times and each time the village refused.

The forest officer, however, did not interpret the villagers' reticence as originating from their own disquiet. Instead he claimed that politically active 'sons of the village' based in Kissidougou town, but affiliated to the opposition party, had been to the village to discourage villagers from participation.[22] By interpreting village reticence in terms of party politics, the forester was able to avoid facing the possibility that hesitancy was 'real', with all that that would imply. Such interpretations raise the complicating importance of party politics in modern engagement with state services.[23]

The project eventually decided to take several villagers to visit an established Forestry Group in another part of the prefecture. They appeared reassured when villagers there explained that when the trees were mature they could fell them and keep the profit.

156 Science, Society and Power

A second village example shows how problems have arisen following reservation. Here, villagers were similarly unhappy about establishing a Forestry Group when approached by an officer from the prefectoral forest service. The forest officer came three times, and according to the village chief, more or less coerced him to coerce others to constitute a Forestry Group.[24] Thirteen people joined, agreeing to do so because the establishment of the Group was linked to a promise of infrastructural improvement (building a bridge or school). After they reserved the forest, the donor project did build a new classroom for the village school. A year later, however, a national NGO separately offered assistance in building a three-classroom school. As is their practice, this project needed inputs of labour and local materials, including timber, from the village. The villagers contracted a chainsaw operator to fell and prepare a tree.

The forest officer who had initiated the Group, knowing that timber would be needed for this new school building, intervened. He asked the chief from whom he had requested authorisation. The chief replied that the forest 'is for us'. The forester objected, claiming that only he could give authorisation. He imposed a large fine on the villagers, and then took the chainsaw operator to the sub-prefecture tribunal where he also had to pay a fine too, leaving the village further in debt to him as well. Prior to the establishment of a Forestry Group, these villagers had never had problems in felling a tree for their own infrastructure improvement. That this was somehow now problematic hugely discouraged the Group members. Two left, and even the committee president no longer has confidence in it. As a senior aid official said in despair of such stories, 'Many forest agents look for money, which breaks the system'.[25]

Villagers' anxieties were notably not voiced during the meeting to establish a Prefectoral Federation of Forestry Groups in Kissidougou in February 1999. This meeting was facilitated by the European Union-funded Niger River Protection Project, and brought together one or two representatives of each village Group established in the prefecture together with several sub-prefectoral forestry staff and NGO representatives who were active in promoting the approach. Each Group reported on its activities, in a relatively standardised way. In all cases they emphasised first, the efficiency and achievements of the management committee in preparing plans and in generating a Group fund (from *per diems*), and second, achievements in preventing tree felling. The Forestry Group representatives were speaking about their expectations of the event, and their perceptions of the conservation-focused goals of the organisations promoting and paying for the approach. No representative described or even envisaged timber exploitation as a current activity or future goal of their Group. Only on one occasion was this issue raised, and then by a representative of the NGO III which narrates its aims in improving villager control over the timber economy.

Thus the organisation and conduct of the meeting favoured conservation objectives over exploitation, favouring one possible meaning of the Forestry

Group approach over others, and institutionalising it within the Federation which was established. In this arena for 'participation' by villagers in a policy process, through democratic election of a prefectoral committee, participation was highly circumscribed. Villager concerns, and their own perspectives on Forestry Groups located in their historical experiences of landscape found no means of expression, exemplifying how project-orchestrated participation can be framed by certain terms of debate which exclude alternative perspectives and the material concerns linked to them.

Conclusions

There are presumably elements of truth in each of the perspectives on the origins of Forestry Groups, and indeed there may well be other explanatory narratives which we do not cover here. Our aim, though, has not been to evaluate them. Each narrative appears to pick out and emphasise different events as significant to the development of the approach, and its character: events which different people have been involved in (and which they are familiar with and benefit from) and which thus emphasise their own centrality. Notably, each narrative presents some actors necessary to the Forestry Group movement rather negatively, and others positively. Nevertheless, each group can find a narrative in which the policy is advantageous to them. It is partly this that explains how Forestry Groups have emerged in a convergence of diverse positions and concerns.

So in one sense, Forestry Groups provide a case of a policy emerging through a discourse coalition, formed – as defined by Hajer – when previously independent practices are being actively related to one another; when 'a common discourse is created in which several practices get meaning in a common political project' (Hajer 1995: 65). 'Practices' as conceived in Hajer's definition would refer here to the diverse activities orchestrated by and important to different actors: NGOs might be 'doing community-based development' or organising meetings to empower villagers vis-à-vis chainsaw operators'; the state forest service 'reserving forests', and so on, yet these diverse practices are able to converge in a single, Forestry Group approach. At the same time, though, we have focused on a common set of practices; that is, the scientific and policy practices that together constitute the dossier, and put into place and monitor forest management plans.

In another sense, however, the diverse narratives reveal that the Forestry Groups approach does not actually constitute a common policy. The Forestry Group approach goes on meaning different things to different people, despite the manuals, procedures and laws which appear to produce it as a unitary phenomenon. The 'origin stories' for the Forestry Groups approach, linked to particular positions on its raison d'être and meaning, are continually played out in the doing of Forestry Groups, and in administrative discussions about them. The different interpretations echo economic-structural differences between

those involved. One policy thus exists as very different policies for those involved in its administration. There is a clear tension between those seeing these
Forestry Groups as 'protecting people from a predatory state' and those seeing them as extending state management and influence; those imaging them
as a devolution or decentralisation of governance, and those seeing them as
a form of centralisation, and between those seeing the policy basically in
terms of revenue generation, and those focusing on forest regeneration and
protection.

The emergence of the approach, the shape it has taken and its momentum has
therefore depended, in part, on a coalition around a set of laws and practices
but not a common interpretation of what these are, and their intent. Equally
it has depended on the particular nature of financial flows; the fountain which
has stimulated the development of the policy (or more properly, policies), but
which has not determined its shape. This paid for the various meetings, studies,
training programmes and so on which have been understood and experienced
very differently by those involved in some, and never in all.

The Forestry Group approach has also interlocked with existing practices, so
sedimented in Guinea's administrative history as to become naturalised: the administrative signature; the forest inventory; the clarification of tenure; the forest
management plan; the classified forest; the monitoring of forest management;
the election of a committee (village, sub-prefecture, prefecture). Others, more
recent and stimulated by the influence of international neo-liberal agendas,
are now repeated across numerous arenas – in agriculture, micro-credit, etc,
inter-animating with forestry to become common expectation: the allocation
of contracts; the creation of 'groupements'; the village development fund; the
village development plan, and so on. The distinction between 'old' and 'new'
practices is very blurred; indeed as Ribot (1999) has argued, contemporary processes of decentralisation and administrative deconcentration in francophone
West Africa are modifications of earlier colonial administrative practices. In
this sense Forestry Groups are a bricolage of existing practices each laden with
meaning for bureaucracy and for populace; existing meanings which shape
contemporary interpretations of them, whether through inheritance or dialogical opposition. So although there can be no overarching narrative concerning
the development of the policy, these relatively 'autonomous' practices – in the
sense of each having their own biography – have shaped the structure it has
taken, and meanings it has acquired.

Despite different administrative interpretations, something is definitely happening. There are more points of authority, more 'techniques of registration' of
tenure, of forest inventory and so on, which bring the village closer to the administration. Villagers may gain in being less exploited by timber contractors,
but in so doing may become more vulnerable to other actions of the state. And
whilst the village is acquiring control, it does so within a committee structure

(with president, treasurer, secretary, fire warden and token women to do the cooking), which is a microcosm of the bureaucratic ideal of statecraft. Such committees are very different from the political networks, kinship and descent groupings, and other forms of association which connect people within and between villages in other socially- and culturally-embedded ways. The committees contribute to an illusion of working 'with community', and of there being yet another state bureaucracy microcosm in the village. But actually a restricted membership 'Group' and its committee is created, composed of a village elite here, a family there, and perhaps elsewhere a press-ganged youth, which might have acquired valuable forest resource claims (or onerous obligations) as the case may be.

From a village perspective, amidst these practices, the state administration and apparently non-governmental organisations tend to fade into one another – after all NGO contracts are monitored by state functionaries, and NGO staff once used to work for state projects. Moreover, all outsiders appear obsessed with forests (a particular vision that the villagers have of them) in a peculiar way, as outsiders have been for generations, and very alien to land users' experiences. Thus however incoherent the approach may be, as we have outlined, it is felt at least initially by villagers as coherence – the state/party/project seeking to reserve the village forest. That villagers considered the project/Forestry Groups movement to be essentially a continuation of forest reservation was clear in their statements to the Federation meeting that 'nobody had felled trees'. This meeting, and its competitive, as well as federative, edge reinforced the social category of the 'good village' defined through its 'good Group' and conservation ethic.

In the 'pilot' and 'experimental' nature of the programmes, in the importance attributed to student memoirs, and in the overt consideration of certain villages as laboratories, the policy process is a broader exercise in the co-production of science and policy. On the one hand, the inquiries into village forests and their management are clearly enabled and framed by the policy structures in which they are elaborated. On the other, the set of policy practices acquires momentum and shape through the experimentation process. One dimension of this experimentality is the capacity it creates for interested donors, government and NGO personnel to present these Group cases – and laboratory findings – as lessons for regional and global audiences, whether through workshops, conferences or publications in the development-network and academic literatures. In this way, 'local' cases speak to internationalised epistemic communities, and the vortex of scientific and policy interest in forest co-management. Those at the 'coal-face' of development – field-level workers – are simultaneously at its centre. This engagement with the international vortex also plays into the scientific and policy dynamic on the ground. Seen through the lens of science and policy, then, the influences on the approach are simultaneously local, national and global. The different weight that these geographical/institutional referents acquire in narratives about the approach are reflective not of any fundamental contradiction, but of the economic and political positions of those forwarding them.

Notes

1. Group discussion, national director and senior staff, National Forest Directorate, Conakry, 12 January 1999.
2. Note from Madame Bangoura Makalé Camara to the Director of Forestry, 'Agrément des forêts collectives au niveau villageois', Ministère de l'Agriculture, de l'Elevage et des Forêts, Conakry, 1996.
3. Group discussion, leader and two members of NGO I, Kissidougou, 30 January 1999.
4. Ibid.
5. It is important to note that at the time of this interview in 1999, consultancy organisations were competing for new contracts under a refinancing of the programme.
6. Interview, leader of NGO II, Kissidougou, 2 February 1999.
7. Ibid.
8. Group discussion with leader and three members of NGO III, Kissidougou, 3 February 1999.
9. Ibid.
10. Interview, European project manager of donor-funded forestry project, Conakry, 8 January 1999.
11. For example, ibid.
12. Interview, European social scientist with donor-funded forestry project, Nzerekore, 15 February 1999.
13. Interview, Prefectoral Director of Forestry, Kissidougou, 20 January 1999.
14. Interview, sub-prefectoral forest agent, Kissidougou, 30 January 1999.
15. Ibid.
16. In a similar way, Wade (1982) has traced the formal and informal financial flows structuring incentives around canal irrigation in South Asia. As yet, Forestry Groups appear to have had rather little impact on Guinea's timber economy. Although not detailed in this chapter, timber operators whom we interviewed are unperturbed by the approach. Those operating in Kissidougou, for example, already consider that they negotiate with villagers, up to their limit, in effect paying them for their timber, accepting that *de facto*, timber already belongs to the village, even if *de jure* it belongs to the State.
17. Interview, European project manager of donor-funded forestry project, Conakry, 8 January 1999.
18. Ibid.
19. Publications, working papers and video material (e.g. the 40 minute video 'Second Nature: Building forests in West Africa's savannas' produced by Cyrus Productions in 1996 with DFID funding) documenting this work are available in the libraries of many local project offices. The findings have, at times, been a talking point amongst project and forest service staff. This may possibly have supported administrators' attention to the forest-building practices recounted in villages.

20. Projects promoting Forestry Groups were going to use the term forest 'classifica-tion', but chose to avoid it because of villager's fear, and these associations. The term 'Groupement', with its more benign associations with development projects, was chosen instead.
21. Group discussion with Forestry Group management committee, village X, Kissi-dougou, 20 March 1999.
22. The forester was also suspicious that certain local figures were sympathetic to the political opposition, and had encouraged dissent from a programme of the existing government.
23. Those working within the state administration are reasonably assumed by villagers to be sympathetic to the party in power (PUP), which has been in government long enough to have had time to favour its supporters in administrative positions. Project staff are often state functionaries and are interpreted in the same way. More significantly, even when not state functionaries, and perhaps not sympathetic to the PUP, villagers generally still assume them to be.
24. Interview, village chief, village Y, Kissidougou prefecture, 23 March 1999.
25. Interview, senior European aid official, Conakry, 10 January 1999.

7 Sustainable timber production and forest management in Trinidad

Introduction

In Trinidad most remaining forest is in government-held reserves (Map 7.1). In this second timber case study, we focus on reserve-based forestry. In international discussions, Trinidad has acquired a rare reputation for the sustainability of its natural forest management. This rests partly on its 'Periodic Block System' (PBS); a 'blueprint' system for selective logging in demarcated forest blocks on a 25–30-year cycle in the forests to the south and east of the island. Here we examine the co-evolution of this system with forest administration, use and ecology, and the scientific and policy practices that it involves.

The PBS is both a timber production system, and a management system regulating forest exploitation by artisanal loggers (known locally as woodworkers) and others. We explore how science and regulation/policy have mutually informed each other in the development and operation of the system. Formal research (or practices formalised as research) have been important to the legitimacy of the PBS and to its surrounding culture of scientific professionalism. Nevertheless, inquiry, innovation, creativity and adaptation by local forestry field staff and daily workers ('field-level bureaucrats') have been significant in shaping the evolution of actual land management practices.

The system has also been shaped by the pressures exerted by others interested in the forest and its resources. Issues of poverty and participation are raised by woodworkers, and concerns with wildlife and biodiversity conservation, aesthetics and economics have been raised by others. In these respects, concerns with Trinidad's south-east region are locked into assorted national and international political and academic institutions.

Despite Trinidad's international and professional reputation for sustainable forest management, many Trinidadians have become deeply concerned by the state of the forest and the logic of degradation which seems to have accompanied so called 'sustainable' practices. This contradiction draws attention to a contrast between certain scientific and policy practices premised on ideas of ecological and social stability, and others which acknowledge and deal with less equilibrial processes.

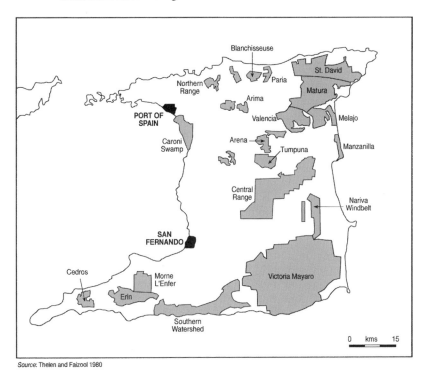

Source: Thelen and Faizool 1980

Map 7.1 Forest reserves in Trinidad

Definitions, criteria and indicators of sustainability used both internationally, and in Trinidad's PBS are premised on ecological and social predictability: that forests and people will respond to rational management in rational, predictable and known ways. Yet forests and people have not been so reliable. Trinidad's natural forest management, despite being the oldest in the tropical Americas, dates back less than eighty years. During this period, management practices have been responding continually to unpredicted ecological developments (failures of regeneration, fire events and so on) as well as social developments (changes in social and economic policy, or at least practice), which were either not acknowledged or excluded from consideration in the development of the system. So while there has been an enduring, professional management philosophy of 'sustainable management' – and the elaboration of structures which give Trinidad's forest management the trappings of 'sustainability' in the view of professional foresters and international organisations – management practices, as we shall see, can also be understood as ad hoc adaptations, responding from one problem to the next. While some forests remain of high quality after two felling cycles, others are highly degraded, swept by fire. Corrective sil-viculture to 'stabilise' and shape the forest have been costly, placing greater strain on both on budgets and on poor, small-scale artisanal loggers coerced into improvement felling. The changing social configuration of the logging sector, in which artisans increasingly lose out to larger enterprises threatens the viability of corrective measures. Added to the socio-political instabilities, the forest itself may display less equilibrial dynamics than assumed in for-est management plans. National foresters nevertheless represent the system as stable, sustainable and productive, and the chapter examines how scientific and policy practices serve to maintain this image of stability in the face of uncertainty.

While our principal focus is on the natural forest management of state lands, we compare it with timber production in state plantations, and on private and non-reserved state land. Exploring contrasts and similarities between the sci-entific and political-economic practices associated with these different types of timber production enables us to locate the PBS better within both the broader culture of the Forestry Division, and the changing political economy of timber production in Trinidad.

Trinidad has acquired an international reputation for sustainable produc-tion. When reviewing tropical forest management in South America and the Caribbean, for example, Synnott (1989) wrote that

From the viewpoint of professional forestry, this author has not identified any case of operational tropical moist forest management for sustainable timber production in any [ITTO] member country except Trinidad and Tobago. . . . It is the only country in which government foresters are carrying out natural forest management, on an operational scale, for timber production, over a substantial proportion of the national forest land (Synnott 1989: 75–76).[1]

Timber in Trinidad currently derives from a range of sources and land types: state forest reserves holding natural forest which are used for production; plantations on reserved and unreserved state land; forest re-growth on abandoned private agricultural land; private areas of natural forest, and new planting on private land (Table 7.1). The PBS has developed and been applied within state forest reserves in the south-east, a highly-forested region where many state reserves are dominated by an astonishingly gregarious natural forest tree, *Mora excelsa*. This species accounts for 60–80 per cent of plants, and still more of the upper canopy. Mora is a high quality timber, used for shipbuilding in the 1800s and subsequently in building, bridge construction and as railway sleepers (Forest Department, 1933).

Our focus on Trinidad's Mora forests also enables us to explore the relevance of modern developments in the theories and practice of forestry science to the way forest composition is understood and hence to sustainable natural forest

Table 7.1 *Silvicultural systems in Trinidad*

Silvicultural system	Area	Remarks
Shelterwood	c. 1,500	Arena Forest Reserve, Compartment system, now suspended
Clearfelling plantation	c. 10,000	Teak
	c. 5,000	Pine
	c. 2,000	Mixed Hardwoods
Selection	c. 130,000	Girth control
Open Range		
Periodic Block	c. 10,000	30 years polycycle

Source: Clubbe and Jhilmit 1992. Note that planting on private land, which greatly accelerated during the 1990s, is not included.

management. The past two decades have witnessed the culmination of a revolution in ecological science both in general, and in relation to forests (e.g. Botkin 1990). Ideas that forests can be treated as stable vegetation communities best understood in terms of plant succession to climax formations have been fundamentally challenged. Analysts of North American and European forests now embrace non-equilibrium theory in ecology, considering forest form and composition as subject to constant variability over space and time, forcing forest management and conservation issues to be reframed (e.g. Sprugel 1991). This perspective itself derives support from research into climatic variability and forest history (Worster 1994), and from revised assessments of the effect of human impacts (e.g. Taylor 1988).

As we shall see, Trindad's Mora forests have long been considered by ecologists as 'invasive', yet at time-scales which enabled Mora forests to be treated as an equilibrial climax. Recently, however, studies by climate and vegetation historians suggesting that drier climates have prevailed in Central America's tropical forests invite new questions to be asked of the status, dynamics and unpredictable responses to management of the Mora forest. Notably, though, these questions have not been taken up within the scientific and policy practices of the PBS.

The emergence of the Periodic Block System

While foresters represent the PBS as a 'system', it combines and builds on earlier practices current elsewhere, and its emergence needs to be considered within the evolution of Trinidad's natural forest management practices more generally.

In the nineteenth and early twentieth centuries, Trinidad imported much of its timber, despite its own timber resources on private land and on the 51 per cent of the island which was forested state land. While the original impetus to establish reserves derived from concerns over climate and soils, discussions in the 1920s instigated a shift towards managing state forests for timber production to offset imports and generate exports (Marshall 1925; Troup 1926; Robinson 1926). The greatest timber resources lay in the two big Mora forests in Mayaro and Matura.[2] These were hardly used until the establishment of Trinidad's first major sawmill in the south-east Mora forest, whereupon it became the most heavily cut timber in the colony (Trinidad and Tobago 1934a: 58) – although nothing approaching the estimated potential annual production. Moreover imports of Mora continued from Guyana, remaining profitable as the necessary port and milling infrastructure had grown up around it.

Colonial forestry began to regulate timber extraction from 1918, and from then on the Forest Department developed and applied a succession of management systems. In 1918, selection felling was introduced. Certain trees could be felled only if over a certain girth, and only if another of the same species over 3 foot in girth grew within 300 feet, to ensure future seed.[3] Selection felling came to be known as a poor management system, as loggers felled trees over 'scattered areas throughout the forest, and trees [were] selected for cutting purely on the marketable value and without regard to regeneration' (Marshall 1925: 11).

Many of these problems were repeated in the 'Open Range System' (ORS) which developed from it, in which 'Individual licensed loggers are licensed to cut a specified volume or number of trees and may select them anywhere in the reserve or range as defined and approved by the Forest Department' (Synnott 1989: 93). In many reserves the ORS 'amounted to a "loggers' selection system"' (ibid). A forest officer could, for silvicultural reasons, prevent the felling of a tree that had attained the required girth, but this was not achieved in practice due to the large territories covered by forestry staff, their frequent transfer and pressure from woodworkers. Woodworkers are small-scale operators who purchase private or state timber under licence, fell the trees, deliver them to the roadside and sell them from there to sawmillers. As licensees, they tended to cream the crop, removing the best timber and leaving the poor (a process known as 'highgrading'). With extraction permitted over the whole range, it was also difficult for the limited forestry staff to police illegal felling. Moreover, today's foresters consider girth limits to have been set too low, geared more to permitting colonial forest 'mining' than long term sustainability.[4]

The ORS remains operational to this day in certain reserves and on non-reserved state land. Yet from the earliest, foresters were proposing improved systems, frequently adapting practices in use elsewhere in the tropics. Marshall (1925) suggested a 'Periodic system' – similar to those long in use in India and

Burma (Troup 1926: 3) – through which a mixed wood of uneven-aged trees would be converted into even-aged woods of a pure crop, amenable to easy management and exploited on a sixty-year rotation. To achieve this, felling by licensees would be limited to annual coupes within a given block for a twenty-year period, with all timber disposed of. In theory, a block of even aged timber regenerates. Second and third blocks are subsequently treated in the same way (Marshall 1925: 11). A variant of this system was introduced in 1929 into Trinidad's Arena forest reserve. There was careful control of logging intensity and the opening of the canopy; careful tending, weeding and select-ing out 'defective' trees within the regeneration, and removal of shelterwood once regeneration had succeeded. This drew on the practices of the 'tropical shelterwood system' pioneered in Malaysia and later popular in West Africa (Synnott 1989). The cutting cycle was also reduced from an expected sixty-year monocycle to a thirty-year polycycle.[5] It is the 'polycyclic' selection system which became referred to locally as the Periodic Block System.

It was not until the 1960s that such a system was applied to Trinidad's Mora forests. When Mora reserves attracted management attention from the late 1940s, they were at first subjected to an ORS focused in blocks,[6] but geared towards converting Mora to more productive and valuable mixed hardwood species (Chalmers 1981). The regeneration of other species under Mora shelter proved poor. This influenced the decision in 1957 to clearfell a block of the northern Mora forests each year, and replace it with pine plantation (*Pinus caribaea*). Globally, at this time, the promise of natural forest management which had influenced 1950s policy was being questioned on technical and economic grounds, and in many countries 'by the beginning of the 1960s, the scales tipped in favour of artificial methods' of plantation (Bertault 1993). Trinidad, too, thus switched to a plantation focus in many areas. Yet the pine plantations also proved unsuccessful due to fire and other factors. After ten years of clear felling, by the late 1960s, 94 per cent of the northern Melajo and Valencia Mora forests had been totally destroyed as a source of timber (Chalmers 1981, citing Bell 1969/71), and the southern forests had narrowly escaped similar destruction. The forester Bell, who studied these forests, suggested halting clear felling, and exploiting Mora under a selective system of management.

It is the management system that developed in the south-east which is presently considered as the PBS. This was first introduced in 1960 in the Rio Claro West range of the Victoria Mayaro reserve, and was subsequently ex-panded into other ranges. Timber management there is now almost completely under the PBS – although only 20 per cent of the land is managed for produc-tion, with the rest set aside within on-shore oil concessions, a wildlife sanctuary (Trinity Hills) or as a strategic timber reserve.

The PBS emerged as a set of practices attempting to integrate the control of Mora forest ecology with the regulation of timber users. At first it was not such a radical departure from the open range system, involving a similar practice of maintaining 'replacement' trees ('take one, seize one'), although felling was confined to and monitored within annually-demarcated blocks. The better trees were still taken, and the poorer ones left standing.

In the early 1970s, an important innovation occurred in the introduction of 'silvicultural marking'. In theory:

> . . . stems are selected for sale by a team of highly skilled markers who go through the block systematically and physically mark trees that should be removed. In principle, the trees that are marked are those which in the next 30 years would not do as well as others that they are shading, or competing with. They may either be mature, or faulty or likely to become so (Clubbe and Jhilmit 1992:5).

Marked trees were sold to licensed woodworkers, who had to buy licences permitting them to fell 500 cubic feet of timber over a two-year period, after which the block would be closed from sales and allowed to regenerate for the cutting cycle of thirty years. In principle, one or two blocks (each of 200ha) is opened each year.

According to those now working as silvicultural markers, it was local forestry staff who were behind its introduction, exemplifying a case of policy innovation by field-level bureaucrats. Indeed markers today accredit Mr. Boysie Rambharat, then a junior forester (Forester 1), and 'a man who lived forestry, he knew everything'.[7] His seniors, they claim, were at first reluctant to recognise an innovation from a junior and the divergence from established procedures which it entailed. Indeed junior foresters narrate that seniors stalled the introduction of the practice by, for instance, refusing to supply Rambharat with the necessary paint to mark trees. Nevertheless, within a few years, silvicultural marking became an established part of the PBS. It was then taken over by a separate specialist branch of the Forestry Division – the Forest Resource Inventory and Management section (FRIM).

PBS practices today

With the shift to silvicultural marking, the PBS became directed not only towards sustainable extraction from the Mora forest, but also to more active ecological management and shaping of it. The Mora tree is often so dominant as to constitute an almost-pure stand. The intent is to harvest the increment from each twenty-five-year period, and to increase quality up to about 80 per cent sound trees.[8]

'Opening a block' involves several operations. First, FRIM conducts an inventory of all species above 20cm diameter, and commercial species above 10cm, recording basal area and estimated volume of timber in each block. In practice this is not always done, as foresters consider themselves able to gauge the likely content of a block by comparison with any neighbouring blocks which have been opened recently, as well as through two small research sites (permanent sample plots), monitored every two years (more recently every four years due to staff and funding shortages).[9] Second, FRIM staff cut vines at their base so they will not pull down the crowns of neighbours when their tree is felled. The block is then compartmentalised, and trees marked for felling by two FRIM officers, each accompanied by a daily paid worker.

Trees are selected on the basis of whether they would be better felled now, or in twenty-five years time. 'Better' refers to the balance of a number of criteria in a process that FRIM officers describe more as an art than a strict science; one where personal judgement and experience count.[10] Criteria include crown form and position; tree size in relation to the officer's knowledge of the species; indicators of decay (e.g. a hollow echo when tapped or active low branching);[11] location (even an unsound or mature tree may be left standing on a river bank or steep slope); form of bole; species rarity, and diversity of valuable timber species (e.g. if a Galba is seen in a Mora forest, one would leave it). Further selection criteria balance timber production with wildlife conservation: trees that are sheltering burrows or nests, certain fruit trees for food, and vines for animal shelter are left unmarked (although wildlife take priority in other parts of the reserve). This balancing is reasonably straightforward in Mora forest which is relatively less diverse in vegetation and animals than other forest types.

A key aim is to avoid opening up the forest too much to let in pioneer species which would impoverish the forest.[12] On the ecotone between Mora-dominant forest and other forest types, foresters tend to mark trees so as to further the expansion of this invasive species. Yet at the same time they emphasise that they are not trying to create a Mora monoculture.

After marking, FRIM makes a logging operation plan detailing vehicle routes and collection points, recalling those from earlier cutting cycles. FRIM then hands over a master list of the marked trees to the local forestry staff who work as sales officers, allocating and selling trees to licensees.

In recent years, silvicultural management in the PBS has expanded into a further period of post-harvest operations. Forest officers had long demanded the introduction of 'improvement felling' in blocks after formal harvest, and this was finally introduced in 1997 with funding from a national Public Sector Investment Programme. This involves felling both marked trees which were left standing after harvest, and defective unmarked trees, including those damaged during harvesting. The operations are supposed to be carried out immediately following the closure of the block, but in practice the demand on FRIM staff frequently imposes a delay of several years. To date, three blocks have been treated in this way. In contrast with the main harvest, forest officers carry out improvement felling themselves, selling trees to licensees from the stumps.

Figure 7.1 Forest officers reviewing felled timber within the periodic block system, Victoria Mayaro Reserve

This is because woodworkers find it unprofitable to fell such trees (they would otherwise already have felled them), but profitable to use the parts they want once the trees felled.

Science and research in the PBS

The knowledge and skills involved in silvicultural marking and the PBS are seen by forest officers as acquired through experience and practice. Thus while students in forestry training school (ECIAF) might learn silvicultural management techniques, 'they only learn the basics: real learning is by apprenticeship, once posted to FRIM'.[13] It is now Division policy for all forest officers to pass through FRIM, where they initially work alongside experienced officers. Once on their own, they work with daily paid workers who as some officers note, 'should never be underestimated; they really know their stuff . . .'; moreover their knowledge base is sustained since today 'forest officers come and go, but workers are always there'.[14] Local officers see the need to create a handbook for silvicultural marking, to ensure maintenance of these accumulated skills. In some senses, then, those working as markers in FRIM have little respect for the Forestry Division's usual hierarchy of ranked forest officers (3, 2, 1). Nevertheless, the officers appreciate the need to follow instruction from their seniors and the 'Division bible', the Forestry Handbook (e.g. Forestry Division 1992), without interpreting these for themselves; otherwise it would 'defeat the purpose of the system'.[15]

Compared with the importance of judgement by those on the ground, 'formal' research seems to have been rather peripheral to the development of PBS practices. For example in 1983 a system of Permanent Sample Plots was established as part of a 'statistically designed sampling programme for forest management', unique in Tropical America (Synnott 1989: 92). Yet while data on species composition and size are regularly collected from the plots, they are not analysed by the Forestry Division, at least partly because of the overstretched staff and limited resources of the central FRIM office. Designed for management use, the only use to which the data have been put is for academic research at the University of the West Indies.[16] Yet the sample plots become significant to forest management through informal practice, as forest officers remark on and discuss the ecology and evolution of trees while collecting plot data.[17] Thus although the data sit unanalysed in offices, the experience of gathering them feeds valuably into the 'art' of silvicultural marking.

The importance that local foresters attribute to knowledge-through-experience in the PBS fuels their cynicism concerning higher-level education in forestry science.[18] Senior staff – those of the Assistant Conservator rank or above – must be graduates in forestry, yet with no degree course available in the Caribbean, they are trained in North American or European universities and inevitably acquire a temperate or Mediterranean bias. A common quip among lower ranking foresters, as well as other critics of the Forestry Division is that such graduates become 'office foresters', not forest officers, increasingly divorced – by their qualifications and the locus of their work – from the everyday realities of Trinidad's forests and field-level interactions with them. This cynicism extends further into international forestry culture, with those graduates who continue field-based work concerned that those they meet with PhDs in the increasingly international world of natural forest management know so little of field-level realities. This cynicism even extends to the Oxford Forestry Institute, which for Trinidadian foresters has been an icon of professional forestry research and education, and which was the colonial focus for emergent knowledge of Trinidad's forest ecology and management. One experienced FRIM visitor who had held the Institute in awe from a distance, was disillusioned after a training visit, astounded by the mediocre knowledge of tropical forests displayed by those who were to train him. But while somewhat disdainful of the way formal forestry science is conducted, then, local foresters are also concerned that their own inputs to it – as data collectors – go largely unacknowledged. And while local foresters may consider themselves to be doing the 'real', on-the-ground research in their daily work, this is neither encouraged nor recompensed. Their field science, as they see it, is increasingly divorced from the 'hard' science of the 'office foresters'.

The formality and 'trappings' of hard science are nevertheless important for policy influence and change, and in maintaining the external reputation of the Forestry Division. For example those FRIM staff who would like the PBS applied in *Carapa guayanensis* (Crappo) forest, have an idea of the approximate rotation age for Crappo – forty years – and feel they could develop appropriate practices on the ground through experimentation. Yet they recognise that formal research would be needed in order to gain legitimacy and permission from the Director of Forestry and the Minister to move ahead. In other words, changing the system needs formal scientific justification. This research has not been done. FRIM lacks analysis of Crappo growth rates, and the Permanent Sample Plot data have not been entered.[19]

Woodworkers, sawmillers and the PBS

The woodworkers, whose livelihoods depend on the allocation of timber in the reserves, have a very different perspective on the PBS. In particular, they critique its practice in the context of national political economy (in which they are disadvantaged), and question the balancing of priorities within the system – especially the trade-off between future quality and current production.

Woodworkers have developed their perspectives and critiques not only in relation to the Forestry Division, but also to sawmillers, within a changing political-economic context. Sawmillers in the south-east vary from small operators working niche markets (e.g. sawing lowest grade timber for disposable pallets) to large-scale lumber industrialists who import timber from Guyana and distribute it throughout the country (Figure 7.2). Although assorted forms of vertical integration between woodworkers and sawmillers exist, woodworkers remain a distinct interest group in Trinidad's south-eastern forests, not least because they have organised themselves.

In 1964 licensed woodworkers formed the Nariva-Mayaro Woodworkers' Association. In 1971 they became a Co-operative Society, stimulated by an ultimately unsuccessful attempt to purchase a communal sawmill. The Association now remains as both a lobbying organisation for woodworkers' rights and interests, and a partner with the Forestry Division (south-east conservancy) in

Figure 7.2 A medium-sized sawmill in south-east Trinidad

orchestrating the allocation of licences. There are seventy-two licensed wood-workers, although a further nineteen aspire to be licensees. New applications are approved by the Association which is in effect 'their union', although their lists are vetted by the Forestry Division.[20] The Association develops a list of licensees with the Forestry Division and revises it annually. The order in which licensees feature on the list – strictly by length of licenseeship – is crucial, dictating which woodworkers can enter the block first to choose the trees they will fell. All seventy-two licensees are entitled to go in turn with a forest officer to locate their trees, but frequently, those after about 20th on the list will obtain little timber of value. No licensee can have more than three licenses open at any time, and theoretically at least, each license must be filled before a new one is allocated.

Representatives of the Woodworkers' Association have a generally positive view of the PBS, with which their organisation has co-evolved. The Forestry Division has a history of protecting woodworkers' rights as part of social policy, and of protecting the forest. As the Association's president put it: 'Without the PBS the whole area would become savanna and our children would not see forest. The PBS is good for both the small man and the state'.[21]

In making such positive remarks, the Association draws comparisons with the Open Range System where there was no woodworker-controlled register of licensees: 'It was a free for all, and the big operators [large sawmillers] just creamed the timber. . . . the license system was open to abuse, and one sawmiller could use ten "decoys" to obtain ten extra licenses . . . It is through organising that we have managed to keep the livelihoods of the poor'.[22] Purchasing wood under licence from the Forestry Division is extremely profitable. The low price at which the state sells timber in effect subsidises the woodworkers.[23] It is not surprising that woodworkers seek as much state licensed timber as possible – and that as we shall see, sawmillers attempt to cash in on the profits to be made.

But while viewing the PBS as a potentially ideal 'socio-technical system' (Pfaffenberger 1992), woodworkers nevertheless critique the actual practice of it, at least in recent years – making this distinction between ideal and practice themselves. They critique the ways foresters balance what to fell and what to leave, complaining that the quality of timber made available to them is very low. FRIM 'mark the sick and the dead – there are very few good solid trees. They care for the forest at the woodworkers' expense'.[24] Woodworkers are naturally hesitant to fell the poorer quality trees which are unprofitable, and those lower down the licensee list, whose licences are filled by such trees, have even more cause to complain. In the 1980s, the Forestry Division attempted to introduce a requirement that licensees fell all marked trees (including the 'sick and the dead'), but this failed to work as the less profitable mopping-up fell disproportionately on those lower on the list. It was this that prompted the introduction of improvement felling.

The basis for these criticisms of silvicultural marking practice are accentuated by recent events in which certain sawmillers have gained priority access to blocks, 'creaming' the best timber before the block is opened to woodworkers. In the case of one recent block, the Woodworkers' Association is actually taking the Forestry Division to court over its privileged granting of access to sawmillers before the block was opened.[25] Worse, once sawmillers have the wood they require, woodworkers have no market for theirs. As the Association president put it: 'Even a year after felling, our wood is still by the road'.[26] The 'government order' is a critical means to such access. When the government needs timber for its own construction projects in bridges, buildings and so on, it passes the order to a sawmiller, who can use it to purchase timber directly from the state, without having to buy it from the licensees. Woodworkers see these government orders as a mechanism by which certain sawmillers with high-level political connections can subvert the authority and market control of the Woodworkers' Association.[27] At the same time, the incentive for sawmillers to oust woodworkers has been greatly accentuated by technological changes, as power saws and tractors now make it economic for sawmillers to do the woodworkers' work.

Woodworkers explicitly critique emerging practices on equity grounds, claiming that sawmillers have many sources of livelihood but they have only one; sawmillers should be made to purchase all their timber from licensees, or licensees will face greater poverty. Moreover the structure of the sawmilling industry has changed. Woodworkers once enjoyed good relations with smaller sawmillers, but the latter have increasingly been pushed out of business by the 'big boys', the lumber industrialists. Only five sawmillers (out of seventy-two in the country) constitute these 'big boys' and they are the main beneficiaries of privileged state timber access. But other sawmillers, aspiring to these same privileges and more profit-oriented than in the past, have also ceased to support woodworkers. The 'big boys', as woodworkers understand it, are also close to the powers of the present government, which is less sympathetic to woodworkers than its predecessor. The government, in turn, is supported by international consultants who have recommended a rationalisation of sawmills for economic efficiency, and to reduce over capacity (Chalmers 1992).

A second area of woodworkers' complaint concerns the time that the Forestry Division bureaucracy takes. Licensees are required to pay up-front for their licences, but the Division is then frequently slow to open the block. Woodworkers sometimes have to provide free labour to ensure that blocks are opened.[28] They see these delays as caused by the Forestry Division's short-staffing for necessary tasks, as well as its slowness in processing the paperwork, with data on the market trees, expected timber volume and so on having to be sent first to Port of Spain, and then San Fernando. Even once the trees are felled, it can take a year before paperwork and measuring by forest officers is complete and the woodworkers are free to remove the trees. During delays such as these, woodworkers' money is tied up, and they are frequently left indebted. If, as is sometimes the case, a marked block is not opened for 3–4 years, further problems arise. The tree marks become invisible, and the Forestry Division may deny that the tree is for sale. Between felling and authorisation, felled trees become hard to find as they have become buried in undergrowth.[29] Woodworkers also argue that they should be allowed to take all unmarked damaged trees, windfalls, broken crowns and so on (including those damaged accidentally during their felling operations) straightaway when first felling in a block, rather than simply letting these trees rot and to be dealt with much later in post-harvest felling.

A third area of complaint refers to radical changes in procedure following forest fires. The major ramifications of these for woodworkers and their livelihoods will be discussed after considering the broader questions of sustainability raised by these fires, and their implications for how Mora ecological dynamics might be understood.

Ecological dynamics in the PBS: relations between equilibrial and non-equilibrial perspectives on Mora forest

The management of Mora forest under the PBS is geared towards maintaining a stable state productive forest: a kind of equilibrium. Yet a major shock – in the form of extensive forest fires in 1987 – has forced system adaptation. The fires, linked to a particularly deep and prolonged dry season, burnt about 20,000 ha of good forest, 10,000 ha under PBS.[30] In response, the Forestry Division re-planned block rotations, promoting the productive use of the fire-burned blocks through 'salvage cuts', and holding back the opening of what came to be called 'green' blocks.

When explaining the fire event, foresters image it as a one-off external variable to an otherwise stable system over the longer term.[31] Such explanations and management practices are configured in accordance with equilibrium ecology. Yet Trinidad experiences very high inter-annual variability of rainfall and dry season length, and in this context one could expect major fire risks to occur several times in the course of a century – as forestry records themselves reveal. Moreover, other scientific perspectives – embracing non-equilibrial dynamics, and increased attention to climate variation and the legacy of historic land use – would question such equilibrial views. In contextualising fire events as part of a path-dependent history of forest disturbance, in effect as part of the system, they question both the premise of stability in Mora forests, and the management implications which flow from this.

The studies of early ecological scientists themselves suggested that over a long time-scale, Trinidad's vegetation was not usefully understood in relation to equilibrium. Marshall (1934, 1939) noted that Mora was an invasive tree, while the failure of Mora boundaries to correspond to obvious soil or physical features, and the presence of saplings in neighbouring associations, suggested its progressive march into these (Beard 1946b: 181). Beard deduced from present distribution and rates of natural advance that Mora arrived 30–50,000 years ago.

Studies in mainland tropical America, however, suggest that non-equilibrium conditions may also apply over much shorter time-scales. Climate historians and paleo-archeologists suggest that a generally drier climate prevailed in the mid-Holocene, c. 6,000BP to c. 4000 BP, with modern conditions returning some 2,000 years ago, but with climate remaining rather variable (with significant dry phases) even since then (e.g. Tardy 1999). This makes sense of the domination of northern South American forests by rapidly colonising species, in a process of 'scarification' since the last dry phase (Tardy 1999: 270; Ramcharan 1980). Thus Beard's idea of a gradual, steady colonisation of Mora over the 30,000 to 50,000 year time-scale begins to look problematic.

Furthermore, research on Amerindian population history and land use suggests the possibility that this had a significant impact on the evolution of vegetation. Beard appreciated that Amerindians used Mora for food (as in contemporary Guyana) and might have been responsible for distributing Mora within Trinidad in small patches (Beard 1946b: 189) but minimised any wider impact, and excluded any more radical suggestion that they might have introduced it and favoured its development. Equally, he minimised the impact of Amerindian agriculture on the grounds of lack of evidence, and the low, largely coastal populations: 'The discovery of kitchen middens along the coast has led to the supposition of widespread shifting cultivation by aboriginals in pre-Columbian times, but there is no actual evidence' (Beard 1946a). Yet historical studies suggest larger populations and far-reaching farming and trade. They suggest that people were shifting cultivators of bitter cassava, sweet potatoes, cotton and a great variety of other crops, in an economy locked into wide reaching water-borne trade networks which stimulated settlement of major river valleys, as well as the coast (Boomert pers.com).

Taken alongside climate history studies, these works might lead to an interpretation of Trinidad's forest vegetation as a scar tissue, two or three generations of trees old, following sixteenth-century Amerindian depopulation. This built on a pre-columbian vegetation history of a complex of anthropogenic management and vegetation response to climate rehumidification from c. 2,000 years ago. From such a perspective, the reasons for particular forest formations appearing in particular locations may relate more to 'path dependent history' than any natural tendency towards equilibrium. The formations found today may not be as long-lived and stable as assumed, and – more importantly – may respond very unpredictably to major disturbance. Quite plausibly, the apparent difficulty for Mora to regenerate following fire could be interpreted as a manifestation of this.

Notably, though, the archaeological studies which would be required to verify population estimates and anecdotal evidence of dense inland settlements have not been carried out (Newson 1976: cf. Boomert 1984: 144–45); nor have vegetation histories and paleoecological studies which would provide actual data on pre-columbian vegetation. The absence of focused study of long-term vegetation patterns in Trinidad, and the related absence (or minimisation) of non-equilibrial perspectives on ecology, in turn relates – at least in part – to the powerful co-production of science, policy and management around views of stability.

In the meantime, ad hoc management changes to cope with unpredictability have been among the factors provoking tension between woodworkers and the Forestry Division.

Socio-political dynamics in the PBS: relations between woodworkers and the Forestry Division

Woodworkers argue that they have borne the brunt of changes in PBS management in response to ecological dynamics – geared ever more towards restoration and improvement following the fires. They complain that the Forestry Division has not kept to its stated policy of opening up two blocks per year. Since around 1996, they have tended to open one instead, or to allow access only to fire-burned blocks in a given year. When two blocks a year were opened, 'one could have a decent livelihood, work six licences a year and eat chicken twice a week like everyone else'.[32] This is no longer the case. Moreover, long delays of up to twelve years have occurred between the burning (in 1987) and the opening of fire-burned blocks. As a result much of the timber is rotten, with larger trunk-hollows. So 'If you buy 100 cubic metres of timber in a salvage block, you might sell only 40–50 cubic metres'.[33] The President of the Association wrote to the Director of Forestry to complain about the reduced number of blocks, and claims to have received a reply that the Division could do nothing over and above the policy that the Minister had made. He interprets this as 'political interference'.

FRIM officers are well aware of these critiques.[34] They acknowledge that more, 'virgin' blocks could be brought into the system, but argue that the licensees cannot be satisfied; to give them a little more would be the thin end of a wedge of expanding, insatiable demand. The officers thus tend to dismiss the woodworkers' perennial claims about insufficient timber: they might complain about fire burned blocks, but they still harvest them . . . They might complain that each license fails to give enough timber, but this is because they think in numbers of trees, not cubic metres . . . Forest officers also run a 'tragedy of the commons' argument, saying that woodworkers want to maximise individual gain, whereas the foresters' duty is to regulate the system and keep everyone's allocation low enough for all to get a share. In many respects, this tension is a microcosm of the broader situation in Trinidad. Nationally, forest officers claim, the demand for timber cannot ever be met: 'Trinidad has imported more than 50% of its timber since the 1940s, and 90% since the 1980s'.[35] In effect, given a perception of insatiable demand, forest officers feel that it would be inappropriate to attempt to close the gap between demand and supply. This in turn allows them to operate on the precautionary principle in forest management and conservation, taking a highly cautious approach to the release of new blocks and keeping large areas of Mora forest unexploited.

Unpredictable ecological events also affect the course of the forester's work, and in interaction with the exigencies of labour and resource availability this places further demands on woodworkers. Demands to perform unexpected timely operations such as surveying fire-burned areas, and substituting for absent labourers, interrupts the normal flow of forestry work. Foresters' performance varies with the weather, and the equally fickle availability of workmen and surveyors. In this context, forest officers see the current Forestry Division system of performance-related salaries and promotions linked to a pre-agreed work programme as invidious. It fails to acknowledge the day-to-day and year-to-year flexibility required to respond to ecological and social contingencies, and the initiative foresters must frequently take to cope with unpredictable field conditions.[36] Foresters' responses frequently create extra delays, and place extra calls on the labour of woodworkers who must assist forest officers in their own work.

At the same time, there is a sense of common purpose between local representatives of the Forestry Division and the woodworkers, a relationship concretised in the organisation of the PBS. This is partly because local forestry staff, too, feel vulnerable to many of the political-economic processes of which woodworkers complain. As one forest officer explained, the government originally aimed to provide employment for rural people, and woodworkers are justified in their claims that sawmillers are now taking their rights.[37] This officer is due to speak for the Forestry Division in the court case brought by licensees against the Division's priority allocation of felling rights to sawmillers. He finds himself highly sympathetic to the woodworkers' plight. Furthermore, large sawmillers are now pushing to be granted forestry concessions of around 400ha. Local forest officers are concerned about the sustainability of timber production under such conditions, given the profit orientation of big business. In this way they see support to the woodworkers and their unionisation as important for maintaining the integrity of the forest and PBS.

Forestry field staff, moreover, frequently feel threatened by large operators. As one put it 'a small forest officer may take them to court, but because of their [political] connections, you find yourself in difficulty and you get a transfer'.[38] Policing the activities of well-connected large sawmillers only magnifies the more general difficulties foresters now face in policing timber theft. Following a recent ministerial ruling, officers are required to take all forest offences to court rather than settling them directly (by 'compounding' – which foresters of rank 3 and above were once entitled to do). 'But unfortunately they find that if they do not have all the evidence and know all the rules, the prosecution case will fail. Moreover, magistrates do not value the environment, consider forests to be wasteland and might impose a trivial 50 dollar fine and a reprimand'.[39]

Conservancy forest officers are thus vulnerable to – powerless in relation to – processes operating at higher levels and in Port of Spain. In some respects it is better for them to work with those less powerful than they, such as licensees. Woodworkers, to a certain extent, acknowledge these conditions, seeing local forest officers as conduits for orders and 'political interference' from above. Indeed their major calls for change are to higher-level policy makers. Oil companies are a further type of 'big boy' with high-level political connections. Neither woodworkers nor local forest officers like their impact on the forest, their profit orientation and their overriding influence on Port of Spain politicians, and are allied in both this dislike and a sense of incapacity to alter the situation.

Yet other remarks and instances suggest persistent tensions between woodworkers and forest officers. Foresters are suspicious that woodworkers were behind the 1987 fires, for example. Woodworkers question the motives of foresters:

for example the Forestry Division had planned to open a block near the Trinity Hills Wildlife Sanctuary, and went as far as silviculturally marking the trees. The Director of Forestry forbade the extraction, erring on the side of wildlife conservation. Woodworkers reinterpret this, claiming that the Forestry Division wanted to give sawmillers half and woodworkers half of this block and that when the woodworkers successfully objected to this allocation, the national Forestry Division withdrew the block to 'get back at them'.

This instance, and others like it, illustrate a general perception that the Forestry Division uses arguments about conservation and sustainability as a 'greenwash' to hide their real political-economic interests; interests which both local and national forest officials are seen to have in developing good relationships with large sawmill operators, and from which they benefit economically or politically. For example, the slow opening of blocks, justified on the grounds of fire damage and sustainability, is seen by woodworkers as an excuse for foresters who want to 'weed the licensees out of the system' and build up their relationships with the 'big boys'.[40] Thus woodworkers critique aspects of PBS science and its local praxis on the grounds that it is politically motivated.

The sense of woodworkers being squeezed out is easily understood given that a decade ago there were ten Woodworkers' Associations in the country, but now there are only one or two in the south-east; and whereas the Nariva-Mayaro Woodworkers' Association now has only seventy-two members, it once had 600. 'The forest used to provide bread in this region, but now this is only for a few'.[41] Woodworkers who cannot make a livelihood from timber are forced to turn to other occupations: to temporary construction work, hunting or squatting – frequently having no choice but to turn to 'illegal' activities.

In the Woodworkers' Association–Forestry Division relationship, then, some degree of alliance coexists with considerable and mutual lack of trust: a lack of trust in an expert institution, balanced by a reciprocal lack of trust in a civil institution. To a certain extent, each side blames problems in the operation of the PBS on the other side's supposed links with politicians, and sees its claims about inappropriate PBS scientific practice as masks for 'unreasonable', individualistic profit-seeking behaviour. Such citizen's mistrust in state institutions can be contextualised more broadly in Trinidad's colonial history and subsequent ethnically-divided politics. Moreover, while there may be real mistrust rooted in material experiences, styles of Trinidadian discourse which emphasise the 'bacchanal' and personalised scandal also tend to amplify images of mistrust.

While at one level, then, the PBS can appear as a 'blueprint' system of science and management – the image given in the Forestry Handbook, and the image around which the Forestry Division has partially constructed its own image of scientific professionalism in forestry – it is at the same time a field of social and political struggle. In this, actual management practices (which trees are marked, when and how; which blocks are opened, when and how) may be responses to the more day-to-day dilemmas forest officers face in dealing with woodworkers, sawmillers and politicians, as well as with the exigencies of ecology. The 'system' as it emerges on the ground is partially an unintended product of these socio-political practices. It is a product balancing social and technical objectives in the use of state reserve land, from producing subsidised wood for woodworkers or sawmillers, and providing surveillance in the forest, to altering its ecological structure and diversity. At the same time the PBS (and particularly, its image as a structured and stable system) is instrumental in maintaining the existence (and justification for) these state reserves themselves, and in maintaining the scientifically-professional image of the Trinidad Forestry Division.

The PBS and timber plantations

The PBS exists among several other modes of forest management in Trinidad. One of the most commercially significant, yet controversial, has been the practice of clear-felling 'degraded' forest, removing all saleable timber, and re-planting with teak, Caribbean pine or mixed hardwoods. Teak was introduced in 1913, some plantations were installed in the 1920s and many more were established in a major wave of teak and pine planting in the 1950s. The Forestry Division is now promoting the establishment of Colombian cedar, which appears to be highly productive in plantations (as was at first the case with teak and pine).

Plantation forestry began in a period when the colonial forest service was re-orienting its aims from forest conservation to production. Plantations epitomised this new focus. Arguably, it fitted into and helped shape a developing professional forestry culture oriented around silviculture and production, which could be studied and promoted in the relatively controlled, uniform environment of the plantation. That plantations and silvicultural experiments within them carried high status in international scientific forestry circles encompassing Europe and Asia, where Trinidadian foresters studied for degrees, contributed to this colonial orientation. By the 1950s further economic concerns influenced policy: notably the need to substitute for high levels of import of construction pine lumber from Honduras and the southern United States.[42] From its establishment until the 1980s, the forest officers' training programme in the Eastern Caribbean Institute of Agriculture and Forestry focused strongly on plantation silviculture.[43] A generation of foresters emerged with skills in plantation forestry, which defined their Division's culture as much as their everyday practices.

At first sight plantation forestry and natural forest management in the PBS appear to work from quite different premises. Yet there are strong similarities in the ways scientific forestry attempts to control 'nature'. In effect, the PBS shapes natural forest to become (more) like a plantation. It is perhaps no accident that the system developed in Mora forest whose homogeneous, mono-specific characteristics already resonated with the monoculture of the plantation, and could be further simplified by encouraging evenness of growth, uniform quality of bole, etc. The particular natural forest ecology of Mora, then, is particularly amenable to the 'scientific culture' of plantations. The similarity between Mora PBS and plantation forestry can also be painted in a different light. Through the mono-specific ecology of Mora, the plantation culture of the Forestry Division finds an easier transition into natural forest management, and a bridge into more complex natural forest management issues, for example in the desire to introduce PBS into more diverse Crappo forest.

At the same time as creating order in the forest, the PBS and plantation forestry 'systems' have also been managing foresters, producing the 'Trini' forester as a particular type of manager and controller of disorder, with specialised technical knowledge and work routines to suit. But just as in the PBS this image of order lies at odds with forester's day-to-day adaptations to unpredictable circumstance, so it is true of plantations. In the 1980s, analysts were still optimistic about the potential of plantations to dominate timber supply:

There is no doubt that within the next 10–15 years, teak will be making a major contribution to meeting local timber requirements, and to the local construction and furniture industries. The implications of the availability of a large volume of highly valuable teak timber will be even greater with the modernization and expansion of the sawmilling complex . . . The forecast is an extraordinary . . increase in the output of sawn timber, to 4.3 million board feet in 1977 and to 7.0 million board feet in 1985 (Chalmers 1981).

Yet the Forestry Division's experiences with teak and pine have failed to live up to technical expectations. First, the plantations succumb regularly to devastating fires and subsequent soil erosion – so frequently as to give rise to a public perception that teak actually needs fire for successful growth, and that foresters set these fires as part of plantation management strategy.[44]

Second, the Forestry Division faces dilemmas at the end of the plantation growth cycle, in how to treat plantation lands after felling. The teak and pine plantations established in the 1950s and 1960s were intended to mature in about forty years' time, so this issue is now becoming pressing. The plantations are clear-felled at harvest, but due to the effects of annual fires nothing will regenerate in teak plantations except teak from coppices. Second-rotation teak has thus become an important land-use possibility and a correspondingly important area of research practice. In a revitalised research effort within FRIM, where staff and funding constraints had otherwise sidelined formal studies during the last twenty years,[45] a senior FRIM officer has been experimenting with growth rates on differently-managed plots.

Third, there are heated debates about access rights to the timber from planta-tions. From 1977, plantation timber of teak and pine was sold to Tanteak, a state enterprise with monopoly status (Symes 1991). Nevertheless, woodworkers could buy teak licences from Tanteak. However since 1996/97 and in response to repeated accusations of Tanteak's inefficiency, plantation timber sales have been liberalised. Despite stipulations in the Forestry Handbook (p.48 paragraph 8), teak is not sold to the public or licensees, but only to sawmillers and manu-facturers, with woodworkers getting only occasional remnants. Woodworkers argue strongly that they should have access, perhaps by grouping together to harvest larger areas: 'It is simple. The teak should be optionable to the working classes, to those who have been depending on wood all these years'.[46] The As-sociation's President who applied for, and was refused, access from the Director of Forestry, now argues the need to 'go political' over the teak issue: 'to start to work by saying vote for him, not him. It has come to that'.[47]

Fourth, monoculture plantations are strongly critiqued by groups who give priority to biodiversity and wildlife conservation. For example, the South-East Hunters' Association sees them as 'creating animal deserts in the interests of commercialisation'.[48] Indeed the Association originated in 1994 to lobby gov-ernment and educate the public on the problems of monoculture plantations, and considers that it influenced the Forestry Division's abandonment of monocul-tural teak planting. The Hunter's Association now criticises the government's turn to cedar for similar reasons, and because the shallow roots leave it vulner-able to hurricane damage. It advocates that if plantation forestry must continue, plantations should at least be mixed, accommodating a greater diversity of trees, plants and animals.

Conclusions

Science and policy as co-produced within the development of the PBS have drawn on and reproduced framings of stability, in social and ecological sys-tems. The premise of stability is important to the institutions involved in forest policy in a number of ways. First, it iconises a form of scientific professional-ism in forestry which has long been central to the Trinidad Forestry Division's image and claims to institutional authority, and is increasingly so as multiply-ing conservation-focused institutions compete – as we saw in Chapter 5 – for national and international funds and attention. Second, the system is a means to justify the continued use of state forest reserves for timber production, against critical NGOs and others who would prefer them devoted to biodiversity pro-tection. Third, the relationship with artisanal loggers can be cast as a form of 'community forestry' – useful to the department's image with NGOs and international donors – without implying loss of state resource control, and si-multaneously preventing timber sales to large concessionaries.

Sustaining this image has depended on several processes less openly acknowledged by national foresters. The dependence of the artisanal community means they absorb much of the work resulting from unforeseen 'externalities' of the system. The system has also received – and may owe its economic viability to – heavy state subsidisation from the oil and gas-rich revenue base. That forestry has not had to be financially autonomous has enabled its science and practice to continue in particular ways, such as intensive PBS management over a relatively small area, and has allowed Trinidad to maintain a culture of scientific and sustainable forestry as opposed to economic forestry.

In contrast, both foresters working at field-level, and artisanal loggers, acknowledge the ecological and social unpredictabilities of the system. They make flexible adaptations to felling practices and agreements that continually subvert the system's 'rules', yet are necessary for it to work. These practices of adaptive management remain unformalised and unacknowledged within the larger forestry bureaucracy, as the latter's required image of scientific professionalism intersects with its strongly hierarchical authority structures which tend to discourage initiative-taking by local staff. The co-production of science and management around notions of stability, and the importance of this to powerful national institutions, serve to exclude non-equilibrial alternatives from being seriously countenanced.

Playing into the co-evolution of science and policy in the PBS is the curious nature of Mora forest itself. The Forestry Division has developed a strong tradition of plantation forestry and associated forest and silvicultural science. Mora forest presents a pre-existing natural monoculture of a valuable tree – a 'plantation' that does not need to be planted – onto which the traditions of plantation science are easily grafted. Practices in the PBS can thus sustain the image of 'scientific forestry' long important both to the identity of Trinidad's Forestry Division, and in internationalised forestry debates.

New pressures on the forest management system may further threaten its sustainability. First, squeezing out the woodworkers may break down the sustainability of the system. International consultants have proposed that an increase in profitability and efficiency would be possible if there was a rationalisation of sawmills to five or so, enabling improved capacity for state regulation of sawmillers. They recommend proceeding with this regardless of the implications for livelihoods – for example of woodworkers who may be undermined. But if it is the case that the woodworkers are self-exploiting at present; have borne the brunt of improvement and have been co-operative with the PBS, there must be serious doubts as to whether their exclusion would help sustainable practice. Larger, more powerful millers may easily be able to apply political pressure to gain concessions – as they have been attempting – and may not be prepared to bear the costs of improvements. This might lead to increased profitability at the cost of loss of such sustainability as there is. Moreover, in as much as woodworkers have contributed to the present quality of PBS forest through their own work, there must surely be a serious ethical question that they should be its beneficiaries.

Lastly, there is pressure in Trinidad from environmental lobbies to stop logging all state forested land due to the impact that it has had on national forests. Their argument is to shift all timber production to plantations and private land. In response, foresters have drawn on the PBS to suggest that natural forest management can balance timber and other (conservation) objectives on state land. Indeed the PBS serves as an icon of scientific professionalism (and indeed of participation, in co-evolution with woodworkers), in an otherwise vulnerable Forestry Division, saddled with an embarrassing history of poorly performing plantation forestry and a less than participatory ethos. In this, practices of 'scientific forestry' are supporting arguments for the Forestry Division as steward, which play into contemporary inter-ministerial struggles over authority and resources.

Notes

1. See also World Bank 1991. That Trinidad has not pursued 'certification' of sustainably produced timber can be attributed to the market for its wood: this is local, where the demand for certified timber is as yet irrelevant.
2. In Victoria Mayaro there are 54,000 acres of Mora in 128,285 acres, and in Matura, 14,000 acres of Mora in 31,734 acres of reserve; Chalmers 1981: 85.
3. Mora, however, was not included among the regulated species, as at that time it was 'barely used at all' (Marshall 1925: 12).
4. Interview, senior forester, Victoria Mayaro reserve, 30 June 1999. As Clubbe and Jhilmit (1992) suggest, low girth limits may also have been necessary early in the century when trees were removed by oxen, but rapidly became unnecessary as tractors came into play; extraction could then have capitalised on the rapid growth increments of larger trees, and afford to leave the smaller girth trees.
5. Most SFM employ polycyclic felling; the term polycyclic refers to the fact that only larger trees are cut during the initial harvest so that smaller trees may provide another crop in 25–40 years.
6. This was introduced into the Mora forest areas in the north-east of the country (Melajo) in 1948 and in the south-east, into Valencia reserves in 1954 (Synnott 1989: 93).
7. Interview, FRIM forest officer, Rio Claro, 28 June 1999.
8. Ibid.
9. Interview, FRIM forest officer, Rio Claro, 28 June 1999.
10. Group discussion with FRIM staff and local forest officers, Victoria Mayaro Reserve, 30 June 1999.
11. Mora has a particular tendency to develop a hollow trunk in certain conditions and at certain stages, frequently limiting the proportion of sound trees to 50–60 per cent.
12. If more than ten Mora per hectare are felled, a new environment is created; ibid.
13. Interview, FRIM forest officer, Rio Claro, 28 June 1999.

14. Ibid.
15. Ibid.
16. Interview, university-based forest ecologist, St Augustine, 4 May 1999.
17. Group discussion with FRIM staff and local forest officers, Victoria Mayaro Reserve, 30 June 1999.
18. Ibid.
19. Interview, senior forester, Victoria Mayaro reserve, 30 June 1999.
20. Interview, Forester I, Rio Claro, 29 June 1999.
21. Interview, President of Woodworker's Association, Rio Claro, 29 June 1999.
22. Ibid.
23. Woodworkers purchase standing Mora at 90 cents + VAT/cubic foot, but sell it for 12–13 dollars per cubic foot as logs at the roadside. Cedar they purchase from the state at 1 dollar 10 cents, whereas for private purchases, they would have to pay 20–40 dollars/cubic foot.
24. Ibid.
25. Interview, member of Woodworkers' Association, Rio Claro, 5 July 1999.
26. Ibid.
27. Group discussion, Woodworkers' Association, Rio Claro, 5 July 1999.
28. Ibid.
29. Ibid.
30. Interview, FRIM forest officer, Rio Claro, 28 June 1999.
31. The Forestry Division even suspected that the woodworkers had burnt the forest deliberately in order to gain access to it, and FRIM's delayed opening of the block until 1991 was in part a strategic response to this. Group discussion with FRIM staff and local forest officers, Victoria Mayaro Reserve, 30 June 1999.
32. Interview, President, Woodworkers' Association, Rio Claro, 29 June 1999.
33. Ibid.
34. Group discussion with FRIM staff and local forest officers, Victoria Mayaro Reserve, 30 June 1999.
35. Interview, FRIM officer, Rio Claro, 30 June 1999.
36. Group discussion with FRIM staff and local forest officers, Victoria Mayaro Reserve, 30 June 1999.
37. Interview, Forester I, Rio Claro, 29 June 1999.
38. Interview, FRIM officer, Rio Claro, 30 June 1999.
39. Ibid.
40. Interview, President of Woodworkers' Association, Rio Claro, 5 July 1999.
41. Ibid.
42. Eden Shand, 'Forestry Division must engage in conservation', *Daily Express* 23 June 1999.
43. Interview, Head of FRIM, Port of Spain, 17 June 1999; Bertault 1999.
44. Some observers claim that these problems stem from the Forestry Division's failure to perform technical management operations such as thinning and pruning to the required standard.
45. Interview, Head of FRIM, Port of Spain, 17 June 1999.
46. Interview, member of Woodworkers' Association, Rio Claro, 5 July 1999.
47. Ibid.
48. Interview, President of South-East Hunters' Association, 30 June 1999.

8   Science and policy in society: mass media and education

Introduction

This chapter moves out of the realm of science, policy and politics to consider how scientific messages about forests and environment play in wider society. We are interested not only in the 'dissemination' of messages to wider publics, but also in the broader ways that mass media and education are interlocked with scientific and policy institutions. Media and education can serve to stabilise scientific and policy perspectives in an unquestioned sense, by embedding them in wider society. Yet as we show, they can also provide vehicles for contestation and critique. They can expose fractures and disagreements between policy-makers, scientists, sections of government and their diverse international sponsors, and provide fora through which publics express dissent from dominant perspectives, and instigate alternatives. Media are thus important to – in fact, part of – the constitution of scientific and policy coalitions and networks. When, how and for whom these different possibilities become apparent needs to be considered empirically, and this chapter does this. It cannot be definitive or comprehensive in its coverage of the wide range of print, audio, visual and online sources that constitute contemporary media. Even for a work focused entirely on media, this would be an impossible task.

For Guinea and then for Trinidad, we explore the history of media and education in their particular settings, and how institutions concerned with environment have come to articulate with these media and education traditions. We are interested in understanding how messages within media acquire stability in relation to educational messages and available readings of the world around. The idea of intertextuality captures this, referring to the way in which different media interact to create and sustain certain images of the world. Intertextuality refers to the continual referencing of other texts in media products, whether horizontally (when images appear in different media and create meaning across them) or vertically (when one text promotes another) (Fiske 1987). Intertextuality has been cast as a postmodern phenomenon, where media images 'relate to and across each other' in a way that Baudrillard refers to as 'implosion', suggesting that postmodern images look in on themselves and similar texts

(Taylor and Willis 1999: 82). We suggest that a similar kind of intertextuality has long operated between media, education and the practices of science and policy, via policy documents, certain research perspectives, meetings and so on. Extending the idea of intertextuality beyond a focus on language alone shows how it can also expand into everyday practices where people engage actively with 'the environment' and advertising about it – whether in buying and eating 'rainforest yoghurts' from a supermarket, taking part in a sponsored run in aid of turtle conservation, or passing a sign for an NGO tree nursery project on a savanna road. The message is linked to experiential phenomena, as the advertised message is combined with the choosing, eating or running. In a similar way educational messages are linked with the experience of being in a particular educational context or environmental festival. As we use it, the concept of intertextuality highlights ways in which diverse thought and sensual practices can become linked in the promotion and absorption of a particular set of environmental messages. It helps one comprehend how the values linked to such messages are put into play, infusing subjectivities and desires.

As work in media studies makes clear, questions of 'message' need to be considered in relation to media production and its political economy, including the identity and agendas of institutions owning, controlling and funding different newspapers, radio programmes or pamphlets; questions of journalistic identity and orientation, and issues of editorial control. Many earlier models of media emphasised the control of media apparatuses in the interests of extending hegemonic power. From this perspective, mass media in developing countries have frequently been seen as promoting the agendas of first colonial, and then post-colonial states and as reinforcing culturally-imperialist 'northern' agendas in the context of international relations and development (Reeves 1993). Debate in the 1970s and 1980s thus called for the establishment of a 'new international information order' which would reverse what was seen as an overwhelming imbalance of information flow from northern industrialised countries to the south, and distorted images of the crisis, poverty and environmental degradation in the latter (Reeves 1993: 102). The international information economy, it is argued, links up with the increasing internationalisation of governance, making 'national boundaries largely irrelevant, with nation-states generally unable to control information movements and the types of information being disseminated effectively' (Reeves 1993: 105). Several factors complicate the picture. These include more rapid information flows in all directions via the Internet (e.g. Miller and Slater 2000); intense struggles within countries over the control and content of different media which inflect their relations with international processes, and increasing debate about folk and alternative media which develop and operate outside the major media apparatuses. Furthermore, as we show here, NGO, government and donor agencies are now producing media and educational materials in ways that are integrated with research and policy actions, through their agendas, personnel and funding. This more complicated scene requires a more disaggregated, practice-based analysis that can resolve how different practices in science, policy, media and education play out in particular institutional networks and relations. This draws attention to ways local and national media practices in the contemporary world overlay and articulate with older practices in media and popular culture, shaping their meanings. Such a perspective, and the lens of science, policy and knowledge problematics, in turn undercuts some of the established distinctions in media studies such as between nationally and internationally-owned media, and state and 'alternative' media.

As will become clear, media and educational materials establish particular images of environmental and forest issues, (re)producing moral images of environment and its management in which certain types of person are vilified as destructive, and others lauded. Aspects of genre and style, such as photogenic, picturesque or crisis stories, the use of simplified narratives, and of iconic characters – heroes and villains – amplify these images (Lowe and Morrison 1984, Chapman *et al.* 1997). Such aspects of style have been identified as features of media reportage in general. In as much as media and education are integral to policy processes, their 'skeletonisations' play into the use of simplified narratives and story lines in policy argumentation (cf. Hajer 1995), and into the social and moral stereotyping which is, as we have shown in earlier chapters, part of scientific and policy processes. Stereotypes are projected larger than life through the particular rhetorical styles of media and their inter-animation.

Mass media are also sites of struggle over representation (Spitulnik 1993: 296). As the third part of the chapter explores, those producing media imagine and project to particular audiences, but in ways which may be contested or subverted at a variety of levels: amongst editors, journalists, teachers, readers/listeners and so on. Exploring this tension between stability and dissent, and the nature of participation in each, helps to discern the relations of power of which scientific and policy processes are a part.

In some respects Guinea and Trinidad echo Chapman *et al.*'s (1997) distinction between India and the UK; the former where the greatest proportion of the population are involved in direct productive/livelihood relationships with the environment; the latter where it is more distant and 'environment' comes to exist as an objectifiable category. Thus, for example, in Trinidad much environmental media and education speak to an urban-based population, not directly dependent on forests for material well-being. The educational emphasis is on creating an 'environmentally literate' citizenry (e.g. Ariasingam 1999), among urban populations who engage with rural environments not through everyday experience but as 'read' from a distance and dipped into as visitors. 'Environmental literacy' suggests creating the ability to write/comprehend according to a particular field of intertextual meaning. In contrast, the emphasis in Guinea is more on reforming the perpetrators of environmental problems. Educational materials are targeted at people and children who are assumed to be interacting with/gaining livelihoods from environment, and as we shall see, much environmental media is co-ordinated with this. This key word is less 'literacy' than the 'sensibilisation' of those already involved, to encourage users to become conscious of the destructive effects of their actions, and to amend them.

Guinea

The production of environmental media and education

In Guinea the production of media and education have long been closely interlinked with science and policy institutions. The newspapers that the colonial state produced derived from, and addressed, the interests of the colonial administration. That the French language dominated, added to social distance. Opposition was found in media outside this arena of state control: whether in the informal oral 'radio trottoir', the roving story tellers and theatre groups which have a long tradition in the region, or in the more formalised oral media culture of Griots, islamic clerics and initiation societies.

The region also has a long-established tradition of literacy, whether in Arabic, linked to koranic education, or in local scripts such as N'ko which was developed in the 1940s expressly for communicating in Guinean languages, as an alternative to French.

The pan Africanist, state socialist regime which won power at independence had its roots in these oppositional cultures. It attempted to harness them in its project of Africanisation on one hand, and modernisation/demystification on the other (Rivière 1969, 1971). The regime took over the national press, and produced, under the authorship of the President, a huge quantity of pamphlets which promoted the cultural and political values of the regime. Yet this was only a part of state media control which extended also into 'traditional' media, education and aspects of popular culture, enabling a more orchestrated field of intertextuality. The language of education and popular discourse was forcibly Africanised.[1] The state favoured Islam and was able to work through it. Roving theatre became a key tool of political 'animation', and youth theatre groups were formed, trained and ideologically aligned to spread the message of 'La Révolution'.

The regime was, by the late 1970s understood by many as a reign of terror, with dissent ruthlessly suppressed. Experience of terror was in part rooted in lack of media space for opposition; even 'radio trottoir' was penetrated by agents of the state, or at least by fears that friends and neighbours might be informers. Demystification – in conjunction with Islam – formally abolished and criminalised initiation societies. Disengaging or dissenting from this intertextual field thus became a very private, not social affair.

Science was central to key agendas of both Africanisation and demystification. There were direct links between political and scientific agendas. Africanised medicine (and veterinary medicine), as we have seen (Chapter 4) harnessed and 'scientised' aspects of indigenous knowledge alongside chemical analysis of plant properties. Around agriculture and environment Africanisation was less evident, as agriculture focused on modernisation through technology (tractorisation), and environmental analysis highlighted the environmentally destructive nature of traditional practices, to be reformed (Fairhead and Leach 1996, 2000).

Following the death of Sekou Touré in 1984, increasing engagement with international donor organisations coincided with prominent international environmental concern, and translated into a range of environmental programmes. It also coincided with the development of new broadcasting and publishing technologies that were appealing to government and donor interests in 'reaching the masses'. Rural radio broadcasting was established and audiences escalated as radios themselves became more affordable. An efflorescence of newspapers emerged alongside state media. Many of these have a critical edge.

Funding for the communication of environmental messages has been central to the development and shaping of new media. For instance, it is the regional EU funded environmental communication programme, Programme Regional d'Assistance Technique à la Communication et à l'Information sur la Protection de l'Environnement (PACIPE)[2] which funds the newspaper *Somaya Silan* which popularises the African N'Ko alphabet. The same programme supports journalists and broadcasting of Rural Radio, and funds and makes environmental programmes to be broadcast alongside government programmes on culture, news and information. It supports journalists to write on environmental issues in national newspapers. A different EU programme instigated rural radio in Kundara prefecture, in order to promote environmental education around the Niokolo-Badiar National Park.[3] Although radio and newspapers address a much broader range of issues, environmental issues loom large. Although not exclusive, the environmental field has been pivotal in the shaping of mass media in form as well as content.

These activities in the development of media in Guinea operate within a strong international context. PACIPE in Guinea, for example, forms part of an EU-funded regional programme linking six countries of the West African forest zone. Equally, the activities of UN agencies, donors and international NGOs are co-ordinated within international and regional programmes, and shape the evolution of national and local activities in interaction with international and regional best practice. On the one hand, this leads to a certain international alignment in the development of their media and educational practices; on the other, it places activities in Guinean localities as experimental or 'pilot', participating in a regional field of emerging best practice.

The way the environmental education project PACIPE engages with rural radio illustrates linkages between policy, education and the broadcast media. PACIPE funds the making and broadcasting of environmental programmes. According to the project, the programmes 'are done by villagers', hence fall into the genre of 'public participation' media – yet the nature of such participation requires qualification. When the project became involved in Rural Radio, there were a few, poorly paid and equipped journalists. 'We recruited a peasant journalist in each Prefecture, giving them a seminar and some back up'.[4] Yet the 'peasant' journalists who were hired were not 'peasants'. They were well-educated, having either been school teachers or ex-development workers. They were people who can speak the language of state education and development projects when it comes to environmental concern. In developing each environment programme, it is the project which chooses the themes, and pays for it to be made and broadcast. 'We give the broad theme, and they elaborate it as they feel fit'.[5] The themes are linked to seasonally relevant issues, and their diffusion is co-ordinated with project campaigns, for example in fire management. In this, their messages (and the stability of intertextual meanings) are co-ordinated with the 'sensibilisation' activities of ministries.

Environmental projects have also sought to work through more 'traditional' media, and in this they build on the political propaganda practices of the earlier regime, for instance in working through Imams and the Friday prayers to 'green' Islam, and with theatre groups, praise singers and hunters. 'Traditional' events and gatherings such as major fishing festivals may be harnessed to communicate modern environmental messages. PACIPE staff seek to incorporate their messages into the events, for instance by asking griots to compose and perform songs which link Mande mythology such as the 'bush law' (*wa ton*) of the Mande hero, Sundiata Keita, and of elders with modern environmental messages. At the same time, environmental programmes on 'modern' media such as radio are interlaced with 'traditional' resonances, whether Guinean music, or the replication of Mande hierarchies of interview order and the customary phrase '*namu*' (That's right, good) within journalists' interviews.

When linking with 'traditional media', modern institutions are linking with media whose practices have been shaped in form and meanings first through opposition to colonial state practices, and then in their incorporation into a state socialist regime. Donors working with essentialist concepts of 'tradition' fail to recognise this. Thus for example in funding roving theatre groups to convey environmental messages, the international cachet of alternative media current in development rhetoric is actually drawn into a field where audiences associate theatre with the political animation of the Sekou Touré period, and their defensive attitudes towards it. Such an association is compounded as many of today's actors and directors also played in earlier political animation. This in turn shapes (although need not determine) interpretative possibilities.

The use of travelling video shows in adult education or environmental project consciousness-raising can also be understood in part within these antecedents. The Niger River protection programme uses video footage of its own project activities in the region to diffuse its environmental protection messages. UN and US-based NGOs funded the production of an adult education video on the causes and consequences of deforestation with similar aims.[6]

These combinations of media forms and their meanings are thus shaped by their particular histories of practice. Such histories in turn shape, but do not determine, interpretative possibilities. They can be modern for youth and traditional for elders, politically loaded for some and liberating for others, depending on which elements are emphasised.

Several of the organisations that have been active in developing environmental education for adults and that have assisted in inserting environmental issues into mass media have also been promoting environmental education within schools. As with adult education and media, involvement has not only been influential in shaping curriculum content, but also innovation in pedagogical practices and the building of educational infrastructure. Indeed many of the primary schools in the region have been built by internationally-funded environment programmes.

From December 1989, UN organisations supported a series of workshops to elaborate a national strategy for developing environmental education in Guinea (UNESCO/UNEP 1989). These built on a pilot project which had commissioned a group of Guinean university researchers, government foresters, educationalists and others to set out Guinea's environmental problems, the necessity for environmental education, and the specific objectives, in an outline national strategy.[7] It contextualised formal education within a wider strategy for national environmental education aimed at all sections of the population, incorporating public campaigns and the mass media.

An experimental project to introduce environmental education into teacher training was launched, focusing on the National Teaching Institute (IPN 1990). By 1993 this developed into a programme (IPN 1993). It was argued that:

Environmental education is one of the most important innovations made in the improvement of Guinea's education system. The pertinence of this new approach for both schools and Guinean society needs no further elaboration. It imposes itself as a vital necessity in a country dangerously menaced by the many dreadful consequences of the deterioration of the ecological system: abusive deforestation, drying-up of water courses, degradation of soils, extinction of plant and animal species and pollution in its different forms . . . (IPN 1993: 1).

The strategy sought to infuse environmental messages into the teaching of sciences, geography and chemistry. The environmental components were also seen as a catalyst to introduce new teaching approaches, based less on the rote learning of the past than on field inquiries, class projects and self-discovery by pupils. The National Environmental Education Project produced primary school teaching materials supported by UNICEF and the EU funded PACIPE, including, for example, a bi-monthly cartoon strip with a chimpanzee character illustrating environmental messages.[8]

The weight given to environmental messages in primary schools is strongly reinforced through the efforts of several donor funded developments including, in Kissidougou, the EU funded Niger River Protection Project, and Plan Guinea (part of the US-based international NGO, Plan International). During the early 1990s, the EU project built schools as part of infrastructural improvements to assist their overall objectives in encouraging villagers to engage in their environmental protection and reforestation activities. The programme developed teaching materials and travelling teachers to support environmental education. As building schools could thus be justified as a direct contribution towards environmental protection, funding their construction has been retained into the second phase of the project, even though other types of infrastructure development have been cut back.[9] As we saw in Chapter 6, villagers have on occasion agreed to create Forestry Groups in the hope of having a school built.

Alongside its school building programme, Plan Guinea also supports an informal educational programme 'Child for Child' which is innovative in pedagogical practices in Guinea, encouraging older children to help teach younger children and their parents in moral and civic issues. Topic-focused 'brigades' create theatre pieces. In 1999 one of the three topics was 'child and environment' (forest environment, fauna, environment and health).

The institutional configuration in which environmental education and media are produced thus indicates a tight interlocking of media and education with each other, and with institutions producing and implementing environmental policies and projects.

Intertextuality in messages

Looking at what is said about forest change, fire and wildlife in different media illustrates an intertextuality of messages in operation – which can be understood in the context of this institutional interlocking in their production. Here, we exemplify how common narratives recur across media.

The National Strategy Workshop for developing environmental education stated in the main workshop report's opening paragraph:

In Guinea, over the last two decades or more, we observe the exhaustion of agricultural soils, the desiccation of watercourses, reduced rainfall, forest retreat, the flight of animal species, and so many other depressing sights which show that our natural environment, barely surpassed in diversity and richness on the African continent, is the victim of a degradation flabbergasting for the future of the country (UNESCO/UNEP 1989: 2).

The report proceeds to go through a list of Guinean agricultural practices, showing their degrading character. Deforestation is further caused by fuelwood collection and 'anarchic' timber exploitation. A section on bush fire accuses the hunter: 'with fire and all his weapons, he kills the fauna and all the flora' (1989: 6). And of cultivators: 'the farmer uses fire to clear his field; thus in satisfying his own interests he destroys the flora of an entire village, of an entire region, of an entire nation'.

These radically simplified narratives of deforestation, fire and blame for this are embodied in the class schedules in secondary-level teacher-training programmes relating to rural environment, illustrated in Table 8.1. The very act of simplification for teacher training and class planning sharpens the singularity of narrative – a narrative so strongly at odds with the more complex people/forest dynamics and frequent landscape enrichment directed, experienced and understood by villagers (e.g. Fairhead and Leach 1996, 1994).

Whereas these lessons are for science and geography classes, similar images are produced in primary level where environment is taught as part of Moral and Civic Education course in third and fourth year primary. The textbook for this has a chapter on 'the struggle against deforestation', with its central exercise reproduced in Table 8.2.

Geography in secondary school gives more detail on vegetation in Guinea. In the tenth year text, for example, it is said that:

South-East Guinea is said to be 'Forest' even though the dense forest there no longer occupies more than relatively small areas: it is maintained in inaccessible mountainous regions, and in protected forest reserves (Ziama and Mt. Nimba, for example). Previously very extensive, it has strongly retreated under the effects of clearance, extensive farming methods and repeated bush fire (INRAP/SERVEDIT 1997b: 189).

And that:

Forest Guinea is the last area where there remain some islands of dense forest, rich in tree species, lianas and epiphytes. Following clearance, 'foret claire' and anthropic savannas increasingly substitute for the original forest (INRAP/SERVEDIT 1997b: 190).

The issue of bush fire and its impact on vegetation and animal fauna is the central story for educational materials produced by the EU Niger River Protection Programme. A brightly illustrated cartoon hardback 'La Grande Découverte' (CENAFOD 1993) pits hunters against an Africanised, anthropomorphised

Table 8.1 *Lessons concerning rural environment in secondary school teacher training material (IPN 1993)*

Lesson: link point with national curriculum	Educational objectives	Content
Natural and agricultural sciences Chapter II: *Study of plants cultivated in the locality*	1. Explain the danger of bush fire in the impoverishment and degradation of soils.	Consequences of bush fire: – desertification – destruction of vegetation cover – erosion
Ecology 3rd year, Chapter I *Knowledge of the environment.* Theme: the food chain	Explain the consequences of overpopulation of consumers in a limited space.	Consequences of overpopulation on environment.
Theme: the ecosystem	1. Indicate on the basis of a survey what the landscape of your region was like 40, 50 and 60 years ago. 2. Determine the causes of the degradation of your region.	– forest, savanna, mountain – deforestation, bush fire, abusive exploitation of natural resources
Chapter II: *People and the environment.* Lesson 1: deforestation	1. Determine the principal causes of forest regression in your region. 2. Indicate the consequences of this deforestation in the life of your region. 3. Propose solutions to conserve the forest.	– abusive timber felling, bush fire, agricultural nomadism, illiteracy – desertification, erosion Re-wooding, improved cooking stoves, reglementation of forest resource use
Lesson 2: soil degradation	1. Identify the consequences of the action of man in the impoverishment of soils in your region in the life of the population. 2. Propose solutions to protect the soils of your region.	Reduced yields, disappearance of certain plant and animal species, malnutrition Re-wooding and improvement of agricultural and herding techniques
Geography 1st year: Chapter II *Geomorphology* Theme: erosion	Determine the bad effects on the soil of the destruction of vegetation cover.	Denudation of soil, mechanical and chemical erosion, laterisation, necessity of protecting trees.

Table 8.1 *(cont.)*

Lesson: link point with national curriculum	Educational objectives	Content
Lesson: Action of man	– Determine the diverse destructive actions of nature by man. – Be capable of participating in the protection and improvement of nature.	– Identification of causes of the destruction of the natural milieu (traditional agriculture, bush fire, poaching, fishing, herding, tree felling, disorganised gathering of medicinal plants) – Identification of different means of protecting the environment: re-wooding, terracing, improved animal husbandry
Chapter III: Climatology Lesson: climate and vegetation	Identify the bad influences of vegetation destruction on tropical nutrition.	Acquisition of notions: rainfall deficit, desertification, sahelisation, fragile ecosystem, ecosystem equilibrium.
Geography 2nd year Problem: deforestation and soil degradation.	Examine environmental problems in each of Guinea's four 'natural regions' e.g. Upper Guinea: characterise the agriculture and herding of Upper Guinea and propose solutions to remedy them	These activities are characterised by old techniques and rudimentary tools which favour the denudation of soil and their degradation.
	e.g. Forest Guinea: determine the advantages of the region due to its latitudinal position	Forest Guinea has a position advantaged by its sub-equatorial situation with a rainy season of 8–10 months. The soil humidity is conserved and agriculture is favoured even though cultivation techniques are archaic; it is a rice granary.

Table 8.2 *Lesson on deforestation in 'Moral and Civic Education'* *(INRAP/SERVEDIT 1997a: 92).*

[Picture of farmers setting field clearance fire]
I observe and I respond
1. Who are the people who set bush fire?
2. Why do they do it? The teacher explains that it is difficult to stop fire when the wind blows.
3. What are the dangers of bush fire?
I reflect
It is important to pay attention to trees to avoid the soil coming to resemble that of the deserts.
The trees protect the soil from the sun's rays and avoid a hard crust forming on the soil surface.
That is desertification.
I react
You want to make your parents understand that it is necessary to protect the forest
What will you say to them?
Choose among these responses
1. Thanks to bush fire, one has much bush meat.
2. Bush fire destroys the fire and advances the desert.
3. Bush fire leads to the massacre of wild animals.
4. Dewooding enlarges fields.
I retain
Bush fire and dewooding are the enemies of trees.
To plant a tree is to stop the desert from advancing.
The forest must be protected.

Bambi-antelope. Children save the baby but not the mother. All come round to see the error of hunting and fire setting (Figure 8.1).

The emphasis in the national curricula and among the projects is on using children as a conduit to teach their rural kin proper farming and hunting methods. This reproduces the idea that parents do not know how to look after their resources, should change their ways, and are certainly not in a position to teach their children.

These messages inter-animate with those conveyed in adult education. For example, the UNESCO supported video connected to the roving adult education programme noted above has a simple narrative structure. There are four phases:

1. The forest before people, shown in images of verdant, tall forest in the rainy season.
2. Forest destruction by people farming, setting fires and gathering fuelwood.
3. A desolate landscape iconised in a just-burnt field in the dry season.
4. What to do about it, shown by tree seedlings in plastic bags for new planting, and improved cooking stoves.

In watching the film, the maker explained, viewers are encouraged to reflect on each phase before moving on to the next.[10]

Figure 8.1 Extract from donor-funded storybook for environmental education

A similar narrative imagery is found in a second video, made by the EU Niger
River Protection Programme and doing the rounds of villages, which follows a
bus tour of villagers from Forest Guinea north to see the Sahel and Sahara. This
spatial transition is presented as a temporal inevitability, with the desiccation of
the land were farmers to continue their destructive practices. As we have argued
elsewhere (Fairhead and Leach 1996), these narratives themselves play into

ethnic discourses which stereotype southern dwelling Kissia as 'forest people' suffering the desolation wrought by savanna-loving Mande immigrants from the north; an ethno-ecological idiom introduced into contemporary political discourse in the early French colonial period (e.g. Adam 1948).

These educational messages of a verdant past endangered by current practices are echoed in rural radio broadcasts, at least in the perspective that the journalists themselves convey. For those who understand French the messages are supported by international broadcasts – principally Radio France International and the BBC World Service in French – which carry comparative and global stories surrounding deforestation and climate change. They echo the visual messages displayed on maps of original forest cover and subsequent decline (now widely diffused following the biodiversity priority-setting exercises of Conservation International and the WorldWide Fund for Nature), and echo project publicity signs – almost the only signs to punctuate the bush and village landscape along arterial roads.

The nexus of education, media and policy/project information and publicity is thus mutually supportive, with co-ordination in message linked to co-ordination in production. The essence of the message is of a rural population requiring reform, and of a knowing elite with the expertise to achieve this.

Trinidad

The production of environmental media and education

Mass media were originally introduced into Trinidad during the early colonial period both as administrative tools and social links for expatriates. Yet in reviewing the emergence of Trinidad's vibrant press, Skinner (1990) notes that already by the 1830s, the papers were being used to express resistance to colonial policy. Although this use of the press was at first limited to the local elite, it 'set the tone for a politically active and argumentative public voice' (1990: 36). Over the next century, the number of papers, breadth of readership and scope of critique expanded, leading to the banning of several of the more extreme papers by colonial authorities in 1919. By the 1930s, Trinidad housed a vibrant anti-establishment intelligentsia, expressed through union newspapers, magazines and fictional literature alike. With the voice of the elite continuing to be expressed through papers such as the *Trinidad Guardian*, the press became central to vibrant political struggle and debate in the ensuing decades leading to Independence, and all the more so after.

Public education also dates from the 1830s, when colonial support to the education of former slaves and children interplayed with Catholic and Anglican rivalry. The number of state-aided religious and secular schools grew, such that by 1900, they provided primary education for most of the island's creole children, though not Indian. Secondary education remained almost the preserve of the fee-paying elite, although not exclusively so due to scholar-ships. As Brereton (1981:126) notes, social mobility through education was not straightforward, and the attractiveness of education remained opaque to many. The ideal progression from primary, to secondary and – through the rare 'island scholarship' to British universities set the tone of the curricula, even though such progression was the exception. Nevertheless, educational op-portunity was part of the religious and education ethic in certain black and coloured families, laying the foundation for an emerging middle class, espe-cially in the expanding urban centres. In this, it also produced publics who could and did engage actively with social and political debate through the mass media.

During the 1960s, British publishers concentrated their ownership of the main flagship newspapers until these titles were acquired during the oil boom by Trinidadian conglomerates. Today, the main daily papers, the *Guardian* and *Express* have wide readership; their Sunday editions are read by a third of the population. Skinner characterises them as conservative and business-orientated socially, politically and editorially, financed through advertising, and 'with editorial positions which support capitalism, middle class consumerism, upper-class social and cultural aspirations' (Skinner 1990: 36). Yet they promote themselves as independent voices. Alongside these papers there are more than ten weekly papers known for their more scandalous critical commentary and bacchanal gossip on local and national political and social issues. These fade into a third genre of community-focused papers.

Virtually all households have a radio, listening to a variety of national and local stations, and already by 1990, 93 per cent had a television (Skinner 1990: 47). The country's three TV stations are dominated by US programmes (Lashley 1995; Skinner 1990). To these can be added increasingly-available satellite channels. A further recent media transformation is the growth in Internet access both from (largely urban) homes and, in particular, via a proliferation of cyber-cafés (Miller and Slater 2000).

Given the long history of national ownership of both press and broadcast media, and the increasingly international orientation of the latter, and a rev-enue base in advertising, media production is less dependent on science/policy institutions than in Guinea. That said, the government, NGOs and research in-stitutions involved in environmental science/policy processes have long played a strong role in shaping media coverage of this issue, interlocking with envi-ronmental education.

Material concerning forests and 'nature' in the elite early media was put out by a variety of organisations such as the Trinidad and Tobago Agricultural Society and the Field Naturalists Club in their own journals, shaping portrayals in the national press. These at times reported on concerns such as the destruction of forests and its consequences (Mootoosingh 1979). The readership was an elite circle of people with international and colonial connections.

The colonial Forest Department produced educational materials and pamphlets directed towards wider audiences, complementing forest conservation and production strategies. The educational focus expanded greatly from the 1970s when Bal Ramdial presided over the Forestry Division and launched a mass publicity campaign to promote popular interest in environmental and forest issues, and the work of his Division, raising its profile in national consciousness. Ramdial himself authored numerous pamphlets for schools and the public, and set in motion a broader campaign orchestrated through television, radio, newspapers, public rallies, a roving exhibition bus, a 'walkathon – journey back to nature', and school public speaking competitions (Chandool nd). In this, a broad intertextual field was created, directed – at this peak period of oil boom industrialisation – as much to informing urban publics about an objectified and threatened 'nature' as to encouraging the land users implicated in its destruction to amend their ways. By 1992 the Forestry Division had produced more than twenty environmental education bulletins aligned to school syllabus topics, linking these to all aspects of the Division's work (Faizool and Ramnarine 1992).

NGOs and private organisations also linked conservation with environmental education. This began with the Pointe-à-Pierre Wildfowl Trust (PPWT), founded in 1966, and has been joined since the late 1980s by several other organisations. The PPWT focuses on wetland conservation within a major petrochemical complex. In 1979 it initiated an environmental education audiovisual outreach programme which was the first to be taken into primary and secondary schools and community groups, linked with school visits to its site.[11] The Asa Wright Nature Centre promotes environmental education as part of the ecotourism programme for visitors to its privately-owned forested site in the Northern Range, specialising in bird watching. Indeed, education and 'interpretation' is seen as a key part of the ecotourism package offered to visitors in Trinidad's various national heritage sites, nature reserves, leatherback turtle-watching sites, and so on, whether run by government, private sector or community groups. Both the content and methods for such 'interpretation' are taught as part of the training programme for foresters and wildlife conservationists at the Eastern Caribbean Institute for Agriculture and Forestry (ECIAF).

Conservation NGOs such as the PPWT have long lobbied the Ministry of Education to incorporate environmental education, at least their vision of it, within its centrally-planned primary and secondary school curricula. Prior to 1994, 'Social Studies' already contained environmental education at primary level, but emphasis on environment in education increased strongly in the 1990s. A 1993 White Paper advocated adopting environmental concerns in the three overarching goals in primary education,[12] suggesting that environmental concerns be infused into subjects (social studies, integrated science) along lines suggested by the Wildfowl Trust (Ministry of Education 1993; Ajodha nd). These goals became part of the primary school mission statement in 1998. Yet a highly competitive examination regime forces teachers to concentrate on core elements of each subject, limiting the attention to environmental issues. Dissatisfaction with the infusion approach, coupled with the concern that teachers lacked relevant knowledge and materials, prompted the Ministry to embark on preparation of a more coherent framework to guide environmental education programmes. This was led by the Curriculum Division and the Faculty of Education of the University of the West Indies, with participation from teachers, educators and resource persons in the relevant disciplines. It has also involved collaboration with the new Environmental Management Authority (EMA). Part of this effort involved the development of EnACT, a teacher's guide for environmental education in primary schools. This originated as part of an MSc in Conservation Biology from the University of Wisconsin-Madison supervised by a professor who – as Chapter 5 described – has been highly influential in scientific and policy debates over national parks. EnACT's creation during 1995–97 involved much interaction with teachers and ministry staff (science education facilitators and co-ordinators), including a key workshop at Asa Wright Nature Centre, Trinidad's prime ecotourism site. The author herself taught at ECIAF, and has spent some time working for the Forestry Division's Wildlife Section. The guide is explicitly building educational materials from the practices of science/policy institutions in Trinidad, by making available and comprehensible to teachers the in-house reports of various research and government bodies. It also aimed to assemble locally produced materials, to balance the much larger collection of materials focusing on foreign environments and contexts.

Trinidad's growing attention to environmental education has a variety of international dimensions. Some of these involve university linkages, such as those with Wisconsin-Madison and its conservation biology. Others involve funders, some of whom bring particular positionalities. For example the PPWT programme has been funded by the OAS, major US foundations, the Dutch and German Embassies, the UN Development Programme and Global Environmental Facility, and a variety of power and gas companies. The Trust president, Molly Gaskin, has been much honoured both nationally and internationally for her environmental lobbying in Trinidad and the wider Caribbean (e.g. winning UNEP awards). Other linkages involve engagement with particular international programmes. For example the Ministry has engaged with the UN- Global Learning and Observations to Benefit the Environment (GLOBE) programme, a worldwide science and education programme co-ordinating the work of students, teachers and scientists to study and understand the global environment through practical experiments. He is working with the support of the Environmental Management Authority, and technical support from UWI to expand GLOBE into schools. Meanwhile, however, the GLOBE teacher's guide has provided inputs to a Trinidadian teacher resource book sponsored by the Royal Bank of Trinidad and Tobago.[13]

There are also strong links between the Curriculum Division of the Ministry of Education and UNESCO.[14] These have been manifested in assorted ways:

for instance the 1997 Year of the Reef and 1998 Year of the Oceans; school twinning and joint projects around environmental issues among other themes.[15] The World Heritage project provides another example in which students are encouraged to: 'develop a strong conservation ethic and responsibility for the environment', and 'approach their life on the planet in a sustainable way to protect species and ecosystem diversity and to ensure that the ability of future generations to meet their needs will not be jeopardized'.[16] In this, environmental education is about developing a broad 'environmental ethic', and a global one at that.

Such linkages between the production of environmental education, and scientific and policy institutions, extend also into the production of environmental commentary in the mass-media. We focus particularly on press media because, despite the growing importance of radio, TV and the Internet, 'the press presents the most important aspects of Trinidad-Tobago media culture' (Skinner 1990: 35) due to its wide readership and longstanding centrality to national political debate.

There is considerable coverage of environmental issues in the quality press and community papers. Coverage largely follows the categories and terms of debate of dominant scientific and policy institutions, and is strongly shaped by their influence. Whilst certain scandals related to forests and environment are covered in the weekly press, concerning the behaviour of corporations and politicians (e.g. in *The Mirror*'s regular column 'I [eye] on the Environment'), environmental coverage is generally less apparent. Apparent absence may, however, conceal 'environmental' reflections rooted in different idioms and experiential concerns which are less recognisable, as they fall outside the mainstream intertextual field which links science, policy and authoritative media coverage of environment.

Links between scientific and policy institutions and environmental coverage in the quality press take several forms. First, government institutions themselves use the newspapers to disseminate public information about environmental issues, such as fire regulations. They advertise environmental bills to invite public comment, and advertise public consultations, as occurred for example over the national biodiversity action plan. In this the quality press (and media more widely) provides the primary route for securing participation in policy processes.

Government institutions also use media to communicate their positions more widely. Thus the EMA has its weekly environmental column in the *Trinidad Guardian*. It holds school essay and public speaking competitions, and publishes winning entries. It garners media during its annual 'GreenLeaf' award ceremony held on World Environment Day, giving awards to individuals and community groups for environmental protection as well as to environmental journalists. These activities echo, in many respects, the public information campaigns of the Forestry Division in the 1970s, although in more media conscious times, greater attention is paid to logo and public image.

Other institutions already involved in science and policy also feature strongly in the print media. Key amongst these are several of the major environmental NGOs whose leaders are regular journalistic contributors, bringing their own organisation's line to bear on public issues of the day. Thus for example, the charismatic and controversial former politician, Eden Shand, the lynchpin of the Caribbean Forest Conservation Association, writes a regular and erudite column for the *Express*. Molly Gaskin, founder of the Pointe-à-Pierre Wildfowl Trust, and the journalist Heather Dawn Herrera, of a nature trailing and conservation NGO, contribute numerous articles investigating habitat destruction and its causes.

Of the articles appearing in the quality press, several are therefore authored by those directly involved in scientific and policy processes. A considerable body of reporting is investigative, considering environmental destruction and its causes. Some of those writing are linked to NGOs. Others are dedicated journalists who specialise to varying degrees on environmental reporting; a few, such as Ann Hilton having acquired strong national reputations for this. Across this reporting, a coherence in perspective can be discerned, at least for rural issues. This is distanciated rather than engaged, from the observer rather than the user, and it emphasises values of stewardship rather than ownership of environment and resources. Community-based organisations, NGOs, and staff of the Forestry Division and EMA generally appear in a positive light, pitted against the social categories of large farmers, small farmers, slash and burn farmers, hunters, loggers, squatters and fire setters. Occasionally state organisations are berated for not doing their jobs.

The extent to which media portrayals intersect with the science/policy world can be gauged from attendance at 'participatory' national and regional consultation meetings on environmental policies and strategies, which is overwhelmingly by those belonging to the former, positive social categories rather than to those portrayed negatively. The latter, as we have seen in Chapter 6, engage through other institutional channels; oppositional politics and as we shall see below, certain (highly circumscribed) uses of the media.

At times it is hard to distinguish between this environmental reportage and writings embodying a tourist aesthetic, in the emotive descriptions of destruction employed, appealing to an (urban) public to become concerned. In this, they overlap with articles that are explicitly aesthetic in their orientation, such as the *Guardian* column 'On Nature's Trail'. The majority of those reporting on environment (and certainly the most famous and frequent contributors), whether from within NGOs or as professional journalists, are strongly identified by readers as part of white, elite culture; the upper echelons of what some have termed Trinidad's 'pigmentocracy'.

A further substantial category of environmental reportage focuses on news of government and NGO activities, ranging from control of fire, logging and squatters, to the training of ecotourism tour guides and the establishment of community based conservation projects. The content here is more descriptive than positioned, tending to adopt the analytic and perspective of the organisation reported on. These contrast with articles with a more 'bacchanal' tone, commenting on controversies involving politicians and corporations, most notably in recent years on beneficiaries of the privatisation of the government's teak plantations.

Those working for government rarely write media contributions, feeling that it would compromise their terms of employment. Many of those serving in the Forestry Division – especially its field-level workers – are concerned with this silence, as it leads to a more impoverished public debate where agendas are set by NGO and activist constituencies unfamiliar with the more economic and user-oriented realities that foresters must engage with in their work. Such foresters can influence journalism indirectly either in drawing journalistic attention to practical problems in implementing policies without broad-based support, or indeed in encouraging citizen's organisations to voice their critiques – a component of journalism which we discuss later in the chapter.

Opportunities for community organisations and their press to receive funding from international environmental sources have assisted the emergence of community media, and shaped their environmental coverage – frequently used as an entry point for addressing a range of local issues. For example, the 'Toco Foundation', centring on a coastal village in the north-east, has received funds from the Global Environmental Facility small grants programme for different aspects of their work, ranging from its radio station and newspaper (*The Eastern Voice: a newspaper dedicated to the protection and advancement of the natural and social environment*), to its tour guiding and its turtle conservation project. UNESCO has provided further funding support and contributed environmental educational materials to the school. The Foundation's fundraising success is linked to the skill of its 'entrepreneurial' leader who speaks the international language of community based conservation – and who has latterly used the organisation to launch his political career. That this bid failed, and the foundation's offices became targets of political opposition in the 2000 elections suggests the conflicts obscured in those images of community.[17]

The production of environmental education and environmental content in mass media, then, involves many of the same institutions and people as those also active in environmental policy processes. The messages embodied in media and education, as we now go on to exemplify, reflect these patterns of social structuration.

Intertextuality in messages

A full analysis of environmental reporting in Trinidad would need to consider a vast range of material. Even within print media, this ranges from the reporting of sophisticated political debate on the pros and cons of the National Trust, national parks and changes in forestry legislation, through to the importance of environment for the economy, health, spirit and ecotourism, through to accounts of the destruction of particular forests and wetlands, to attempts at forest protection and conservation. There are articles which focus on local events, and others which relate Trinidad's experiences to regional discussions of the timber trade or the global implications of deforestation for climate. Indeed the very variety at times defeats characterisation, encompassing as it does 'high theory' articles on the domino effect as a motif for environmental destruction, and pieces focusing on the daily work of field-level game wardens.

Yet within this diversity, it is possible to discern certain textual elements which recur across and thus align articles. Here we pick out a few among innumerable exemplars, taking as a focal case the *Trinidad Guardian* between 1993 and 1999.

A first key element in these narrative structures is evocation of a recent and wondrous past:

Once on the hill large pregnant iguanas crawled across the sand or dug themselves into nests . . . the surrounding swamp was dotted with tall and stately moriche . . . an integral part of the Nariva wetlands.[18]

In the 1960s, from the Jagruma River into the Nois Neuf, all that area was covered in forest. There was an abundance of wildlife, . . . There was lots of game – agouti, lappe, tattoo, iguana, porcupine, wild hog, a few ocelots. Birds and more birds.[19]

Against this, there are descriptions of a destruction visible today, couched in emotional terms of sadness, anger and disbelief, and labelling social categories responsible for destruction:

Today going to the Sand Hill area is a totally different experience. . . . Where moriche palm had long since been illegally cut and replaced by melon gardens . . .[20]

'In areas where there is no human intervention you get birds galore', Lal says of the still untouched areas of TT. Unplanned forest and oil exploration are major factors resulting in the depletion of the wildlife stocks. So, too, is squatting. Squatting is a problem: with slash and burn agriculture, the forest is destroyed, and the dense regrowth depletes the soil.[21]

It was terribly distressing to discover in a recent drive between Sangre Grande and the Valencia road junction on the Toco Main Road that the magnificent Mora forest has totally vanished . . . it is all evidence of filthy, uncaring people, steadily destroying the lifelines and mental restoratives around us.[22]

A further narrative element highlights continuing threat:

. . . in two instances it was alarming to discover fresh [hunting activity] both on and around the hill Wildlife in Sand Hill.[23]

. . . producing a map, Cross showed where heavy deforestation caused by logging has now encircled the Northern Range foothills and is moving upward.[24]

Problems are identified with current protection measures:

> Though regular patrols are performed within the area, the Forestry Division does not have the manpower . . .[25]

> It does not appear that the forestry laws are enforced . . . the Forestry Division appears incapable of doing anything . . .[26]

> The north coast . . . is a paradise for illegal logging; a nightmare for the Forestry Division. Faizool said while reports in the press about illegal logging in the North Coast were true, in most cases the logging was being done on private lands. 'There is no legislation in the Forestry Act to stop a private landowner from selling his trees', he notes.[27]

Proposed solutions are seen to lie in new forms of management. It is here that narrative elements are at their most diverse, variously recommending increased state rigour, community ecotourism projects, or voluntary action through inspiring calls hailing individual members of the public to environmental literacy and responsibility. This illustrates how journalism interlocks intertextually with policy processes. Nevertheless, a common denominator is the call for intensified surveillance and management, whoever is to provide it:

> It should be an eventuality that the Northern Range be declared a national treasure and designated a national park . . . in order to save it from the ravages of the super predators.[28]

> One wonders (at least I do) why it has taken so long for conservationists to realise that only the local communities, the people on the spot who know what's going on from day to day, can effectively protect a remote rural natural environment.[29]

> Volunteers battle forest fires.[30]

> During the dry season, many uncaring persons may carelessly set fire to the bushes which can spread out of control. We must discourage such persons from those acts and encourage them instead, to put out fires which may seem dangerous. Please tell your friends about this; encourage them to avoid bush fires to save our vegetation and thereby, to keep our country clean, healthy and beautiful.[31]

In other articles, these various narrative elements are collapsed into summary statements:

> A major concern, noted the EMA, is the loss of forest from steep slopes, watershed protection areas and water production areas as a result of quarrying, farming and forest fires . . . the Pawi's survival is threatened by hunting and destruction of its forest habitat.[32]

These processes in Trinidad are in some representations seen to echo international concerns:

> Because of their value to the world environment, in fact the destruction of tropical and sub-tropical rain forest has become a matter of serious international concern. And yet we learn that the forests [of Trinidad] have been disappearing at the rate of 300 ha a year through the uncontrolled operations of loggers on both state and private land.[33]

Readers are thus invited to make links between what is purportedly happening in Trinidad, and the global processes they see and hear on imported television and radio programmes.

These narrative elements are by no means confined to the quality press. They recur in most educational materials, contributing to a broader field of inter-textuality. For example the Pointe-à-Pierre Wildfowl Trust produces a series of 'theme sheets' for teachers.[34] While most focus on wetland conservation and wildfowl, a few cover more general topics such as 'Wildlife in Danger' (theme sheet 9) and 'Saving Wildlife' (theme sheet 10). The latter emphasises conflicts between land use and development, and conservation; and advocates community-based management approaches. 'Wildlife in Danger' draws out local-global connections, stating that:

Habitat destruction [is] by far the greatest cause of wildlife loss – the natural places where wildlife can live are disappearing at an alarming rate . . . In Trinidad and Tobago we have lost about 1/3 of our top soil, most of it has been washed away in floods and man made erosion. Of the area of the planet's surface that is exposed only 6% is land that is cap-able of growing food and that 6% we continue to throw away through constant misuse.[35]

In these materials, Trinidad's population is very much located as part of the global 'north' – or at least environmental education is directed towards ur-banised, globally-connected citizens, rather than those depending on environ-mental resources for their livelihoods:

Our development has taken us through various stages – from hunter/gatherer to farmer and from farmer to trader; from trader to manufacturer, industrialist and technologist. We have, at least in the north, overcome our basic "needs" and we have added a whole list of "wants" – luxuries that make our lives more comfortable . . . it is these which are causing the most damage to the natural world. [36]

The environmental education bulletins produced by the Forestry Division are extremely wide-ranging and thorough. The overall framing is within a distan-ciated aesthetic, evident for example in the first principles of a highly extensive curriculum framework (Box 8.1).

Box 8.1 Environmental education curriculum framework, Part 1 (in Faizool and Ramnarine 1992:20:2)

- Instil a deep appreciation (love) for the diverse forest environment.
- The maintenance of a varied and beautiful life-support system is essential to both physiological and psychological health.
- Contrast and variety that are important to mental health are available in the forest and elsewhere.
- A recognition of beauty and quiet in the forest environment is necessary for a feeling of well-being in many people.
- Opportunities to experience and enjoy nature are psychologically rewarding to many, and important to mental health.

Despite this framing, however, other elements of the curriculum are very different. As we consider later, they emphasise the need to understand diverse interests, values and knowledges as they affect the use of, and decision making about the forest. Indeed they invite citizens to reflect critically on the values and processes through which forest and conservation policies are made.

Journalistic and educational materials inter-animate with wider textual and non-textual fields. Exemplary of this, perhaps, could be the sponsored 'Fun Run/Walk' advertised in a full-page newspaper spread in aid of Nature Seekers Incorporated. Here the literally 'green' advertisement linked to environmental conservation interlocks with physical activity and symbolism that embodies the experience of health. Even if you were not on the walk the connections are made. Such connections make the event appealing to commercial sponsorship; the walk advertisement bears the logos of leading Trinidadian financial and broadcasting institutions.[37]

Walks in aid of environment have a longer history. When 1987 fires provoked the Forest Division into intensified environmental education programmes, they organised a Walk-a-thon: citizens were invited 'clad in t shirts and sun visors to commemorate the fire event . . . to walk 10km as a visible reminder to their compatriots that uncontrolled fires can be devastating ecologically, socially and economically' (Chandool 1990).

Messages are reinforced when people cross into the ecotourism sites during visits, when they drive over mud flows and inhale the smoke of dry season fires, and look up to the hills. It is such inter-animation and the common sense it shapes which enables journalistic and everyday images to be adopted uncritically into the discourse and writings of academics; into the writing of Trinidad's history and society.

Many of the ideas sedimented through texts and experiences are thus simultaneously of a nature threatened by certain social categories (loggers, slash and burn farmers) which needs to be more intensely managed; and of an environmentally responsible citizen, literate in the language of global environmental concern and its applicability to the island. In this, environmental users (destroyers) and environmentally-literate citizens are objectified as distinct, while nature is objectified as dislocated from daily practice, to be appreciated and protected. However sensitive journalists and educators may wish to be to the details and cultural nuances of Trinidadian localities, this takes place within prevailing presuppositions and patterns of objectification.

This is not the only way in which these issues might be construed. As the case of hunters in Chapter 5 described, for instance, forest decline was linked to the alienation of protected areas from land users, opening them to the ravages of illegal uses and turning them into trap-gun protected, no-go areas. Equally the rather singular narrative about the destructive effects of 'slash and burn farming' and 'squatting' overlooks farmer's own perspectives on their interactions with biodiversity, and the highly diverse tenure arrangements under which small farmers live and work, shaping very varied interactions with ecological processes (e.g. Cropper 1997; Driver 2002). Although certain, particularly focused articles do touch on aspects of these experiences[38] they are generally dwarfed by the recurrence of articles evoking the simplified and singular narrative context.

Contestation, critique and its management

There are circumstances in which the stability of environmental messages and linked moral commentary cannot be easily sustained. Sometimes this takes the form of open critique appearing within the media/educational nexus. While this is at times the case in Trinidad, it is much less evident in Guinea. Here, however, critique can still be discerned where messages are destabilised in practices of expression. Our focus here remains on the media/educational nexus, rather than on its audiences,[39] but shifts particularly to those who are implicated actively in constructing and transmitting media/educational messages, whether as teachers, journalists, letter-writers to newspaper editors, or those implicated in journalistic encounters. Such an emphasis on interfaces (Long and Long 1994) in a media context in turn takes the focus off the established distinction in media studies between those who 'produce' and those who 'consume' media as its audience. Rather, it focuses on social relations of active engagement in media, and on how they are shaped through social relations in broader scientific and policy domains.[40]

Trinidad

In Trinidad, direct critique of science and policy, and of shaping of media can be found within the media itself. That it is expressed in an overt and oppositional way (at times in anger) suggests both that the intertextual field is experienced as coherent, and that it is opposed – at least by some:

The Editor: From the many articles in the press lately, one would get the impression that the world is over-populated and this is causing rapid and permanent destruction to the environment. I would like to state that these views are not unanimous among the scientific world. . . . The question is not whether we are overpopulated or destroying the environment; but who wants to get rid of us, and why. When one considers that it is mainly the well to do pushing doom and gloom propaganda, the answers become clearer.[41]

Curiously, the coherence of the intertextual field and its capacity to deceive is even drawn into reflexivity by mainstream environmental writers. Thus the environmental feature journalist Rory Rostant writes an article 'Will you believe the next environmental scare?' drawing on analysis in *The Economist* magazine showing the poor track record of the predictions of environmental doomsayers. Such critiques are drawing international debates and questioning of environmental orthodoxies into a Trinidadian field where they are used to question (and express lack of trust in) the edifice of environmental/journalistic analysis. But they are not, it should be noted, used to question the actual statements about local deforestation, degradation and so on in Trinidad which this edifice generates.

In contrast, other writings draw alternative local experiences of environmental change (and the impact of policy processes) into critical engagement with dominant portrayals. This is exemplified in the series of letters from (and press interviews with) hunters in the mid-1990s around the proposed National Parks and Wildlife Bill. These report hunters' views that the Bill 'is a most pernicious and alarming piece of legislation' and that if 'it is not withdrawn then he and his Association are prepared to step up protest action to ensure that this threat to democracy . . . is stopped'.[42] The Bill is likened to the work of oppressive dictators,[43] 'brutal, wicked, nasty and shades of the reincarnation of a Hitler and Idi Amin all in one'.[44] Hunters also contest the extent of wildlife depletion:

. . . there are agouti all over the country and deer too. Most deer hunters have problems with their packs chasing two deer at one time. And every agouti hunter will tell you invariably Sunday after Sunday they have problems with their agouti dogs chasing sometimes as much as three deer in a day's hunt in the big forest.[45]

Hunters have been particularly adept at using their Associations to gain journalistic coverage and through this, access to institutional channels to influence public debate. Nevertheless this particular issue also incited angry voices from wider members of the public. A letter to the *Guardian* from a taxi driver asked:

On the National Parks and Wildlife Bill the secret police may already be in place. Check out the brand new fleet of Mitsubishi jeeps with heavily tinted windows and painted Civilian Conservation Corps. The new bill can give this now invisible civilian army powers of search and seizure. Is this the new CIA of the Rising Sun?[46]

That these are largely protests against surveillance can be taken to indicate how environmental policy processes are being experienced as extensions of surveillance and control.

It is difficult for analysts and public alike to ascertain the level of orchestration and political engagement in the use of media for dissent. The strategic use of media (spin) by scientific and policy factions in encouraging public opposition might certainly be tactical, for example in the internal disputes between the factions opposing Forestry and Wildlife. It is striking that those (such as the hunters) who engage with media to express alternative perspectives on environment have also been those pioneering 'citizen science'. And as in the citizen science arena, the perspectives of smallholder farmers, and those who depend on rural resources for their livelihoods are conspicuous by their absence. Their perspectives on landscape and its transformations appear not to have engaged with the intertextual world in media and education that we have described.

An appreciation of both disparate interests and knowledges, uncertainty, and the need for a critical and informed understanding of policy processes actually appears within the Forestry Division's own environmental educational curriculum. Indeed, a striking list of points proposed to convey to students could be taken to presage and justify the research agenda which has informed this book, and indicate a receptive readership for it (Box 8.2).

Box 8.2: Environmental education curriculum framework, Part 4 (in Faizool and Ramnarine 1992:20:5–6)

Acquaint students with the perspectives from and by which various interest groups judge contemporary forest/environmental issues, the mechanisms by which these issues are resolved, and ways in which their outcome may be influenced. [Points include:]

• People vary widely in their perception of the forest environment: consequently language and other media used to influence them must be based on knowledge of their values and interests.

• Words and phrases relative to forest/environment issues carry connotative and emotional impact as well as denotative value and must be used and understood in light of this fact.

• Citizenship assumes an informed an understanding as possible of the decision-making process; this necessitates knowledge of the values that enter into a decision, the persons and institutions which are influential and how the decision may affect long-term policy.

• Effective citizens need to be informed about pressures and a variety of institutional structures (such as agencies, interest groups, money) which influence the planning and management of the forest resources.

• Citizenship influences the opportunity to participate freely in helping to make and change public policy.

• Conservation policies come about as a result of interacting social processes, science and technology, government operations and private and public interest and attitudes.

• Management of natural resources requires the flexibility to respond to changing human needs, technological advances, new scientific knowledge, governmental policies and unusual conditions.

Statements such as these imply strong appreciation for more inclusive forest policy and management. To date, however, there is less evidence that they have infused actual strategies and practices either for education or in forest policy.

Guinea

Open, overt critique is less evident in Guinea's media. Nevertheless, messages emanating from the media/education nexus are sometimes destabilised in the very practices of their expression, revealing that critique is present, even though it finds few formalised channels for open expression.

A clear example of such destabilisation occurs in an interview on rural radio with charcoal makers who deny accusations levelled at them concerning deforestation. While rural radio programmes are supposedly 'done by villagers', with 'about 70% reserved for citizens to express themselves freely' (PACIPE 1997: 1), in practice citizens must negotiate such expression with interviewers. Here, these focus on the environmental problems caused by charcoal makers, a social category that is vilified for their wood use and fire-setting, and that epitomises the impact of modernity and commercialisation on 'forest nature'. When the journalist visited a village renowned for its year-round supply of charcoal, sold at the roadside to vehicle passengers, the conversation turned oppositional. Yet as we shall see, the interviewer managed the potential threat by turning dissent into ridicule.

Dear listeners, welcome. Rural radio has come to find out what we must protect. We know that there are several things around us which cannot be used, which can be destroyed, which should be our heritage. Among them we can cite our forests. There is terrible damage from fire. Charcoal makers. Many among them fell wood to make charcoal, many among them leave the fire burning after them, and it is these fires which cause large scale destruction. We have contacted people from the village of Dalabani about this problem. We have exchanged ideas with elders, the way to burn charcoal, the different stages that we do not know. But we know it destroys vegetation . . .

Q: *Mr. Nankouma Keita, you are living at Dalabani . . . how do you obtain charcoal, being a specialist in this?*

R1: I am happy about your question. We make charcoal when we make fields on the slopes. The trees are cut, we collect them. We make the fire. On market day we sell it to buy the things we need. We cut it, put it in the earth, fire it, and sell it to meet our needs.

Q: *You know, to burn charcoal is not bad, but it is the way of doing it. There are those who do not know. There are some who cut green wood. And you?*

R1: We, we do not cut green wood, we use the wood from our fields.

Q: *You, have you never cut it?*

R1: Me, I have never cut it. I have not yet seen anyone cutting it.

Q: *Keep quiet a moment. I will ask someone else. Come here sir, I have heard that you are competent in this charcoal affair.*

R2: Me, I am not great in that.

Q: *But you burn.*

R2: I do it among other jobs.

Q: *Like what?*

R2: I do it alongside the cultivation of rice. Once the real rice work is over, I make charcoal.

Q: *What species of wood do you use?*

R2: The wood I use is the wood from my fields, the dead wood. I don't cut green wood. Charcoal from dry wood is better than from green wood.

Q: *How is charcoal from green wood?*

R2: Green-wood charcoal does not do well. Dry-wood charcoal is good.

Q: *Where have you seen green-wood charcoal?*

R2: I saw it in another village. You know that everyone in the region makes charcoal.

Q: *But you do not use green-wood.*

R2: We, in any case, do not . . .

Q: *And those people?*

R2: Those . . I don't understand.

Q: *They say they learnt from you.*

R2: Not all. They have lied to you.

Q: *They say that they make charcoal all year round.*

R2: They lied. As here, at the time of cultivation, you will not see anyone do it. Only after, if you do not want hunger. After work, you do charcoal. They know too . . .

Q: *Chief, and you. Each year you make new fields as each year one sees sacks of charcoal at your place.*

R3: The wood that we fell in the fields is not all used at once, if you see that we keep at it. If you fell one or two trunks, you burn them. Another time, you cut up a trunk and burn it. It is because of that, that we take time. We can't use it all at once. One does not fell trees to use all at once.

Q: *Charcoal makers are accused a lot. One says that they set the destructive fires, and destroy the bush that everyone destroys, one says that it is them. If one asks you about these problems, how would you reply?*

R3: Me, I can say to that all who set fires are not charcoal makers. It is not charcoal makers, as they also need dry grass. It is dry grass that we cut to put on the wood. If you burn these grasses, where will you get more to put on the wood? It is travellers who set fires, not charcoal makers . . .

Q: *Dear listeners. You have just heard that charcoal makers do not set bush fires, but that they are made independently of them. Yes?*

R4: That depends on your work. If you work badly, you might cause a fire. If you work well, you won't.

Q: *Dear all, let us hear another person.* Can you say that those here do not cut wood?

R5: They do not touch the trees. The wood is plentiful.

Q: *That is why you devastate wood all the time?*

R5: We don't devastate the woods. Where we cultivate, it is there that we fell trees.

Q: *Where you cultivate, it is there that you devastate? There that you destroy?*

R5: One does not destroy. If you don't believe us, come with us to our home.

Q: *What you fell, you replace?*

R5: They are replaced . . .

Q: *Mr. Kourouma. We do not make charcoal without a new field. The rotation of fields does not destroy or impoverish the soil?*

R5: It does not weaken it.

Q: *It does not diminish the cultivable land?*

R5: There is not shortage, as the land is plentiful.
Q: Here, you have too much land.
R5: There cannot be too much. Good land is sufficient though.
Q: The huge devastation that you make does not tire your soil?
R5: We do not cut everywhere.
Q: Where do you cut?
R5: Where we cut does not do any harm. If you leave the place, the trees grow.
Q: They grow just like that?
R5: Yes.
Q: Ah the magician. You think that the wood and the grasses are the same. That the way the grass grows, is the same as the trees?
R5: Just as grass grows, so do the trees.
Q: How long does it take for a tree to grow large?
R5: The wood you use to make charcoal, about 7 or 8 years, before they are large.
Q: If you cut them, for 7 or 8 years you will no longer need the land?
R5: You could use it.
Q: And why do you abandon it?
R5: If it is not good for you, you leave it for a long time before returning. The trees do not weaken the soil. Trees do not harm the soil. A ground without trees is not good for farming. It is for that that we forbid felling trees everywhere. But you can use the wood from your fields until it is finished.
Q: Nankouma, tell me the importance of trees, as Mr. Kourouma does not know their importance. Only destruction . . .

What emerges, then, is a stand-off between the knowing journalist, and the rather differently knowing villagers. This is not confrontational journalism designed ultimately to reveal the perspective of the farmers interviewed (although for some audiences it might have had this effect); rather it is a discussion designed to get the interviewer's message over (the interviewer being answerable to the project for doing precisely this). As one of a few moments where the intertextual world we have outlined engages with the world of land users, this interview served more to perpetuate than to break self-referentiality, failing to generate new research questions and inquiry. Within the programme, and especially in its evaluation, any humour it may have raised through real engagement was effaced as a socially problematic stand off. The dissent of Mr. Kourouma was first turned back on him in dismissive scorn, and was finally trivialised. At the end he too was given the chance to save face by eulogising trees. So stigmatised is the symbol of being a charcoal maker in this encounter, that those who make charcoal were at pains to suggest that they are farmers first, and charcoal makers second.

A second example concerns the reinterpretation of school curricula in the practice of teaching. Primary school teachers working in rural schools and teaching materials provided by environmental projects still have to make a living. Like other resident 'strangers', many teachers also farm on land provided by their village hosts and through similar social arrangements, and use pupil labour. At times they find it problematic to reconcile their environmental teaching with their farming practice. To deal with these contradictions, one teacher in Kissidougou prefecture emphasised a strong distinction between field fires and wild fires in his teaching.[47] He drew selectively on ambiguities in the curriculum course to match his own experience. A Kissi man, and farming actively on land lent by the village, he himself appreciated the value of fire in field clearance, and had seen that following farming, savanna areas had become more wooded. In this way, his teaching differed from a teacher in a nearby village who did not farm. His pupils developed a theatre piece (under Plan Guinea's education programme) which showed villagers valuing fire for farming but the forest service disapproving. As the sketch developed, the forest service was shown to be right. Thus teachers vary in the extent to which they concur with, and reproduce stabilised environmental messages. Yet the extent to which those who have serious doubts about the curriculum can express them in their teaching is ultimately constrained by their need to prepare their children for standardised exams.

A third illustration of how messages can be undermined concerns the use by hunters of a radio interview (and project practice) to further quite different socio-political agendas. As we saw in Chapter 4, PACIPE and the EU have actively supported the revitalisation and arming of 'traditional' hunter's organisations as guardians of both nature, and the moral order required to protect it against the depredations of 'poachers', undisciplined fire-setters and so on. In this context, several rural radio interviews have given hunters voice to explain their organisation and work. Yet, in discussion, a range of socio-political agendas important to hunters, but quite different from the environmental ones which form the ostensible subject of the programmes concerned, are expressed. For example, in one programme, discussion ranged from hunters' regulated use of early fire to their co-operation with PACIPE which – as a hunter put it – 'has come here to protect the environment, water; when the bush is burnt it is not good for the soil; that which is not good for the soil is not good for the trees'. They discuss hunters' laws concerning the regulated killing of animals and the social hierarchies of hunters. But then the benign, conservationist, project-aligned vision of the hunter is destabilised by the non-distinction the hunters draw between this, and military action – the antithesis of participatory conservation.

Q: *What do you say to today's youth concerning obedience to hunter's laws?*
R: Hunting, we have done a little of that, but one does not kill many animals. We have learnt that from our ancestors. In Manding territory, we are all gun hunters. We are the same as soldiers. They are in town and we are in the bush. But we have the same work. So our friends who are outside. We invite you to unite, to come together, to do hunting as it should be done.[48]

On one hand, the hunter's analogy speaks to the long established inseparability of hunters and warriors in Mande myth and history. On the other, it also speaks to the contemporary activity of hunters in regional warfare, either in counter-insurgency, or as rebels. In a country where Mande have been politically marginalised, but where the state itself is threatened by cross border rebels this is a potent analogy.

We have chosen these three examples to indicate different ways in which stabilised messages concerning the environment and how to manage it are destabilised in communication events.

Conclusions

In this chapter we have tried to expand the field of inquiry around science and policy relations to sketch out the wider informational realm of which they are a part, including media, education and aspects of popular culture. Close linkages appear between the social and institutional framing of science and policy, and of this wider field, in the mechanisms of production, and the shaping of content. As in the rest of this book, we have been concerned to highlight the history of practices which have shaped not only messages, but also media and educational forms and their significance, and the ways audiences might interpret them.

Hall has argued that mass media (and here, read mass media in their intertextuality with education and policy) increasingly provide the basis on which groups construct an image of the lives and practices of other groups, and provide the images around which a social totality can be grasped (1997: 340). What we have explored are ways in which this is linked to science and policy, and how the projection of social and moral categories in relation to environmental issues 'feeds back' to naturalise the moral order.

In Guinea, there is a remarkably closed, mutually-referential field of interlocked institutions, which severely constrains public debate about environment through the media. This echoes, in an environmental context, the kind of propaganda machine which was put into effect during the state socialist era, but now also involving international networks, and orchestrated through the more diffuse processes and practices that this book has been exploring. It also echoes Chapman's (1997) analysis of mass media in India as speaking to global framings of environmental problems, while overlooking the more located perspectives of a silent majority. In Trinidad this is less the case, given both ongoing conflicts between institutions, and the more 'participatory' history and character of media in this highly literate society. Yet although it may be true to characterise the contemporary media in Trinidad as participatory, as many commentators do, what we have tried to show here is the nature of this participation and its limits; the institutional configuration within which values and agendas get set, which includes some, but excludes others.

What has not appeared in either country are dialogues in media that inform scientific agendas. Rather, the broader informational realm can be understood to shape scientific activity in its capacity to reinforce the values and framing assumptions already embodied in certain strands of scientific inquiry – primarily those strands which have been co-produced with policy and through the institutional links that we have sketched out. The net effect is to construct an intertextual field of self-evidence; a world of taken-for-granted truth in which the need to assert its 'Scientificity' is absent – accounting perhaps for the (initially surprising) lack of resort to Science as an appeal to authority. Equally, media accounts of scientific process or of debate are absent. At least in Trinidad there is reportage of controversy over policies, or between government and certain public perspectives; perspectives which as earlier chapters have shown are rooted in different research practices and findings – different 'sciences'. Yet the 'Science' frequently remains hidden in reports which seem to be about politics, personal and institutional conflicts and turf battles, or broader values.

No matter what the particular takes of particular hunters, farmers, teachers or journalists, the very volume of material makes the sum greater than parts; the critic is dwarfed by the common denominator. Furthermore, in both Trinidad and Guinea the amplification of dominant science/policy perspectives and their associated moral categories through the requirements of media/educational reporting – the need for simple, catchy narratives and lessons, often with polarised heroes and villains – itself marginalises contestation. The diverse, fragmented perspectives and experiences, and expressions of social and environmental uncertainty, which would critique aspects of dominant science and policy do not lend themselves to easy formulation as a strong 'counter-narrative', even were the social and institutional arrangements in place to unite their proponents.

Notes

1. The language of primary education was exclusively the five major national languages: Susu, Malinke, Peul, Kissi and Guerze; secondary education taught French, and universities taught in French, although it worked towards an Africanisation of this. French was a permitted language only in administrative settings.
2. *http://elodia.intnet.bj/pacipe/pacipe.htm*
3. Interview, European consultant, EU programme, Conakry, 7 January 1999.
4. Interview, Director of PACIPE Guinea, Conakry, 13 January 1999.
5. Ibid.
6. Interview, lecturer in environmental education, CERE, University of Conakry, 13 March 1999.
7. The main third and four year primary school geography textbook (Niane 1986) which predates these discussions does not enter into analysis of vegetation change, or use the words environment and degradation in discussing the country's four regions and vegetation types.

8. *Ecole Propre, Ecole Verte: Bulletin d'Education Environnementale destiné aux élèves du Primaire*. PACIPE, Guinea.
9. Interview, European consultant, EU programme, Conakry, 7 January 1999.
10. Interview, lecturer in environmental education, CERE, University of Conakry, 13 March 1999.
11. Of a population of 1.3 million, 19,500 visit Pointe-à-Pierre annually, of whom 15,200 are schoolchildren (*http://www.users.carib-link'net/~wildfowl/educate.htm* 8 September 1999).
12. Out of fifteen primary education goals, goal 3 is: 'to identify the historical and contemporary environmental processes which contribute to the formation of the society'. Goal 12: 'to develop an understanding of the problems caused by the degradation of our planet', and 13 'to put into practice habits that demonstrate care for the environment'. The main subject areas for these goals are in social studies (with no. 13 also including science) (Ministry of Education 1993: 170–71). In 1998, a further goal was introduced: 'To be provided with the opportunity to acquire the knowledge, values, attitudes, commitment and skills needed to educate, protect the environment and act appropriately'. In secondary school, the 13th goal is 'to demonstrate an appreciation of the value of a healthy environment, avoid any personal action that would contribute to its degradation, and appreciate the importance of conserving and recycling available resources'. Social studies, sciences and geography were to cover this (1993: 180).
13. H. Saunders, 1997, country report – Trinidad and Tobago, West Indies, paper presented at second annual GLOBE conference, July 1997, Airlie, Virginia; *http://www.*globe.gov/fsl/html/templ_airlie1997. *cgi?rep_tt&lang=en&nav=1 3 September 1999*.
14. Interview, secretary to sub-regional co-ordinator, UNESCO, Port of Spain, by Keisha Charles, 12 July 1999; Interview, Secretary General of the National Commission for UNESCO, Port of Spain, by Keisha Charles, 13 July 1999; Interview, Sub-Regional co-ordinator, UNESCO, Port of Spain, by Keisha Charles, 13 July 1999.
15. *http://firewall.unesco.org/education/educprog/asp/aspnet.htm* 3 September 1999.
16. *http://www.norssi.jyu.fi/a-aste/unes.html*, 19 July 1999.
17. For debate over this, see for example: 'Michael Als pulls a fast one on the Toco Community', by Petra George, *Newsday*, 6 September 2000 *www.trinicentre . . . goNews/Sept/MichaelAlsandToco.htm* 24 July 2001.
18. 'Wildlife in Sand Hill', *Trinidad Guardian*, 10 May 1999.
19. 'Lal's country', *Trinidad Guardian*, 24 March 1996.
20. 'Wildlife in Sand Hill', *Trinidad Guardian*, 10 May 1999.
21. 'Lal's country', *Trinidad Guardian*, 24 March 1996.
22. 'Distressing destruction', Letter to the Editor, Lloyd Cartar, *Trinidad Guardian*, 12 June 1993.
23. *Trinidad Guardian*, 10 May 1999.
24. 'Call to make Northern Range a national park', Rory Rostant, *Trinidad Guardian*, 28 April 1997.
25. 'Wildlife in Sand Hill', *Trinidad Guardian*, 10 May 1999.
26. 'Call to make Northern Range a national park', Rory Rostant, *Trinidad Guardian*, 28 April 1997.

27. 'Night raiders ravaging our forests', Rory Rostant, *Trinidad Guardian*, 31 March 1997.
28. 'Call to make Northern Range a national park', Rory Rostant, *Trinidad Guardian*, 28 April 1997.
29. 'Continuing battle to save environment', Ann Hilton, *Trinidad Guardian*, 3 January 1996.
30. Rory Rostant, *Trinidad Guardian*, 13 March 1998.
31. 'Our Forests', Al Ramsawack, *Trinidad Guardian Sunday Supplement*, 27 October 1996.
32. 'EMA reports on wildlife in danger', Rory Rostant, *Trinidad Guardian*, 5 January 1998.
33. 'Save our forests', Editorial, *Trinidad Guardian*, 8 April 1997.
34. *http://www.users.carib-link_net/~wildfowl/educate.htm* 8 September 1999.
35. Pointe-à-Pierre Wild Fowl Trust, 'Wildlife in Danger', Theme Sheet 9.
36. Ibid.
37. In Features section, *Trinidad Guardian,* June 1999.
38. For example 'Carrots for squatters', Ann Hilton, *Trinidad Guardian*, 21 July 1993.
39. In other words, we are not following the audience ethnography tradition in media studies, which has itself generated a large literature. For a critical review see, for example, Alasuutari 1999.
40. This approach might be seen to inflect Alasuutari's 1999 'rethinking' of the media audience, moving beyond reception studies and audience 'to get a grasp of our contemporary media culture, particularly as it can be seen in the role of the media in everyday life, both as a topic and as an activity structured by and structuring the discourses within which it is discussed', in the increasingly globalised mediascape within which people live their lives.
41. Letter to editor from Mario Fortune, Trincity, *Trinidad Guardian*, 10 July 1993.
42. 'Wildlife Bill a threat to democracy', *Trinidad Guardian*, 22 June 1997.
43. Letter to the editor from EPM, Chaguanas, *Trinidad Guardian*, 9 June 1997.
44. Letter to the editor from Lystra Lythe, Sangre Grande, *Trinidad Guardian*, 23 June 1997.
45. 'Throw that wildlife bill in the trash can', Vensee Ali, *Trinidad Guardian*, 4 June 1997.
46. Letter to editor from Maxi Taxi driver, D'Abadie, *Trinidad Guardian*, 28 May 1997.
47. Interview with schoolteacher by Dominique Millimouno, Kissidougou Prefecture, 15 February 1999.
48. 'Discussions with Senior Hunters', Interview, Kankan Rural Radio, 29 August 1999.

9 Reflections on science, society and power

This book has identified how emergent relations between science and policy internationally have been engaging with science and policy traditions and conduct in Guinea and in Trinidad. We have been particularly interested in the social relations of which science and policy are a part, and which they help structure. We chose forest issues because they have been the subject of science and policy traditions in each country for over a century, and concern resources central to many people's livelihoods there. We chose to compare Trinidad and Guinea because they have similar ecologies and colonial forestry experiences, although Trinidad has subsequently become industrialised and urbanised, while highly-rural Guinea now ranks among the most impoverished nations of the world. In each country, we have detailed how particular policies unfold in engagement with particular types of scientific inquiry in specific cases linked to biodiversity and its conservation, and to forest exploitation. We have contextualised this unfolding within each country's broader political and economic history and modes of public engagement. What emerges is how new international scientific and policy configurations play into struggles for authority between political and administrative institutions nationally, and struggles for control over the rural world and its resources. They are integral to processes of enrichment and legitimation for some, and impoverishment and disqualification for others. The roles of science and policy in processes of social objectification and the shaping of subjectivities, and their relationships with forms of media and education, are central in this.

In focusing on the social relations of science and policy and of their coproduction, we have not intended to deny the physicality of landscape processes: the real changes taking place in African and Caribbean ecologies as people interact with them. And in pointing out the partiality of co-produced scientific and policy perspectives on environmental problems, we have not intended to deny that 'problems' exist. How those who depend on forests and their resources interact with ecological processes, and evaluate outcomes within particular social and cultural frames – sometimes as 'problems' – has been the subject of our earlier work, and we have not dwelt on this here. Instead, we have sought to illuminate the processes through which scientific and policy debate engage with it.

This has been a study, then, of contemporary governance and of resource control, but through an empirical analysis of the practice and social relations of science in engagement with policy. With the analytical focus on science and policy, a set of power relations emerges which stands in contrast with analysis rooted in the vocabularies of 'governments', 'international organisations', 'NGOs' and local 'communities', and which questions the analytical salience of these popular distinctions in the contemporary world. Cutting the cake in a different way, we have discerned how alliances and discursive coalitions form around particular issues and positions in scientific and policy debate.

That governance and science are increasingly both internationalised, but also 'localised' in the form of decentralisation, with appeals to citizen voice and local 'participation,' no longer appears as a contradiction. The discussions of biodiversity and forest exploitation in Guinea and Trinidad have repeatedly illustrated both these processes and shown how epistemic alignments and institutional alliances can link international and local processes towards particular forest management agendas. Rather it is distinctions between types of management and governance – and the shaping of science in relation to these – that have emerged as overriding themes across the cases. Internationalisation-localisation distinctions might be better re-cast as between forms of governance, according to the ways they conceptualise and attempt (or do not attempt) to impose order on 'nature', and the distributions of social responsibility and resource control that they imply. Science becomes part of efforts both to impose particular forms of governance, and to contest them.

Treating environmental science and policy together and from a practice perspective begins to resolve how knowledge of 'nature' is framed in relation to institutional and managerial conditions. What has emerged is a mutuality between certain policy aspirations and practices to manage forests, and the imaging of nature and society as both separate from each other, and as stable and predictable – thus manageable. At the same time it is possible to identify less equilibrial models in forest ecological science, as well as lay knowledge and perspectives which both understand the world as inherently unpredictable, and which break down nature–society distinctions. The perspectives of Trinidad's hunters and Guinea's farmers are examples – but many others can be found worldwide (e.g. Descola and Palsson 1996, Croll and Parkin 1992). Indeed the history of environmental knowledge is littered with non-equilibrial perspectives challenging the particular stabilities of the day (e.g. Scoones 1996), and hailing more flexible, adaptive approaches to engaging with socialised ecologies. Viewed within a frame attentive to the co-production of science and policy this is not simply 'knowledge moving on' but the framing of 'knowing nature' within a dialectic of 'management of nature' and dissent. We have been able to explore how ideas of nature and of society are thrown up within specific forms of political engagement. When, as we shall see, attempts are made within institutions of science and policy to engage with 'local perspectives' or to incorporate non-equilibrial views, without questioning the overall premise that nature can be managed to achieve predictable outcomes, inconsistencies arise which generate further instabilities and forms of dissent, and which widen the gulf between such forms of governance and the daily realities of many people's lives in unpredictable landscapes.

Re-considering theories of science, society and modernity

Appreciating this dialectic and the patterns structuring it adds to contemporary theorisation in the relationship between science, society and modernity. In particular, it can be taken to qualify the 'Risk Society' thesis and its subsequent elaborations by Beck (1992, 2000). He has been arguing that in late modernity the institutions of industrial society both produce and legitimate hazards that they cannot control. The scientific and bureaucratic apparatus charged with knowing and managing risk continues to operate according to ideas of predictability, which the contemporary nature of risk defy. Emerging public scrutiny, debate and dissent draw attention to ways that public institutions with inadequate procedures more legitimate than counter hazard – they are part of the problem, not part of the solution. Thus Beck identifies a mismatch between the character of hazards 'manufactured' by late modernity, and the prevalent apparatus of science and policy, which he terms 'relations of definition': the legal, epistemological and cultural power matrix in which risk politics is conducted (Beck 2000: 224).

Several qualifications have been made to this thesis. First, dissent and lack of trust may not be so new; they are not uniquely a feature of late industrial modernity in the west (Latour 1993; Lash 1996). Experiences and public critique of science and of risk-framing, as part of the legitimation of powerful institutions, dates back to early colonial times. They are currently thriving in places and around issues very far from the European hi-tech which dominates Beck's work. Yet this makes reflections on the relationship between science and policy, and the generation of risk and of public dissent, even more, and more widely, pertinent. Second, Beck's work can overstate the novelty of the risks faced by late industrial society, and the incapacity of relations of definition to recognise them. Risks and hazards have long been experienced in the constant interplay of ecological processes, capricious markets, government politics and international engagements – and have long been inadequately appreciated by the sciences informing management. Third, the world is too connected to characterise 'late industrial society' as specific to certain geographical locales.

Relations of definition and responses to them are quintessentially locked into global scientific and policy fields of which African and Caribbean scientific and policy institutions are a part.

Fourth, our ethnography supports the view that public responses are rooted in diverse and located lay knowledges, perceptions and cultural understandings of environmental issues and risks; a dimension little attended to by Beck (who at times even denies such knowledges in his portrayal of a universal 'world risk society'), but which his critics have theorised in varied ways (e.g. Wynne 1996; Lash *et al*. 1996; Caplan 2000). A key dimension is how both lay and official expressions of risk are shaped by experience – or indeed as Douglas argues, by culture imbricated in social structure (Douglas 1992; Lash 2000).

Fifth, the risk society thesis barely problematises the availability or otherwise of fora for the expression of public critique and dissent. Assumptions are made about the capacity for new forms and institutions of public engagement to emerge and have influence. This focus largely precludes attention to forms of public reflexivity, critique and alternative lived experiences which do not find such expression. Here, Beck perhaps mistakes apparent silence for acquiescence, and treats the emergence of critique as reflecting the emergence of risk rather than the emergence of voice. Arguably, it is this slippage (more than the eurocentrism which critics have levelled at the thesis) which allows Beck to restrict 'risk society' to late industrial contexts.

These critiques only show, however, the broader pertinence of the attention Beck gives to the problematic nature of contemporary 'relations of definition' concerning environmental problematics. This pertinence applies not just to issues of risk, but to the range of social and environmental problematics thrown up by science and policy. The broader concerns raised by the risk society thesis are thus relevant to colonial and post-colonial contexts, and to any contemporary setting influenced by the reach of globalising science and policy practices. How diverse knowledges come to interact, and how and to what extent public critique of the scientific and policy practices of powerful instututions comes to be expressed, must remain as questions for ethnographic and comparative investigation of the kind we have attempted here.

Our purpose in drawing on works in the risk society tradition, and in arguing for this expansion in the arenas of inquiry to which these debates are applied is also driven by related practical concerns: with the inadequate consideration given to the forms of mediation which have been outlined as ways forward. Risk society debates explicitly link theory and practice, exploring potential institutional and analytical transformations needed to move from the impossibility and pseudo-security of expert calculation to mediation (Adam *et al*. 2000). Such a shift is required, it is argued, where issues are pervaded by complexity, uncertainty and multiple, partial perspectives. Much literature considers this shift in relation to hi-tech developments around biotechnology, nuclear power and so on (e.g. Wynne 1992). As we have argued, similar parameters of uncertainty also characterise the world of tropical forests, as non-equilibrial ecological, socio-political and economic processes interact, and as people understand these from fundamentally different perspectives. What is suggested is the provision of channels for public engagement in scientific and policy processes through various forms of participation and what have come to be termed deliberative and inclusionary processes, ranging from stakeholder involvement in planning to citizen's juries, consensus conferences and others.[1] This chimes with longer established traditions of participation and participatory learning and action in development praxis (e.g. Chambers 1997; Holland 1998).

Whereas risk society analytics take one to a position where new processes and forms of institution are suggested, an analytics of science and policy can extend further. It can help address the subsequent questions which Beck himself acknowledges as programmatic: asking how the democratisation of decision making and discussions about it are themselves constrained by 'the epistemological and legal systems within which they are conducted' – and moreover at a transnational and potentially global level (Beck 2000: 227). In this, it can also engage productively with critical debates about power and participation in development (e.g. Nelson and Wright 1995; Cornwall 2001; Cornwall and Gaventa 2001). What has become clear in our case is how the internationalisation of environmental governance, in articulation with both national social relations and practices of science and with mass media and education, shape the framings of all scientific and policy processes, mediative or otherwise. This means that far from being a panacea, mediative processes have, paradoxically, sometimes extended the influence of the existing analytics and managerial forms of powerful institutions. Our ethnography reveals structural reasons why this sometimes occurs. This also means that 'successful' public challenges and advocacy of alternative analytics and governance forms cannot occur through confined local events, but must engage critically with these broader national and international framings and processes. Our ethnography also reveals cases of this. Without such broader reflection on scientific and policy processes the praxis programme of the risk society thesis and related contemporary debates may prove self-defeating, part of the problem rather than part of the solution. In the rest of this conclusion, we review some key dimensions of these processes from this book's examples, but which also bear broader relevance for envisaging alternative social relations of science in other domains.

Science and the governance of tropical forests

The cases of biodiversity and timber production have exemplified the configuration of science in relation to diverse attempts to govern forests, their resources, and the people with interests in them. Scientific practices and their social relations are deeply implicated in the progress of intensified forest governance in general, and in the particular forms it takes. In this context, apparent processes of 'localisation' of forest governance frequently become means to pursue goals defined nationally or globally, and to further internationalised approaches. New market-based mechanisms, decentralised and community-based approaches, and research and experiments in projects and programmes can all – in practices of implementation – imply more intense and centralised management of forests in conformity with internationally-standardised objectives.

That market-based mechanisms can, in practice, involve greater state and international regulation is exemplified in 'sustainable forest management'. Certification and marketing of sustainably-produced forest products, and conformity to international marketing standards, requires detailed forest management plans. In this, existing imperatives to control and manage forests associated with national forest bureaucracies are reinforced both by the weight of international debate and pressure for 'management' in general, and by pressure for management in particular ways to harmonise with internationally-agreed principles. Such management plans are only a small part of broader efforts to monitor and authenticate sustainability. This involves new research programmes, technologies and systems, such as satellite and computer-based systems to track forest products. It encompasses social and economic criteria, and calls up a gaze of surveillance, albeit in the guise of indigenous rights, community relations and worker's livelihoods. In this, 'market-led' stewardship of forests is orchestrating a much broader surveillance of the rural world.

That apparent moves towards decentralised forestry can in practice become moves towards more centralised management is exemplified in 'community forestry'. As in Guinea, where people have lived with and used forests relatively autonomously from the state, or in circumstances of weak or ineffective state control, moves to create 'village forests' with management plans imply (and are perceived as) extensions and strengthenings of state bureaucracy. Ribot (2001), who makes this point, contextualises this extension in the deeper genealogy of policies towards political and administrative decentralisation, and attempts at community-based development. As he argues, these bear strong similarities and connections with colonial policies of Indirect Rule. These were driven largely by agendas of national integration and rural control. More generally, anthropologies of development show how seemingly a-political development practices extend state bureaucracy into rural areas (e.g. Ferguson 1990).

At the same time, locally-based, community forestry can in practice become vehicles for the vortex of international tropical forest governance. International organisations and deliberations advocate decentralisation and forest co-management, within which 'local' experiences come to intersect with and be categorised in relation to the global in particular ways, as vehicles for common 'lessons', and means to achieve globally-defined forest conservation and management goals. In this, non-conforming aspects of the ways people live with located forest landscapes are obscured. As the examples illustrate, and as reviews in Africa more broadly note, limits are placed on community autonomy: 'permits are required all over Africa once a villager wants to make commercial use of forest products' (Dubois and Lowore 2000). Kerkhof's (2000) point that 'in France barely 1% of the French forest estate has a management plan, which does not mean that the remaining 99% are "not managed"' eloquently evokes the contradiction. Rural people and their ecological relationships in tropical countries apparently need formal 'management' in a way that the French do not. This policy 'need' has generated a large social science literature on the 'design principles' which should inform 'effective' local institutions for natural resource management (e.g. Ostrom 1990). In this way, managerialist traditions have been influencing the representation of society (and hence administration of it) in social science; representations which can then feed through to shape society in their image through the administrative practices of committee formation, management plans and so on.

The science underlying community-based approaches is conducted at least partly in engagement with users in those localities, yet the cases illustrate how the practices and processes of science and policy inflect the terms of this engagement. Whether local resource users have alternative framings may not be asked, or the implications of these may not come to the fore. In these circumstances, decentralisation can come to be the mirror-twin of internationalisation. A focus on the linkages between science and policy thus helps explain a paradox: that while those involved in such initiatives frequently present them as local innovations, they appear to be springing up over the same time period across the world and taking a remarkably similar form.

Discourses of innovation characterise much policy implementation and many project activities. How this blurs the boundaries with 'research' has been exemplified frequently in the Guinea and Trinidad cases, whether in community forestry, biodiversity conservation or national parks. 'Experimentality' has liberating potentials, implying an eschewing of blueprint plans in favour of learning processes which can engage with local users' perspectives as well as with nature's unpredictable agency. When projects are cast as experimental (as 'pilot', and even as 'laboratories'), project staff become as much 'scientists' and research managers as administrators, pursuing research questions framed by project goals. Neo-liberal contexts encourage experimentality, creating entrepreneurial economies in which contractualised NGOs, donor-funded projects and researchers compete for funds. The international vortex also encourages them: experimental 'findings' can be written up and publicised through international networks, where they contribute to the accumulation of 'lessons learned' and to the 'cutting-edge', globally-relevant reputations of those who designed them.

Nevertheless casting project activity as experimental can also have a range of depoliticising effects. It can mask the political nature of project interventions by casting them as scientific, experimental and temporary. It is largely confined to projects with their artificial, limited and hence non-threatening character towards broader political structures, distancing projects from the state, as well as from international political relations. It also constructs forest users themselves as continual experimental subjects, deferring potential critique and learning into the next phase of trial, and deferring the production of knowledge so that it cannot be so firmly contested. For research and learning to open up productive debate about forest governance approaches, it needs to be expanded beyond technical project remits and pre-defined forest-managerial goals. It could also be expanded to incorporate reflection – by both project staff and citizens – on the broader scientific, policy and political processes which shape governance.

Tropical forest management continually confronts limits. Some arise because first, as the analyses of Guinea and Trinidad have shown, internationally or nationally-legitimated plans rarely work out as such on the ground and in particular settings. Instead they come to interlock with the diverse concerns, strategies and practices of the people and institutions they implicate, with a host of unintended consequences (cf. Long and Long 1992). Second, management runs up against uncertain social and ecological realities: the path-dependent, unpredictable ecological dynamics of tropical forest environments with their varied and lagged responses to disturbance of climate, species availability, and so on, and the equally unpredictable dynamics of forest use, interlocked with shifting socio-political relationships and market forces. Where field-level workers are faced with such contradictions between plans and realities, they have sometimes responded through innovative practices: adapting timber management to cope with fire events in Trinidad's Mora forests, for example, or adjusting school teaching to reflect the realities of local fire ecology in Guinea. Indeed the creativity and agency of such field-level bureaucrats in scientific and policy processes is a theme emergent across all the cases. To influence forest governance, however, these forms of adaptation need to be better recognised by national and international institutions. Otherwise there is a danger that such adaptations – by enabling existing management systems to continue – rescue the viability of and hence reinforce established approaches based on ideas of stability and predictability. More fundamental questions about whether management is pursuing illusory goals based on untenable principles are avoided, as are questions about how approaches and institutions could be reconfigured to embrace the flexibility to ride uncertainties.

That the globalised world of contemporary science and policy frequently operates in highly self-referential ways is amply illustrated by 'Tropical Forest International', with its mass of international networks debating forest issues. Within this, many natural and social scientists emphasise local specificities, and ecological and social dynamics. Equally, many international organisations and staff are at pains to incorporate the perspectives of land users, especially 'the poor', and 'the marginalised', and the perspectives of poorer governments. These emphases, their institutionalised acceptance at the highest levels of international debate, and the fact that virtually all donor funding for tropical forest initiatives requires them, open up important opportunities for forms of forest governance that are responsive to the knowledges and concerns of local users. Yet these commitments also sit alongside emphasis on strengthened and internationally-harmonised management systems to ensure forest sustainability, with its heroic and a-political assumptions about capacities to manage and abilities to regulate. They also sit in some contradiction with procedures in international deliberation, where biases embedded in attendance, agenda-setting, definitions and consensus building processes tend towards conformity to an international order of social and moral valuation of forest. At least to date, there are few procedures in these which allow perspectives from local settings to feed upwards into and shape terms of debate; procedures which would require greater reflexivity and inclusiveness amongst international institutions and networks. At the same time, articulation with national scientific and policy processes and social relations of science means that the international order sometimes contributes to processes which undermine its stated values even in promoting them – in ways that are beyond the influence of any individual or organisation.

Science, policy and social objectification

It is easy to be cynical about the capacity of international deliberations and agreements to have any serious direct effect. Yet here we have traced the broader, more indirect ways in which they shape epistemic communities and coalitions around the ideas they embody. In this sense the institutional aspects of these agreements are only a small part of a much more extensive field of transformation. In the field of environment, international deliberations in articulation with national scientific and policy communities alter the questions that are posed about the environment, and influence the social categories through which it is understood, serving to naturalise and stabilise those social categories within readings of nature and livings of a landscape.

Those who argue that 'environmental policy is about politics, not science', or that 'scientific research is divorced from the realities of policy-making' – as some of our interviewees did, echoing popular views – overlook these ways that the social and ecological categories and logics deployed in political debate are themselves shaped by and shape scientific inquiry. In this vein, studies of the public understanding of science have tended to focus on how publics think about the contents and methods of 'science' and its forms of institutionalisation, patronage and control (Wynne 1992). They can overlook how the practices of science and its mediation with wider society contribute to the production of social and natural categories in which people frame any such reflection. We have used the metaphor of a vortex to capture this alignment of a broader field, bringing even those who are hardly involved and barely sense the operation of the institutions at its centre into the patterns of its circulation. In this sense of configuring cultural categories framed in relation to globalised images, whether in conformity or opposition, science is central to cultural globalisation.

Our environmental cases illustrate the broader point that scientific and policy processes create and sustain social categories and forms of objectification, or labels (cf. Wood 1985). Both in Guinea and in Trinidad, scientific and policy arguments stereotype people in relation to environmental behaviour. Some categories carry strongly negative connotations, associated with 'problematic' environmental behaviour, such as the 'squatter', 'poacher' or 'drug cultivator' of Trinidad, or the 'charcoal-maker', 'shifting cultivator', or 'commercial hunter/poacher' of Guinea. These are contrasted with positive social categories which people claim or find assumed upon them, such as the 'traditional hunter', the 'indigenous person', the 'organised community' or the more distinctly modern 'environmentally literate citizen'. Such caricatures play into elaboration and enaction of policy processes, shaping subjectivities and desires, and opportunities for agency. In so doing they also shape and sharpen social fault lines which have a far wider bearing on politics and governance.

The ways in which ideas of ethnicity have been constructed and reproduced in relation to the environment exemplify such seepage of social objectification between the environmental policy domain and wider society. In Guinea environmental debate has long been ethnicised, with colonial and post-colonial administrations distinguishing between 'forest people' (Kissia, Loma and Guerze) with cultural proclivities towards forest conservation, and 'savanna people' (of Mandinka origin) responsible for supposed southwards savannisation (e.g. Adam 1948). Kissia sometimes draw actively on such ethnicised stereotypes in constructing their capacities for local forest management. As we have described elsewhere, such stereotypes have also been co-opted and reinforced in contemporary ethnic politics as 'forest people' unite, and find unity in the idea of forest, and 'savanna people' draw on savanna as a metaphor of social and political openness and clarity (Fairhead and Leach 1996). In Trinidad, long-embedded scientific and policy stereotypes of 'roving African squatters' as compared with 'diligent Indian farmers' have inter-animated with other social and political processes constructing ethnicity throughout the twentieth century. In the last few years, these labels have been joined by those linking 'surviving' Amerindian identity with ecological-friendliness. Emergent groups claiming Carib ancestry, for example, now claim 'green' knowledge and nature-harmonious lifestyles as among their defining social features (as well as a means to place their cultural artefacts in an ecotourism marketing niche) (Forte 2000). Likewise, novel performances of Hindu river festivals explicitly forge connections between cultural/religious identity, 'ancient attitudes and solutions to a modern environmental crisis'.[2] Such claims about cultural characteristics can be, and are, used creatively by local groups in both Guinea and Trinidad when they jostle for recognition and resources from national and international agencies. In this, scientific and policy processes also play significantly and more broadly into the (re) surgences of performative cultural particularisms and local identity politics that have been identified as associated with globalisation (Appadurai 1996).

The objectification of ethnicity through environmental stereotypes also exemplifies how local and national processes of objectification interplay with international ones. In drawing environmental imagery into their repertoire of social features, local groups forge alliances with other 'indigenous peoples' regionally and worldwide, and with international organisations and networks promoting them. The construction and reproduction of globally-recognised, environmentally-friendly categories of 'indigenous people' in international debate may be a well-known case in point. The 'traditional West African hunter' appears to be emerging as a regional stereotype with similar international salience (Leach 2000). Many 'negative' labels also recur in international discussions, whether the 'slash-and-burn farmer' or the unregulated hunter-poacher. In turn, the global salience of such stereotypes contributes to their adoption in environmentally-focused mass media and education – much of which, as we saw in the last chapter, is produced itself through the intersecting influences of national, donor and international scientific and policy organisations. Environmental communication through media and education does not just reproduce social stereotypes, but also amplifies them: the institutional practices, narrative styles and visual images in media, education and the popular culture they inform frequently make the social categorisations emerging from the scientific and policy field appear larger than life. This is as true in West Africa where media and education are so often directed to reforming the perpetrators of rural environmental problems, as in Trinidad where it more frequently creates environmental literacy among urban based and other populations less directly dependent on forests – but who should know about the squatters, poachers and timber merchants destroying them. These same features simultaneously make media a powerful means by which certain local groups project desired self-images – with Guinean hunters' highly effective use of rural radio as a case in point.

Social categories (re)produced through scientific and policy debate and entrenched in wider society through media come, in turn, to influence its conduct. Those eulogised or stigmatised come to occupy or be assigned certain privileged or marginalised positions in scientific and policy processes. 'Indigenous people', for instance, have acquired a privileged status as virtually the only forest users who can participate 'directly' in the international Convention on Biodiversity meetings (even though this participation is mediated by international NGOs). At the other extreme, 'squatters' in Trinidad – stereotyped in effect as 'non-citizens' in terms of environmental debate – have been conspicuous for their absence in national parks planning and orchestrated policy critique alike. Trinidad's hunters have achieved recognition for their citizen science partly by organising and distancing themselves assiduously from being 'poachers'. This is not to say that people categorised or stigmatised in one policy domain cannot escape such categorisation and find voice in others. Squatters may be silenced in Trinidad's environmental debates but have achieved vocality, recognition and political status around housing, for instance. At times, then, those stigmatised can escape critique or find routes to influence policy process by taking up other subject-positions, and engaging in alternative forms of alliance.

Science, 'participation' and public engagement

Trinidad and Guinea furnish numerous examples of institutionalised attempts to introduce public participation in environmental research, policy and planning processes. These are illustrative of some (though by no means all) of the range considered in the growing literature on participatory, deliberative and inclusionary processes in science and policy. Yet as has become apparent, such attempts are shaped by – become part of – the interplay of scientific and policy processes with wider fields of social categorisation. Science and policy contribute to social stigmatisation and eulogisation in 'participatory' public consultation, just as in 'top-down' planning, influencing the inclusivity and effects of participatory processes.

Our ethnography reveals, for instance, how so-called participatory processes have sometimes excluded the stigmatised or framed the terms of discussion to limit the expression of their perspectives and close off inquiry into broader agendas they might have. Thus press-advertised public consultation meetings in Trinidad concerning biodiversity and conservation issues have tended to include ministries and departments, parastatal research institutions, university staff, conservation and scientific NGOS, CBOs involved in conservation, some commercial organisations, and members of the international community. Absent have been forest users such as farmers, hunters, sawmillers and woodworkers – and 'squatters'. In West Africa, Conservation International's biodiversity priority-setting workshop was framed in such a way that national representatives could voice neither their own nor land user's concerns in an authoritative way. In Guinea, 'community' meetings around national park planning and the creation of biodiversity action plans have notably included 'traditional' hunters and herbalists, but not charcoal-makers and bush-meat sellers. Interested and knowledgeable parties find themselves excluded or silenced in expressing certain aspects of their identities and the knowledge, political and material interests associated with them. Apparent consensus in such circumstances can conceal much conflict.

Different levels of livelihood dependence on forests have affected the scale and manner of inclusion or marginalisation of forest users from 'participatory' scientific and policy debates. In Trinidad, the relatively small number of people directly dependent on forests for their livelihoods – and the dominance of community-based conservation agendas by outward and urban-looking eco-tourism issues – seems to have contributed to the marginalisation of rural forest users from research and policy debates. In Guinea, by contrast, the large numbers of small farmers using forest resources have been a key subject of research, and state and donor agencies are obliged to involve them. However, in practice, such 'invited' participation has frequently come to mean invitation to comply with pre-set environment and development objectives – echoing a pattern prevalent in much so-called participatory development (Cornwall 2001) – and within frames of debate which obscure their own perspectives and interactions with ecology. The tendency is thus always present for 'technologies of participation' to delegitimise and stigmatise the very social groups which, perhaps, most need to be included; a tendency exacerbated when agendas are set and meetings hosted by authoritative scientific and policy institutions. To overcome this would require taking consultation a vital stage further back, into the very concepts and ideas informing policy, and the conduct of the science on which these are based.

In Trinidad, several attempts have been made to conduct environmental research within different social relations. For example the Wildlife Section has begun working with hunters to understand their knowledge and perspectives on wildlife population dynamics, and employing them as honorary game wardens. The instigator of this work, from a new position in the United Nations Development Programme, has also been supporting community members to conduct their own research into the economics of eco-tourism, with the aim of showing that visitors would pay more for turtle watching than they currently do, in order to lobby the Forestry Division to permit higher fees. In this, 'citizen research' is being seen as a direct route into citizen engagement in policy dialogue. This example is seen as a pilot or test for a broader approach to community research and policy dialogue which could be developed more widely,[3] and which carries much potential for transforming processes in the co-production of science and policy. In a different vein, the woodworkers in the south-east have been able to draw on ourselves and another social science researcher (Guenter 1998) to help articulate their rather different perspectives on the ecology and socio-politics of Mora forest, to articulate a user-based critique of the current operation of the Forestry Division's periodic block system, and to forward a rather different vision for the timber sector. That, in our case, it was conservancy staff in the Forestry Division who kindly established our contacts with the woodworkers indicates their support of broader patterns of inclusion, even if this is not shared further up the Forestry hierarchy. Further 'experiments' involve taking science into arenas for public debate. Again, in Trinidad, the Environmental Management Authority has made the Environmental Court a cornerstone of the development of environmental regulation. A key aim is to bring scientific debate out of the university, into a public field where contest is feasible.[4] Whilst remaining expert driven, this does provide a very different forum for the adjudication of environmental issues from the usual mode of public environmental consultation in Trinidad, within an open court forum in which commoners will also sit.

These forms of public engagement within the institutions of science and policy in Trinidad contrast with engagement, including contestation, outside them. The case material provides examples ranging from citizen science, to uses of the media to express and publicise dissent, to political and legal action to derail policies. Citizen science involves attempts to contest policy agendas through engaging in critique of the scientific principles and methods underlying them, as well as forwarding alternative agendas linked to alternative scientific practices (see Fischer 2000; Irwin 1995). We saw both aspects in the case of hunters in Trinidad, who have been conducting research to contest debates over national parks, and to forward alternative conservation visions centred on biodiversity in lived-in-landscapes.

Within Guinea, what appears is a more radical incommensurability between scientific and policy institutions and villagers concerning environmental problematics and analysis, and indeed epistemology (what constitutes knowledge and what it is for). Forms of knowledge developed in experiential interaction with local landscapes, and embedded in their socio-cultural milieux and forms of local political authority, appear strong and vibrant, but relatively autonomous from the sciences of state, university and donor institutions. Rural publics seem more frequently to distrust scientific and policy institutions, interpreting their activities more as political or extractive than as environmental (see also Fairhead and Leach 1996, 2000). Direct engagement of 'indigenous knowledge' in science and policy has tended to involve the incorporation of particular 'stocks' of knowledge – or interpretations of the skills and status of their bearers – into alignment with existing policy directions, to help achieve their aims. This is the case, for example, for the herbal medicinal knowledge now brought into biodiversity conservation, and the versions of traditional hunting lore brought into national parks protection. As has been observed elsewhere, local knowledge is repackaged in terms of foreign science, losing local legitimacy in the process (e.g Thrupp 1985; Fairhead 1992; Agrawal 1995). The social and political relations of knowledge in such engagements are less about contest than co-optation and reinterpretation to fit expert-scientific agendas.

Meanwhile, local knowledges underlie radically different agendas, and positive means of living and working with socialised landscapes, which people continue to pursue as far as they can in their daily lives.

Several contrasts between Guinea and Trinidad can help comprehend different forms of public engagement (or non-engagement) with science and policy. Different formal education histories and literacy levels undoubtedly have an influence, as does Trinidad's longer-embedded tradition of community-based activity as a vehicle for the organisation of citizen-scientific perspectives. More specifically, the way social relations of science have developed in Guinea through colonial and post-colonial practices and agendas is such as to produce a high degree of disengagement between expert institutions and local perspectives. These contrasting cases highlight, then, how citizen science implies a certain engagement with, and dominant role for, the science of expert institutions. They also highlight that there are circumstances where people maintain entirely different positionalities – 'uncaptured' by these scientific and policy configurations – while nevertheless having to deal with the material effects of policy discourses.

Field-level bureaucrats – whether in government or NGOs – occupy ambiguous positions in their engagement with scientific and policy processes. In Guinea, for example, they – like rural schoolteachers – face contradictions between the scientific and policy agendas they are trained and mandated to promote, and the perspectives of resource users. At times resource users themselves (as farmers, members of hunters' associations, or herbalists), they are in certain respects brokers between farmers' and hunters' knowledges and the perspectives of state and international institutions. Many individual field-workers are highly interested in and dedicated to such roles. At times they are very effective, as for example in the Trinidad Wildlife Section's experiments in working with community based organisations, and in supporting new social relations of research, which emerged in part from field-worker initiative. However, our ethnography also highlights how particular structural openings may be important to enable such field-worker agency to be effective. In the case noted, field-workers were supported by a charismatic leader at a time of considerable autonomy from the broader forest administration. In the contrasting case of timber production, involving Trinidad's rigidly hierarchical Forest Department, lower-level forest staff are expected to take directives from above, placing greater limits on the scope of field-workers to pursue new styles of research and action.

Mass media also provide a potential vehicle for contestation of the perspectives of powerful institutions, and for forwarding alternative agendas. In Trinidad and Guinea, contemporary media and educational practices are claimed to be highly 'participatory', and a number of examples have suggested that media can be important not just for the amplification and reinforcement of current scientific and policy perspectives, but for critique, commentary and public reflection. Nevertheless, our ethnography also reveals ways in which such contestation is contained. In Trinidad, the mutual framing of values in scientific and media inquiry is clearly exposed in the distanciated vision of environmental literacy and aesthetics, divorcing nature from economy. Contestation of this broader agenda (as opposed to debate within it) is easily made to look foolish, immoral or ignorant; or at best iconoclastic and certainly marginal. In Guinea, the example of charcoal-makers illustrates how those who dissent more fundamentally are made to look foolish, and their critiques contained. To move beyond these constraints, media strategies could be directed to making explicit the evidence, values, and uncertainties underlying particular scientific and policy positions, enhancing and empowering public capacity to critique and engage in scientific and policy debate.

A further arena for public contestation of powerful perspectives outside the invited participation of state and donor agencies has involved political and legal action. In the multi-party democracies of both countries, voting behaviour – or the threat of it to politicians – offers a potentially important route to de-rail unpopular policies. This has been a significant influence on the policy process in Trinidad, where the threat of public dissent through political action has in effect put a brake on national parks development. This case exemplifies how, if social biases in scientific and policy process are not reflected in wider political structure, policies can emerge on paper which are politically impossible to ratify or implement. Indeed, certain politicians in Trinidad see the country's finely-balanced dual-party system as contributing to a more generalised political populism, in which repressive or coercive environmental measures have little place. In Guinea, by contrast, the more stably-entrenched regional-ethnic character of party politics, and the sense of distance for most rural dwellers from a 'Politics' that happens in Conakry – lessens the significance of such routes to dissent.

Citizens' platforms for expression of interests, demands and perspectives on policy on their own terms might thus be built in diverse ways. But where there is no available platform or coalition for expression, publics also find ways to 'contest' science and policy. These have been particularly apparent in Guinea. They include calculated acceptance of and acquiescence to elements of policy in exchange for other benefits, as where villagers agree to create forestry groups with NGOs linked to school-building programmes. They also include everyday forms of resistance by villagers whose knowledge and values are excluded or incommensurable with those in science and policy, and perhaps – at times – political sympathy with aspects of the armed insurgency that has beset the region.

To draw out the comparison, then, in Trinidad, vibrant local and national NGOs, citizens' organisations and national media are used as forums for public mobilisation, debate and for citizen science around environmental issues, amongst a highly literate population. Public dissent and its threat have at times put a brake on policy development, while alliances between certain publics, state and international interests have successfully forwarded alternatives. In some respects, contemporary Trinidad exhibits patterns of civic engagement around science and policy which correspond with those identified for Europe and North America by many researchers working on science and society there. In Guinea, by contrast, different educational, cultural and political histories have shaped less overt forms of public engagement which have had less impact on policy processes, yet socio-culturally and politically-embedded knowledge and ways of life have continued more autonomously. The inter-country differences should not, however, be allowed to obscure similarities in the experiences of certain people in each, in contexts where 'participation' – whether inside or outside managed processes – has rarely overcome pervasive forms of social objectification. Many poorer land users in Trinidad – such as certain 'squatters' who have found it hard to organise, mobilise, and find channels of expression – remain as marginalised in scientific and policy debates as the larger majority of land users in Guinea. Put another way, these country cases illustrate that in a globalising world common social experiences of science and policy may link people across distant geographical divides.

Articulating international, national and local science and policy

In this era of international environmental regimes, political differences are increasingly played out through scientific analysis and monitoring, stimulating emergent international competition over analytical capability and authority. Scientific debates and political claims linked to them are played out in a globalised field of trans-political and epistemic communities. In this respect, this book shows why studies of science and society need to consider questions of globalisation – and likewise, that work on globalisation needs to address science, overcoming a significant lacuna in studies of globalisation to date.

Our case studies show how scientific practices shape relations between national institutions, whether sections of government, NGOs or research institutions. Science linked to policy shapes fractures and alliances that cross-cut any singular notion of 'the state'. In Trinidad, for example, particular sciences of production forestry have been central to the institutional identity, personal subjectivities, and territorial and budgetary claims of the Forestry Division. Different, conservation-biology and participation-led premises and practices have forged the institutional identity of the Wildlife Section with which it is in tension. This scientific dimension is rarely heeded in most political science or ethnographic works which 'deconstruct' the state to explore the structuring and daily practices of inter-departmental rivalries.

Importantly, however, the shaping of national institutional relations through scientific practices increasingly interlocks with – and is amplified by – scientific and policy processes operating transnationally. This amplification is shaped by the particular political-economies concerned, including – in our case studies – the balance of institutional revenue from timber, national budgets and donor financing, and the procedures of expenditure. For example, international institutions taking decentralised, community-based approaches in Trinidad build coalitions with the Wildlife Section, with its traditions in community-based conservation, while those involved in sustainable natural forest management build coalitions with the Forestry Division. Central state subsidisation has shaped 'scientific forestry', and the Forestry Division's mandate to control forest as a national asset. The Wildlife Section, starved of state funds, competes for funds from international sources, shaping other practices. In Guinea, we have seen how a case of forest reserve management has involved one donor (a bank seeking capital returns) in support of timber reserve management and conservation, and another (a development donor) in support of participatory resource management in the reserve's buffer zone. Particular scientific problematics and perspectives are associated with particular funding flows and the allocation of particular personnel. In this way, science and policy co-produced at the nexus of international and national institutions plays into schisms and 'turf battles' between national institutions. The amplification of these schisms, and the amplification of polarities in research agendas and styles, feed each other.

As international research and policy institutions interact with particular national and local research traditions, the scientific and policy field is transformed into complex processes of global-local connection (cf. Robertson 1992; Appadurai 1996). In Guinea, for example, international concerns with biodiversity conservation have revitalised and funded older research traditions of ethno-botanical research into plant-based medicines, yet the meanings of existing practices have been radically transformed. In Trinidad, international biodiversity concerns have stimulated interest in integrating research traditions around natural history, species-focused university studies and botanical work in the national herbarium, in a nascent biodiversity umbrella institution. Again, older research practices are revitalised but also transformed, hitched to meanings cast within a globalised, universal, rather than a national or local frame.

Funding from international sources is only one dimension of privilege to particular research traditions, and not necessarily the most significant. Indeed the very different levels of foreign aid dependence for supporting national research and development found in Guinea and Trinidad appears to make less difference to the emerging research agendas than one might expect. Research structures in each country are being transformed to become more 'relevant', and in each case, relevance is defined largely by international problem-framings, despite Trinidad's relatively low, and Guinea's relatively high, levels of dependency for research funding on international organisations. University staff in Guinea who do not pursue, through research, their anecdotal, experiential, transitory interests in old settlement sites within national parks, for example, are not just constrained by a lack of funding. They are also constrained by the perceived absence of a wider epistemic community – among their in-country peers, foreign visitors, and the international networks whose publications they receive – who might see this as important, reputable research, and research with policy relevance.

Research institutions in poorer countries are widely perceived as hampered in the international world of knowledge generation and transmission, forced to respond to the agendas of richer nations by structural constraints such as funding and the organisation of international negotiating forums. Yet as our analysis of the vortex of 'Tropical Forest International' illustrates, the structures which reproduce global scientific inequalities are epistemic as well as political-economic. Moreover they are structures which are reproduced through scientific and policy practices extending across global, national and local sites, when they enrol the latter in reproducing internationally-harmonised perspectives. Localised moves towards mediation and public engagement can become part of such multi-sited scientific and policy practices, ventriloquising internationally-configured environmental knowledge and power; becoming part of the problem, rather than part of the solution. But while making explicit these articulations complicates any argument that de-centred, global 'Empires' (Hardt and Negri 2001), scientific or otherwise, can be straightforwardly challenged through located social movements, it is also a critical basis for configuring alternatives. Our cases have exemplified this, showing forest users creatively forging and using multi-sited processes and networks in forwarding their perspectives, and in critiquing powerful agendas. Coupled with greater critical reflexivity in national and international processes, such instances give grounds to envisage transformed science-society relations based on broader, more open and genuinely locally-engaged debate about scientific and governance futures.

Notes

1. There is a large and rapidly growing literature on these approaches, addressing both contexts and methods. This is not the place for a review, but for some overviews by others see, for example, Bloomfield *et al.* 1998; Button and Mattson 1999; Fischer 2000; Healey 1997; Holmes and Scoones 2001; Munton 2002.

2. 'Hindu river festival celebrates environment', Natasha Coker, *Express*, 23 June 1999.
3. Interview, Manager of GEF Small Grants Programme, UNDP offices, Port of Spain, 25 May 1999. In other Trinidadian examples, the community-based organisation Nature Seekers Inc. are conducting their own research (linked with the Institute of Marine Affairs, and other universities) on turtle ecology which may challenge earlier ideas on which present turtle protection legislation is based.
4. Interview, Head of Environmental Management Authority, St Augustine, 7 May 1999.

References

Abrahams, R., 1983, *The Man of Words in the West Indies: Performance and the Emergence of Creole Culture*. Baltimore: Johns Hopkins Press.

Adam, B., U. Beck and J. Van Loon, 2000, *The Risk Society and Beyond: Critical Issues for Social Theory*. London, Thousand Oaks and New Delhi: Sage Publications.

Adam, J.G., 1948, 'Les reliques boisées et les essences des savanes dans la zone préforestière en Guinée francaise', *Bulletin de la Société Botanique Française* 98: 22–26.

1968, 'Flore et végétation de la lisière de la forêt dense en Guinée', *Bulletin d'IFAN Série* A 30(3): 920–952.

Agnew, J.A., 1982, 'Technology transfer and theories of development', *Journal of Asian and African Studies* 17: 273–292.

Agrawal, A., 1995, 'Dismantling the divide between indigenous and scientific knowledge', *Development and Change* 26: 413–439.

Ahmed, B. and S. Afroz, 1996, *The Political Economy of Food and Agriculture in the Caribbean*. Kingston: Ian Randle Publishers Ltd and London: James Currey.

Ajodha, B.A., n.d., Environmental education: Identification of environmental topics in the school curriculum. Port of Spain: Forestry Division.

Alasuutari, P., 1999, 'Introduction: Three phases of reception studies', in P. Alasuutari (eds), *Rethinking the Media Audience*, 1–21. London, Thousand Oaks and New Delhi: Sage Publications.

Amanor, K.S., 1994, *The New Frontier: Farmer Responses to Land Degradation*. London: UNRISD and Zed Books.

Anderson, D. and R. Grove, 1987, *Conservation in Africa: People, Policies and Practice*. Cambridge University Press.

Appadurai, A., 1996, *Modernity at Large: Cultural Dimensions of Globalisation*. Minneapolis: University of Minnesota Press.

Arcin, A., 1908, 'La propriété indigène et les concessions en Guinée francaise', *Actes de l'Institut Colonial de Bordeaux*, Congrès Colonial de Bordeaux, 312–331.

Ariasingam, D.L., 1999, 'Empowering the civil society to monitor the environment: education for students, awareness for the public, and functional literacy for targeted groups', *World Bank Departmental Working Paper* 16. Washington DC: World Bank.

Asquith, P.J., 1996, 'Japanese science and western hegemonies: primatologies and the limits set to questions', in L. Nader (ed) *Naked Science*, 239–258. London: Routledge.

Aubréville, A., 1949, *Climats, forêts et désertification de l'Afrique tropicale.* Société d'Edition de Géographie Maritime et Coloniale, Paris.

Bacon, P.R. and R.P. Ffrench, 1972, *The Wildlife Sanctuaries of Trinidad and Tobago.* Port of Spain: Forestry Division.

Barry, M.S., 1999, Identification, hierarchisation des pressions humaines et analyse de la durabilité des systèmes d'exploitation des ressources sur la diversité biologique terrestre et de causes principales de pressions en Haute Guinée. Report of Project GUI/97/G32/A/1G/99, Strategies Plans d'Action Diversité Biologique. Conakry: Direction Nationale de l'Environnement.

Barzetti, V. (eds), 1993, *Parks and Progress: Protected Areas and Economic Development in Latin America and the Caribbean.* Geneva: IUCN/IADB.

Bass, S., C. Hughes and W. Hawthorne, 2001, 'Forests, biodiversity and livelihoods: linking policy and practice', in I. Koziell, I. and J. Saunders, *Living Off Biodiversity: Exploring Livelihoods and Biodiversity Issues in Natural Resources Management,* 23–74. London: International Institute for Environment and Development.

Baum, G.A. and H.J. Weimer, 1992, Participation et développement socio-économique comme conditions préalables indispensables d'une implication active des populations riveraines dans la conservation de la forêt classée de Ziama. Conakry: Deutsche-Forst-Consult/ Neu-Isenburg/RFA/KfW.

Bauman, Zygmunt, 1998, *Globalization: The Human Consequences.* Cambridge: Polity Press.

Beard, J.S., 1946a, *The Natural Vegetation of Trinidad.* Oxford Forestry Memoirs 20, Oxford: Clarendon Press.

1946b, 'The Mora forest of Trinidad, British West Indies', *Journal of Ecology,* 33, 2.

Beck, U., 1992, *Risk Society: Towards a New Modernity.* London: Sage.

1995, *Ecological Politics in an Age of Risk.* Cambridge: Polity Press.

1998, *World Risk Society.* Cambridge: Polity Press.

2000, 'Risk society revisited: theory, politics and research programmes', in B. Adam *et al.* (eds), 2000, *The Risk Society and Beyond: Critical Issues for Social Theory,* 211–229. London, Thousand Oaks and New Delhi: Sage Publications.

Beinart, W., 1989, 'Introduction: the politics of colonial conservation', *Journal of Southern African Studies* 15(2): 143–162.

Bell, T.I.W., 1969, An investigation into some aspects of management in the Mora (*Mora excelsa Benth*) forest of Trinidad with special reference to the Matura Forest Reserve. PhD thesis, University of West Indies, 1969.

1971, *Management of the Trinidad Mora Forests With Special Reference to the Matura Forest Reserve.* Port of Spain: Trinidad Forestry Division/Government Printers.

Berry, E.W., 1925 in *Studies in Geology* 6, 71–161.

Bertault, J.G., B. Dupuy, and F.F. Maitre, 1993, 'Silviculture for sustainable management of the tropical moist forest', *Unasylva* 181.

Bird, P.J., 1996, *Synthesis of Findings of ODA's Review of Participatory Forest Management.* London: Overseas Development Administration.

Bledsoe, C. and K.M. Robey, 1986, 'Arabic literacy and secrecy among the Mende of Sierra Leone', *Man* 21: 202–226.

Bloomfield, D., K. Collins, C. Fry and R. Munton, 1998, 'Deliberative and inclusionary processes: their contributions to environmental governance', Paper presented at Economic and Social Research Council seminar on 'DIPs in environmental decision-making', London, 17 December 1998.

Boemer-Christiansen, S., 1996, 'The international research enterprise and global environmental change: climate change policy as a research process', in J. Vogler and M. Imber (eds), *The Environment of International Relations*, 171–196. London: Routledge.

Bonneuil, C. and M. Kleiche, 1993, *Du Jardin d'essais colonial à la station experimentale 1880–1930: Eléments pour une histoire du CIRAD*. Paris: CIRAD.

Boomert, A. 1984, 'The Arawak Indians of Trinidad and coastal Guiana, ca. 1500–1650', *Journal of Caribbean History* 19, 2, 123–188.

Botkin, D.B., 1990, *Discordant Harmonies: A New Ecology for the Twenty-first Century*. New York: Oxford University Press.

Bourdieu, P., 1977, *Outline of a Theory of Practice*. Cambridge University Press.

1990, *The Logic of Practice*. Cambridge: Polity Press.

Bourque, J.D. and R. Wilson, 1990, Rapport de l'étude d'impact écologique d'un projet amenagement forestier concernant les forêts classées de Ziama et de Diecké en République de Guinée. Conakry: IUCN.

Braithwaite, L., 1975, *Social Stratification in Trinidad*. Port of Spain: Institute of Social and Economic Research.

Brechin, S., 1997, *Planting Trees in the Developing World: A Sociology of International Organisations*. Baltimore: Johns Hopkins University Press.

Brereton, B. 1981, *A History of Modern Trinidad 1783–1962*. Oxford: Heinemann.

Brooks, R.L., 1942, 'The regeneration of Mixed Rain Forest in Trinidad', *Caribbean Forester* 2, 4, 164–173.

Brosius, P., 2002, 'Seeing natural and cultural communities: Technologies of visualisation in contemporary conservation', Paper presented at Society for Conservation Biology 16th Annual Meeting, University of Kent at Canterbury, 14–19 July 2002.

Brown, D., 1999, 'Principles and practices of forest co-management: Evidence from West-Central Africa', *European Union Tropical Forestry Paper 2*. London: Overseas Development Institute.

Brown, P., 1990, 'Popular Epidemiology: Community response to toxic waste-induced disease', in P. Conrad and R. Kern (eds), *The Sociology of Health and Illness in Critical Perspective*, 77–85. New York: St Martin's Press.

Brown, P. and E.J. Mikkelsen, 1990, *No Safe Place: Toxic Waste, Leukemia, and Community Action*. Berkeley: University of California Press.

Bryant, D., D. Nielsen and L. Tangley, 1997, *The Last Frontier Forests: Ecosystems and Economies on the Edge*. Washington DC: World Resources Institute.

Button, M. and K. Mattson, 1999, 'Deliberative democracy in practice: challenges and prospects for civic deliberation', *Polity* 31 (4): 609–637.

Callon, M., 1986, 'Some elements of a sociology of translation: domestication of the scallops and the fishermen of St Brieuc Bay', in J. Law (eds) *Power, Action and Belief: A New Sociology of Knowledge?* London: Routledge.

Callon, M., J. Law and A. Rip (eds), *Mapping the Dynamics of Science and Technology: Sociology of Science in the Real World*. Houndmills: Macmillan.

Caplan, P., (eds), 2000, *Risk Revisited*. London and Sterling, Virginia: Pluto Press.

CARICOM/FAO/ODA, 1993. Tropical Forests Action Programme: National Forestry Action Programme Trinidad and Tobago. Main Issues, Summary of Main Report, Priority Project Profiles. Port of Spain: FAO.

Carlozzi, M. 1964, 'Report on the development of parks, nature reserves and outdoor recreation areas in Trinidad and Tobago'. Unpublished report to Forestry Division, Port of Spain.

Carter, J., 1996, *Recent Approaches to Participatory Forest Resource Assessment*. Rural Development Forestry Study Guide 2. London: Overseas Development Institute. *Recent Experience in Collaborative Forest Management Approaches: A Review of Key Issues*. Washington DC: World Bank.

Castells, M., 1997, *The Information Age: Economy, Society and Culture*. Volumes I and II. Oxford: Blackwell Publishers Ltd.

CENAFOD, 1993, *La Grande Découverte: Livre de lecture*. Conakry: Centre Africain de Formation pour le Développement, for Programme Régional d'Amenagement des Bassins Versants du Haut Niger et de la Haute Guinée, Projets KISS 1 and KISS 2.

Chalmers, W.S., 1981, 'Forests', in Cooper, St G.C. and P.R. Bacon (eds.) *The Natural Resources of Trinidad and Tobago*, 78–104. London: Edward Arnold.

1990, FAO Technical Forestry Action Plan for Nine Caricom Countries. Report on Preparatory Mission. Rome: CARICOM/FAO.

Chalmers, W.S. and Faizool, S. 1992, FAO/CARICOM Tropical Forestry Action Programme: Trinidad and Tobago National Forestry Action Programme. Report of the Country Mission Team. Port of Spain: CARICOM/FAO.

Chambers, R., 1997, *Whose Reality Counts? Putting the First Last*. London: Intermediate Technology Publications.

Chandool, N., n.d., 'Environmental education programs in Trinidad and Tobago', Paper prepared for Department of Resource Recreation and Tourism, University of Idaho, USA.

Chapman, G., K. Kumar, C. Fraser and I. Gaber, 1997, *Environmentalism and the Mass Media: The North-South Divide*. London: Routledge.

Cherif, El-Hadj Amadou and L. Conde, 1998, Allah, l'homme et la nature. Kankan: Programme Regional d'Assistance Technique à la Communication et à l'Information sur la Protection de l'Environnement (PACIPE).

Chevalier, A., 1911, 'Essai d'une carte botanique forestière et pastorale de l'AOF', *Comptes Rendus de l'Academie des Sciences*, 152(6).

1928, 'Sur la dégradation des sols tropicaux causée par les feux de brousse et sur les formations végétales régressives qui en sont la conséquence', *Comptes Rendus de l'Academie de Sciences* CLXXXVIII: 84–86.

Clements, F.E., 1936, 'Nature and structure of the climax', *Journal of Ecology* 24: 253–283.

Clubbe, C. and S. Jhilmit, 1992, 'A case study of Natural Forest Management in Trinidad', unpublished paper presented to 'Wise Management of Tropical Forests', Oxford Forestry Institute, 1 March 1992.

Coleman, W., G. Skogstad and M. Atkinson, 1997, 'Paradigm shifts and policy networks: cumulative change in agriculture', *Journal of Public Policy* 16: 273–301.

Cornwall, A., 2000, *Beneficiary, Consumer, Citizen: Perspectives on Participation for Poverty Reduction*. Stockholm: SIDA.

Cornwall, A. and J. Gaventa, 2000, 'From users and choosers to makers and shapers: re-positioning participation in social policy'. *IDS Bulletin* 31(4): 50–62.

Cozzens, S.E. and T.F. Gieryn (eds), 1990, *Theories of Science in Society*. Bloomington: Indiana University Press.

Cozzens, S.E. and E.J. Woodhouse, 1995, 'Science, government and the politics of knowledge', in S. Jasanoff *et al.* (eds), *Handbook of Science and Technology Studies*, 533–553. Thousand Oaks, London and New Delhi: Sage Publications.

Croll, E. and D. Parkin (eds), 1992, *Bush Base: Forest Farm: Culture, Environment and Development*. London: Routledge.

Cropper, J., 1997, 'Regreening the foothills of the Northern Range Part 1: first assessment of the potential for implementation of a programme of revegetation of squatter and other low income communities on the hillsides of the East-West corridor in Trinidad', Unpublished report submitted to UNDP, Port of Spain.

Crush, J. (ed), *Power of Development*. London: Routledge.

DFID, 2001, *Biodiversity – A Crucial Issue for the World's Poorest*. London: Department for International Development.

DNFF, 1998, Presentation du projet BIODIV lors de l'atelier de planification du projet 'Reserve partielle de Kankan'. Conakry: Direction Nationale des Forêts et Faune.

Dahl, R., 1961, *Who Governs? Democracy and Power in an American City*. New Haven: Yale University Press.

Dapper, O., 1668, *Naukeurige beschrijvinge der Afrikaensche gewesten . . .* Amsterdam 1668.

Davies, J. and M. Richards, 1999, 'The use of economics to assess stakeholder incentives in participatory forest management: a review.' *European Union Tropical Forestry Paper* 5, EC and London: Overseas Development Institute.

D'Azevedo, W.L. 1962, 'Some historical problems in the delineation of a Central West Atlantic Region', *Annals, New York Academy of Sciences* 96, 513–538.

De Leener, P., 1995, 'La méthode MARP fait-elle 'participer' les forestiers aux dynamiques paysannes? Rapport d'un evaluation collégiale Paysans + Forestiers + Consultants dépuis sa conception jusqu'à sa réalisation', ENDA/GRAF, Dakar, CENAFOD and DNFF, Conakry.

Descola, O. and G. Palsson (eds), 1996, *Nature and Society*. London: Routledge.

Devenish, S., 1875, 'Paper on Trinidad Timber in answer to certain questions put by Her Majesty's Commissioners of Woods and Forests', in Hart, J. H., 1891, *Trinidad: Report on Forest Conservation*. London: Waterlow and Sons, 6–8.

Diallo, T.D., 1999, Etude de la diversité biologique en Guinée Forestière. Study for UNBIO. Conakry: Direction Nationale de l'Environnement.

Dopavogui, G. and M.M. Kourouma, 1993, Etude ethnobotanique des bas-fonds de la prefecture de Faranah, Memoire de fin d'études, ISAV, Faranah.

Douglas, M., 1992, *Risk and Blame: Essays in Cultural Theory*. London and New York: Routledge.

Doumbouya, M., 1974, Etude de pharmacognosique de *Cassia sieberiana* – plante utilisée en médicine populaire comme purgative. Memoire de diplome de fin d'etudes superieures, Institut Polytechnique Gamal Abdel Nasser, Conakry.

Driver, T., 2002, 'Watershed management, private property and squatters in the Northern Range, Trinidad', *IDS Bulletin* 33(1): 84–93.

Driver, T. and A. Kravatsky, 1998, 'Community institutions for natural resource management in Brasso Seco-Paria, Trinidad and Tobago', *SEDU Working Paper*. St Augustine: SEDU.

Drysek, J., 1990, *Discursive Democracy: Politics, Policy and Political Science*. Cambridge University Press.

Dubois, O. and J. Lowore, 2000, The journey towards collaborative forest management in Africa: lessons learned and some navigational aids. An overview. *Forestry
and Land Use Series* no. 15. London: International Institute for Environment and
Development.

Dubow, S., 2000, *Science and Society in Southern Africa*, Manchester University Press.

Dudley, N., J-P. Jeanreneaud and F. Sullivan, 1995, *Bad Harvest? The Timber Trade and
the Degradation of the World's Forests*. London: Earthscan.

Dupuy, B., H.-F., Maitre and I. Amsallen, 1999, Tropical forest management techniques:
a review of the sustainability of forest management practices in tropical countries.
Working paper: FAO/FRIRS/04 prepared for the World Bank Forest Policy Implementation Review and Strategy, CIRAD, FAO Forestry Policy and Planning
Division, Rome.

Eisemon, T.O. 1982, *The Science Profession in the Third World*. New York: Praeger.

Escobar, A., 1995, *Encountering Development: The Making and Unmaking of the Third
World*. Princeton University Press.

Evans-Pritchard, E.E., 1937, *Witchcraft, Oracles and Magic Among the Azande*. Oxford:
Oxford University Press.

FAO, 1998, 'Forestry Policies in the Caribbean: Volume 2: reports of 28 selected countries and territories', *FAO Forestry Paper* 137/2. Rome: Food and Agriculture
Organisation.

FAO, 1999a, 'FAO and the international forestry agenda', *Forestry Information Notes*,
Rome: Food and Agriculture Organisation.

   1999b, 'National forest programmes', *Forestry Information Notes*, Rome: Food and
Agriculture Organisation.

   1999c, 'Support to forestry research', *Forestry Information Notes*, Rome: Food and
Agriculture Organisation.

   1999d, *State of the World's Forests*, Rome: Food and Agriculture Organisation.

   1999e, Sustainable Forest Management: Issues Paper. Paper prepared for the World
Bank Group Forest Policy Implementation Review and Stategy Development:
Analytical Studies. Rome: Food and Agriculture Organisation.

FRAP, 1999, World Forest Survey: Draft programme component plan. Mimeo. Rome:
Food and Agriculture Organisation.

Fabig, H. and R. Boele, 1999, 'The changing nature of NGO activity in a globalising world: pushing the corporate responsibility movement', *IDS Bulletin* 30(3):
58–67.

Fairhead, J., 1992, 'Indigenous technical knowledge and natural resources management
in Sub-Saharan Africa: a critical review', Paper prepared for SSRC project on
African Agriculture, USA.

Fairhead, J. and M. Leach, 1994, 'Contested forests: modern conservation and historical
land use in Guinea's Ziama reserve', *African Affairs*, 93: 481–512.

   1996, *Misreading the African Landscape: Society and Ecology in a Forest-Savanna
Mosaic*. Cambridge: Cambridge University Press.

   1997, 'Webs of power and the construction of environmental policy problems: forest loss in Guinea', in R. Grillo and J. Stirrat (eds), *Discourse of Development:
Anthropological Perspectives*, 35–58. Oxford: Berg Press.

   1998, *Reframing Deforestation: Global Analyses and Local Realities – Studies in
West Africa*. London: Routledge.

2000, 'Fashioned forest pasts, occluded histories? International environmental analysis in West African locales', *Development and Change* 31(1): 35–59.

Fairhead, J., T. Geysbeek, S. Holsoe and M. Leach, 2003, African-American Exploration in West Africa: *Four Nineteenth Century Diaries*. Bloomington: Indiana University Press.

Faizool, S. and Ramnarine, R., (eds), 1992, *Some Environmental Education Bulletins*. Port of Spain: FRIM, Forestry Division.

Ferguson, J., 1994, *The Anti-Politics Machine: 'Development', Depoliticisation and Bureaucratic Power in Lesotho*. Minneapolis: University of Minnesota Press.

Ferme, M., 1992, 'Hammocks belong to men, stools to women': constructing and contesting gender domains in a Mende village (Sierra Leone, West Africa). PhD Dissertation, University of Chicago.

Fischer, F., 2000, *Citizens, Experts and the Environment: The Politics of Local Knowledge*. Durham and London: Duke University Press.

Fiske, J., 1987, *Television Culture*. London: Methuen.

Fofana, S., *et al.*, 1990, Monographies des Bassins Kan I, Kan II, Kiss II. Conakry: European Union.

FRIM, 1989, *The National Forest Resources Plan*. Forest Resource Inventory and Management section. Port of Spain: Forestry Division, Ministry of Environment and National Service.

Forest Department, 1933, *Trinidad Mora*. Port of Spain (Trinidad): Government Printing Office.

Forestry Division, 1981, *Forest Resources Policy*. Port of Spain: Forestry Division, Ministry of Environment and National Service.

1992, *Forestry Handbook*. Port of Spain: Forestry Division, Ministry of Agriculture, Land and Marine Resources.

Forte, M., 2000, 'The contemporary context of Carib 'revival' in Trinidad and Tobago: creolization, developmentalism and the State', *KACIKE: Journal of Caribbean American History and Anthropology* 1(1): 18–33.

Foucault, M., 1973a, *The Birth of the Clinic: An archaeology of Medical Perception*. London: Tavistock.

1973b, *Discipline and Punish*. Harmondsworth: Penguin.

1980, *Power/Knowledge: Selected Interviews and Other Writings 1972–77*. New York: Pantheon.

Franks, P., 2001, 'Poverty and environmental degradation in the context of Integrated Conservation and Development Projects: What makes an ICDP integrated?' Paper presented at Danish Environment and Development Network seminar on 'Rethinking Poverty-Environment relations', Copenhagen University, 23 May 2001.

Frazer, J.G., 1911–1915, *The Golden Bough: A Study in Magic and Religion*. London: Macmillan.

Funtovicz, S. and J. Ravetz, 1993, 'Science for the post-normal age', *Futures*, 25: 739–755.

GECP, 1999, *The Politics of GM Food: Risk, Science and Public Trust*, ESRC Global Environmental Change Programme Special Briefing no. 5. Brighton: ESRC Global Environmental Change Programme.

GECP, 2000a, *Risky Choices, Soft Disasters: Environmental Decision-making Under Uncertainty*. Brighton: ESRC Global Environmental Change Programme.

GECP, 2000b, *Who Governs the Global Environment?* Brighton: ESRC Global Environmental Change Programme.

GFA, 1998, Mission d'Appui: conservation de la biodiversité. Rapport de Mission. Gessellschaft für Agrarprojekte MBH for Direction Nationale des Forêts et Faune (DNFF), Conakry, and KfW, Frankfurt, October 1998.

Gaillard, J., 1991, *Scientists in the Third World.* Lexington: University Press of Kentucky.

Gardner, K., 1997, 'Mixed messages: contested "development" and the "plantation rehabilitation project"', in R. Grillo and J. Stirrat (eds), *Discourse of Development: Anthropological Perspectives*, 3133–3156. Oxford: Berg Press.

Germain, J., 1984, *Peuples de la Forêt de Guinée.* Paris: Académie Sciences Outre-Mer.

Ghimire, K. and M. Pimbert (eds), 1997, *Social Change and Conservation.* London: Earthscan.

Giddens, A., 1984, *The Constitution of Society: An Outline of the Theory of Structuration.* Cambridge: Polity Press.

1990, *The Consequences of Modernity.* Cambridge: Polity.

1991, *Modernity and Self-identity: Self and Society in the Late Modern Age.* London: Polity Press.

Gieryn, T., 1995, 'Boundaries of science', in S. Jasanoff *et al.* (eds), *Handbook of Science and Technology Studies*, 393–443. Thousand Oaks, London and New Delhi: Sage Publications.

Gledhill, J., 1994, *Power and its Disguises: Anthropological Perspectives on Power.* London: Pluto Press.

Gordon, C., 1980, 'Afterword', in M. Foucault, *Power/Knowledge: Selected Interviews and Other Writings 1972–77*, 229–259. New York: Pantheon.

Grillo, R., 1997, 'Discourses of development: the view from Anthropology', in R. Grillo and R. Stirrat (eds), *Discourses of Development: Anthropological Perspectives.* Oxford: Berg Press.

Grillo, R. and R. Stirrat, 1997, *Discourses of Development: Anthropological Perspectives.* Oxford: Berg Press.

Grindle, M. and J. Thomas, 1991, *Public Choices and Policy Change.* Baltimore: Johns Hopkins University Press.

Grove, R., 1998, *Nature and the Orient.* Cambridge University Press.

Guenter, M., 1998, 'Report on the implementation and testing of social criteria and indicators for sustainable forest management and development in small island states', Unpublished paper for ECLAC, Port of Spain.

Guijt, I. and M. Shah, 1997, *The Myth of Community.* London: IT Publications.

Guinée Ecologie, 1998, 'Plantes Medicinales et Communautes Locales', Project Bulletin no. 1, Conakry: Guinée Ecologie, COFEG and Club Traditions et Dévéloppement.

Gunther, A.E., 1942, 'The distribution and status of mora forest (*Mora excelsa*) in the Ortoire Basin, Trinidad', *Empire Forestry Journal* 21, 123–127.

Haas, P., 1990, *Saving the Mediterranean.* New York: Columbia University Press.

1992, 'Introduction: Epistemic communities and international policy coordination', *International Organisation* 46: 1–36.

Haas, P., R. Keohane and M. Levy (eds), 1993, *Institutions for the Earth: Sources of Effective International Environmental Protection.* Cambridge, Massachusetts: MIT Press.

Hajer, M., 1995, *The Politics of Environmental Discourse: Ecological Modernization and the Policy Process*, Oxford University Press.

Haraway, D., 1988, 'Situated knowledges: the Science Question in feminism and the privilege of partial perspective', *Feminist Studies* 14: 575–609.

Haraway, D., 1989, *Primate Visions: Gender, Race and Nature in the World of Modern Science*. New York: Routledge.

1991, *Symians, Cyborgs and Women: The Reinvention of Nature*. London: Free Association Books.

Haraway, D., 1997, *Modest Witness@Second_Millennium.FemaleMan©Meets_Onco-Mouse™: Feminism and Technoscience*. New York: Routledge.

Harcharik, D.A., 1997, 'The future of world forestry: sustainable forest management', *Unasylva* 190/191 (48): 4–8.

Harding, S., 1986, *The Science Question in Feminism*. Ithaca: Cornell University Press.

1991, *Whose Science? Whose Knowledge? Thinking From Women's Lives*. Buckingham: Open University Press.

1998, *Is Science Multicultural? Postcolonialisms, Feminisms and Epistemologies*. Bloomington and Indianapolis: Indiana University Press.

Hardt, M. and A. Negri, 2000, *Empire*. Cambridge: Harvard University Press.

Harrison, E., 1995, Big fish and small ponds: Aquaculture development from the FAO, Rome to Luapula Province, Zambia. DPhil Thesis, University of Sussex.

Hart, J.H., 1891, *Trinidad: Report on Forest Conservation*. London: Waterlow and Sons.

Hawthorne, W.D., 1996, 'Holes and the sums of parts in Ghanaian forest: regeneration, scale and sustainable use', *Proceedings of the Royal Society of Edinburgh*, 104B: 75–176.

Healey, P., 1997, *Collaborative Planning: Shaping Places in Fragmented Societies*. London: Macmillan.

Higman, B.W., 1999, *Writing West Indian Histories*. Warwick University Caribbean Studies.

Hoben, A., 1995, 'Paradigms and politics: the cultural construction of environmental policy in Ethiopia'. *World Development* 23(6): 1007–1022.

Hofrichter, R., (eds), 1993, *Toxic Struggles: The Theory and Practice of Environmental Justice*. Philadelphia: New Society.

Holland, J. with J. Blackburn (eds), 1998, *Whose Voice? Participatory Research and Policy Change*. London: Intermediate Technology Publications.

Hollick, A., 1924, A review of the fossil flora of the West Indies. *Bulletin of the New York Botanical Gardens* 12, 259–323.

Holmberg, J., K. Thompson and L. Timberlake, 1993, *Facing the Future: Beyond the Earth Summit*. London: IIED/Earthscan.

Holmes, T. and I. Scoones, 2000, 'Participatory policy processes: lessons from North and South'. *IDS Working Paper*. Brighton: Institute of Development Studies.

Hooper, E.D.M. 1887, *Report Upon the Forests of Tobago*. Madras: Lawrence Asylum Press.

Horton, R., 1967, 'African traditional thought and western science', *Africa* 37: 50–71, 155–187.

House of Lords, 2000, *Science and Society*. Third Report of the Select Committee on Science and Technology, Session 1999–2000. London: HMSO.

IIED, 1994, *Whose Eden? An Overview of Community Approaches to Wildlife Management*. London: International Institute for Environment and Development.

INRAP/SERVEDIT, 1997a, *Morale et instruction civique: 3ème et 4ème années*. Paris: Maisonneuve et Larose.

1997b, *Morale et instruction civique: 5ème et 6ème années*. Paris: Maisonneuve et Larose.

IPN, 1990, Project pilote d'introduction de l'education relative à l'environnement à l'école normale d'instituteurs: Programme de formation. Conakry: Institut Pedagogique National, Ministère de l'Education Nationale.

1993, Programme d'education environnementale à l'école normale d'instituteurs. Conakry: Institut Pedagogique National, Ministère de l'Enseignment Pre-Universitaire et de la Formation Professionnelle.

IUCN, 1980, *World Conservation Strategy: Living Resource Conservation for Sustainable Development*. Gland, Switzerland: IUCN, WWF and UNEP.

Irwin, A., 1995, *Citizen Science: A Study of People, Expertise and Sustainable Development*. London: Routledge.

Irwin, A. and B. Wynne, 1996, *Misunderstanding Science?* Cambridge University Press.

Irwin, A., S. Allan and I. Welsh, 2000, 'Nuclear risks: three problematics', in B. Adam *et al.* (eds), *The Risk Society and Beyond: Critical Issues for Social Theory*, 78–104. London, Thousand Oaks and New Delhi: Sage Publications.

Jackson, M., 1988, *Paths Toward a Clearing: Radical Empiricism and Ethnographic Inquiry*. Bloomington and Indianapolis: Indiana University Press.

James, C. (eds), 1983, *Highlighting Wildlife: Basic Information on Wildlife Conservation in Trinidad and Tobago*. Port of Spain: Forestry Division.

James, C., and K. Fournillier, 1992, Enhancing the conservation status of the leatherback turtle through eco-tourism at Matura Beach, Trinidad. Report, Forestry Division, Ministry of Agriculture, Land and Marine Reosurces, Port of Spain, 15 May 1992.

Jasanoff, S., 1996, 'Beyond epistemology: relativism and engagement in the politics of science', *Social Studies of Science* 26: 393–418.

Jasanoff, S., G.E. Markle, J.C. Petersen and T. Pinch (eds), *Handbook of Science and Technology Studies*. Thousand Oaks, London and New Delhi: Sage Publications.

Jasanoff, S. and B. Wynne, 1997. 'Science and Decisionmaking', in S. Rayner and E. Malone (eds), *Human Choice and Climate Change: An International Assessment, Vol. 1 The Societal Framework of Climate Change*. Battelle Press.

Jeanrenaud, S., 2002, 'Changing people/nature representations in international conservation discourses', *IDS Bulletin* 33(1): 111–122.

Johnson, N. and B. Cabarle, 1993, *Surviving the Cut*. Washington, DC: World Resources Institute.

Jordan, G., 1990, 'Sub-governments, policy communities and networks: refilling old boots', *Journal of Theoretical Politics* 2: 318–319.

Joshi, A., 1997, *Progressive Bureaucracy: An Oxymoron? The Case of Joint Forest Management in India*. Delhi: Institute of Economic Growth.

Kamano, M. and S.II Kpoghomou, 1995, 'Plan simple d'aménagement de la forêt péri-villageoise de Fourdoukoura, Bassin de Bodoro, Projet Kiss II, Kissidougou', Memoire de Diplome de Fin d'Etudes Superieures, Institut Superieur Agronomique et Veterinaire Valery Giscard d'Estaing de Faranah.

Keeley, J. and I. Scoones, 1999, 'Understanding environmental policy processes: a review', *IDS Working Paper* 89. Brighton: Institute of Development Studies.

Kerkhoff, P., 2000, *Local Forest Management in the Sahel: Towards a New Social Contract*. London: SOS-Sahel.

Kientz, A., 1996, *Le groupe-cible et ses problèmes spécifiques, intervenants institutionels et acteurs de développement, zones d'intervention prioritaires et partenariats préconisés*. Projet de Gestion des Ressources Rurales, Mesures Riveraines. Conakry: GTZ and DNFF.

Kingsbury, B., 1998, '"Indigenous peoples" in international law: a constructivist approach to the Asian controversy'. *American Journal of International Law*, 92(3): 414–457.

Kolie, H.Y. and S. Mara, 1993, 'Conception des ruraux ou paysans en matière de notion du terroir villageois de Dawa-Bassin de Kambo, Préfécture de Kissidougou'. Memoire de Diplome de Fin d'Etudes Superieures, Institut Superieur Agronomique et Vetérinaire Valéry Giscard d'Estaing de Faranah.

Koziell, I., 2001, 'Diversity not Adversity: Sustaining livelihoods with biodiversity'. *DFID Issues Paper*. London: International Institute for Environment and Development.

Koziell, I. and J. Saunders, 2001, *Living off Biodiversity: Exploring Livelihoods and Biodiversity Issues in Natural Resources Management*. London: International Institute for Environment and Development.

Knorr Cetina, K., 1999, *Epistemic Cultures: How the Sciences Make Knowledge*. Cambridge and London: Harvard University Press.

Lackhan, N.P. and Ramnarine, R., 1996a, *History of the Forestry Division in Trinidad and Tobago (1901–1996): National Parks Section* (Chapter 56). Port of Spain: Forestry Division, Ministry of Agriculture, Lands and Marine Resources.

1996b, *History of the Forestry Division in Trinidad and Tobago (1901–1996): Progress Reports*. Port of Spain: Forestry Division, Ministry of Agriculture, Lands and Marine Resources.

Lash, S., 'Risk culture', in B. Adam *et al.* (eds), 2000, *The Risk Society and Beyond: Critical Issues for Social Theory*, 47–62. London, Thousand Oaks and New Delhi: Sage Publications.

Lash, S., B. Szerszynski and B. Wynne (eds), 1996, *Risk, Environment and Modernity*. London: Sage.

Lashley, L., 1995, 'Television and the Americanization of Trinbagonian youth: a study of six secondary schools', in H.S. Dunn (eds), 1995, *Globalization, Communications and Caribbean Identity*, 83–97. Kingston: Ian Randle Publishers Ltd.

Last, M., 1980, 'The importance of knowing about not knowing', *Social Science and Medicine* 15B: 387–392.

Latour, B., 1987, *Science in Action*. Cambridge: Harvard University Press.

1993, *We Have Never Been Modern*. Hemel Hempstead: Harvester Wheatsheaf.

1999, *Pandora's Hope: Essays on the Reality of Science Studies*. Cambridge and London: Harvard University Press.

Leach, M., 1994, *Rainforest Relations: Gender and Resource Use Among the Mende of Gola, Sierra Leone*. Edinburgh: Edinburgh University Press for the International African Institute.

2000, 'New shapes to shift: war, parks and the hunting person in modern West Africa', *Journal of the Royal Anthropological Institute* 6(4): 577–595.

Leach, M. and R. Mearns, 1996, *The Lie of the Land: Challenging Received Wisdom on the African Environment*. London: James Currey and New York: Heinemann.

Leach, M., Mearns, R. and Scoones, I., 1997, 'Challenges to community-based sustainable development: dynamics, entitlements, institutions', *IDS Bulletin* 28(4): 4–14.

1999, 'Environmental entitlements: dynamics and institutions in community-based natural resource management', *World Development* 27(2): 225–247.

Levi-Strauss, C., 1966, *The Savage Mind*. University of Chicago Press.

Li, T.M., 1996, 'Images of community: discourse and strategy in property relations', *Development and Change* 27: 501–527.

Lipsky, M., 1979, *Street Level Bureaucracy: Dilemmas of the Individual in Public Services*. Russell Sage Foundation, New York.

Lodge, F., 1900, *Report on Forest Conservation in Trinidad and Tobago*. Port of Spain (Trinidad): Government Printing Office.

Long, N. and A. Long (eds), 1992, *Battlefields of Knowledge: The Interlocking of Theory and Practice in Social Research and Development*. London: Routledge.

Long, N. and J. van der Ploeg, 1989, 'Demythologising planned development: an actor perspective', *Sociologia Ruralis*, XXIX (3/4): 227–229.

Long, N. and J.D. van der Ploeg, 1994, 'Heterogeneity, actor and structure: towards a reconstitution of the concept of structure', in D. Booth (eds) *Rethinking Social Development*.

Lowe, P. and Morrison, D., 1984, 'Bad news or goods news: environmental politics and the mass media', *The Sociological Review* 32(1): 75–90.

MALMAR/LTC (Land Tenure Center, University of Wisconsin-Madison), 1992, Land Rationalization and Development Programme. Final Report. Port of Spain: Ministry of Agriculture, Lands and Marine Resources.

MLCVE, 1998, Recommandations de la Réunion Préparatoire Ouest-Africaine de la IVème Conference des Parties à la Convention sur la Diversité Biologique (COP4), Abidjan, 26–27 March 1998. Abidjan: Ministère du Logement, du Cadre de Vie et de l'Environnement, Côte D'Ivoire, and WWF.

Maley, J., 2002, 'A catastrophic destruction of African forests about 2,500 years ago still exerts a major influence on present vegetation formations', *IDS Bulletin* 33(1): 13–30.

Malinowski, B., 1925 (1948), *Magic, Science, Religion and other Essays*. Garden City, New York: Doubleday Anchor.

Marcus, G., 1995, 'Ethnography in/of the world system: the emergence of multi-sited ethnography', *Annual Review of Anthropology* 24, 95–117.

Marshall, R.C., 1925, *Report on Forestry in Trinidad and Tobago*. Port of Spain (Trinidad): Government Printing Office.

1934, *The Physiography and Vegetation of Trinidad and Tobago: A Study in Plant Ecology*. Oxford Forestry Memoirs 17. Oxford: Clarendon Press.

1939, *Silviculture of the Trees of Trinidad and Tobago, British West Indies*. Oxford.

Martin, E., 1994, *Flexible Bodies: Tracking Immunity in American Culture From the Days of Polio to the Age of AIDS*. Boston: Beacon Press.

Martin, E., 1997, 'Anthropology and the cultural study of science: from citadels to string figures', in J. Ferguson and A. Gupta (eds) *Anthropological Locations*, 131–146. Berkeley: University of California Press.

Marx, K. and F. Engels, 1964, *The German Ideology*. London: Lawrence and Wishart.

Mason, P. 1998, *Bacchanal! The Carnival Culture of Trinidad*. Temple University Press: Philadelphia.

Miller, D. 1994, *Modernity: An Ethnographic Approach: Dualism and Mass Consumption in Trinidad*. Oxford: Berg.

1997, *Capitalism: An Ethnographic Approach*. Oxford and New York: Berg.

Miller, David, 1999, 'Risk, science and policy: definitional struggles, information management, the media and BSE', *Social Science and Medicine* 49: 1239–1255.

Miller, D. and D. Slater, 2000, *The Internet: An Ethnographic Approach*. Oxford and New York: Berg.

Millimouno, S. and T.S. Telliano, 1997, 'Constitution d'un groupement forestier de la forêt péri-villageoise de Kissiyallankoro, Projet d'aménagement des Bassins Versants Kissidougou', Memoire de Diplome de Fin d'Etudes Superieures, Institut Superieur Agronomique et Vetérinaire Valéry Giscard d'Estaing de Faranah.

Ministry of Education, 1993, *Education Policy Paper (1993–2003) (White Paper)*. National Task Force on Education. Port of Spain: Ministry of Education.

Mittermeier, R.A., P. Robles-Gil and C.G. Mittermeier, 1997, *Megadiversity: Earth's Biologically Wealthiest Nations*. Mexico: CEMEX.

Mittermeier, R.A., N. Myers, J.B. Thomsen, G.A.B. de Fonseca and S. Olivieri, 1998, 'Biodiversity hotspots and major tropical wilderness areas: approaches to setting conservation priorities'. *Conservation Biology* 12(3): 516–520.

Mittermeier, R.A., N. Myers, P. Robles-Gil and C.G. Mittermeier, 2000, *Hotspots: Earth's Biologically Richest and Most Endangered Terrestrial Ecoregions*. Mexico: CEMEX.

Moore, D., 1983, *Forest Management in Trinidad and Tobago: A Case Study of Forest Management in Tropical Forests*. Rome: Food and Agriculture Organisation.

Mootoosingh, S.N., 1979, 'The growth of conservation awareness in Trinidad and Tobago (1965–1979)', *Occasional paper no.3, Dept. of Zoology*, St Augustine: University of the West Indies.

Munton, R., 2003, 'Deliberative democracy and environmental decision-making', in F. Berkhout, M. Leach and I. Scoones (eds) *Negotiating Environmental Change: New Perspectives From Social Science*. London: Edward Elgar.

Murdoch, J. and J. Clark, 1994, 'Sustainable knowledge', *Geoforum* 25: 115–321.

Murphy, W.P. and C.H. Bledsoe, 1987, 'Kinship and Territory in the History of a Kpelle Chiefdom (Liberia)', in Kopytoff, I. (eds) 1987, *The African Frontier: The Reproduction of Traditional African Societies*, 121–148. Bloomington and Indianapolis: Indiana University Press.

McNaughton, P.R., 1988, *The Mande Blacksmiths: Knowledge, Power and Art in West Africa*. Bloomington: Indiana University Press.

McNeely, J.A. (ed), 1992, *Parks for Life*. Proceedings of the IV World Congress on National Parks and Protected areas. Gland, Switzerland: IUCN

McNeely, J.A., 1993, 'Foreword' in Barzetti, V. (eds) 1993, *Parks and Progress: Protected Areas and Economic Development in Latin America and the Caribbean*. Geneva: IUCN/IADB, ix–x.

1999, 'The ecosystem approach for sustainable use of biological resources: an IUCN perspective', in Proceedings of the Norway/UN Conference on the Ecosystem Approach for Sustainable Use of Biological Diversity, September 1999, Trondheim,

Norway. Norwegian Directorate for Nature Management and Norwegian Institute for Nature Research.

McNeely, J.A. and K.R. Miller (eds), 1984, *National Parks, Conservation and Development: The Role of Protected Areas in Sustaining Society*. Washington DC: Smithsonian Institution Press.

NECC, 1973, 'Preliminary report on proposed national parks in Trinidad and Tobago', Prepared by the Sub-Committee on National Parks of the National Environment and Conservation Council. 26 February 1973, Port of Spain.

Nader, L., 1996, *Naked Science: Anthropological Inquiry into Boundaries, Power and Knowledge*. New York and London: Routledge.

Nelson, H., 1996, Ecological studies of forest mammals in the West Indies, with a focus on Trinidad. M.Phil thesis, University of the West Indies.

Nelson, N. and S. Wright (eds), 1995, *Power and Participatory Development*. London: Intermediate Technology Publications.

Newell, P., 1999, 'Introduction: globalisation and the environment: exploring the connections', *IDS Bulletin* 30(3): 1–7.

Newson, L., 1976, *Aboriginal and Spanish Colonial Trinidad*. London: Academic Press.

Niane, D.T., 1965, *Sundiata: An Epic of Old Mali* (English version). London: Longman.
    1986, *Géographie: 3e and 4e années primaires*. Republic of Guinea. Paris: Editions Nathan.

ODA, 1996, *Sharing Forest Management: Key Factors, Best Practice and Ways Forward*. London: Overseas Development Administration.

Oates, J., 2000, *Myth and Reality in the Rain Forest*. University of California Press.

Olson, D. and E. Dinerstein, 1998, 'The Global 200: A Representation Approach to Conserving the Earth's Most Biological Valuable Ecoregions', *Conservation Biology* 12 (3): 502–515.

Olwig, K.F., 1993, *Global Culture, Island Identity: Continuity and Change in the Afro-Caribbean Community of Nevis*. Chur, Switzerland: Harwood.

Ostrom, E., 1990, *Governing the Commons: The Evolution of Institutions for Collective Action*. Cambridge University Press.
    1999, 'Self-governance and forest resources'. *CIFOR Occasional Paper* No. 20., February 1999. Bogor, Indonesia: CIFOR.

Oxaal, I., 1982, *Black Intellectuals and the Dilemmas of Race and Class in Trinidad*, Cambridge, Massachusetts: Schenkman.

PACIPE, n.d., 'Environnement, savoir traditionnel et communautés locales: le PACIPE pour le retour à l'ordre naturel des choses', Conakry: Programme Regional d'Assistance Technique à la Communication et à l'Information sur la Protection de l'Environnement (PACIPE).

PACIPE, 1997, Radio Rurale Kankan: Appréciations Générales. Kankan, Conakry: PACIPE.

PROGERFOR, 1995, Proces-verbal d'aménagement des forêts de Ziama et Diecke, 1996–2015. Volume 1, présentation générale. Conakry: DNFF.

Paulme, D., 1954, *Les Gens du riz*. Paris: Librairie Plon.

Pemberton, R, 1996, The evolution of agricultural policy in Trinidad and Tobago, 1890–1945. PhD Thesis, University of the West Indies.

Person, Y., 1968–75, *Samori: une révolution Dyula*. vol. 1 (1968), vol. II (1968), vol. III (1975). Dakar: Mémoires d'IFAN.

Pfaffenberger 1993, 'Social anthropology of technology', *Annual Review of Anthropology* 21: 491–516.

Pickering, A. (eds), 1992, *Science as Practice and Culture*. University of Chicago Press.

Pickering, A., 1995, *The Mangle of Practice*. University of Chicago Press.

Pigg, S.L., 1992, 'Constructing social categories through place: social representation and development in Nepal.' *Comparative Studies in Society and History* 34(3): 491–513.

Pimbert, M. and J. Pretty, 1995, 'Parks, people and professionals: putting 'participation' into protected area management', *UNRISD Discussion Paper* 57.

Porter, G. and J. Brown, 1991, *Global Environmental Politics*. Boulder, Colorado: Westview Press.

Premdas, R., 1993, 'Ethnic conflict in Trinidad and Tobago: Domination and reconciliation', in K.A. Yelvington (eds), *Trinidad Ethnicity*, 136–160, Tennessee University Press.

Prior, L., P. Glasner and R. McNally, 'Genotechnology: three challenges to risk legitimation', in B. Adam *et al.* (eds), 2000, *The Risk Society and Beyond: Critical Issues for Social Theory*, 105–121. London, Thousand Oaks and New Delhi: Sage Publications.

Projets Bassins Versants 1997, Guide pour la constitution des groupements forestiers (Expérience des Projets Bassins Versants de la Haute Gambie et du Haut-Niger), Working document. Conakry: June 1997.

Rabinow, P., 1996, *Making PCR : A Story of Biotechnology*. University of Chicago Press.

Ramcharan, E.K., 1980, Flora history of the Nariva Swamp. PhD Thesis, University of the West Indies.

Ramdial, B.S., 1975, The social and economic importance of Caroni Swamp in Trinidad and Tobago. PhD Thesis, University of Michigan.

1980, *The Role of Forests and Trees in Maintaining a Quality Environment*. Port of Spain: Forestry Division, Ministry of Agriculture, Lands and Fisheries.

1983, *Forestry and Agriculture: Rivals and Partners with Special Reference to Trinidad and Tobago*. Port of Spain: Ministry of Agriculture, Lands and Food Production.

Ramnarine, A.R., 1997, *Forest Policy: Trinidad and Tobago*. Port of Spain: Forestry Division/FAO.

Ravesloot, S., 1999, 'Sur la politique de la création de groupements forestiers et la foresterie communautaire envisagée', Report of a workshop, Projet de Gestion des Ressources Rurales, Nzerekore.

Reddock, R., 1974, 'Survey of Private Parks – Existing and Potential', National Environment and Conservation Council Research Paper No. 2/74. Port of Spain: Ministry of Planning and Development.

Reeves, G.W., 1993, *Communications and the 'Third World'*, London: Routledge.

Ribot, J., 1995, 'Local forestry control in Burkina Faso, Mali, Niger, Senegal and The Gambia: a review and critique of new participatory policies', *RPTES Discussion Paper*. Washington: The World Bank.

1999, 'Decentralisation, participation and accountability in Sahelian forestry: legal instruments of political-administrative control', *Africa* 69(1): 23–65.

2002, 'African Decentralization: Local actors, powers and accountability', UNRISD Programme on Democracy, Governance and Human Rights Paper No. 8. Geneva: UNRISD.

Rice, R., C. Sugal and I. Bowles, 1999, 'Sustainable forest management: a review of the current conventional wisdom'. Paper prepared for the World Bank Forest Policy Information Review and Strategy. Washington DC: Conservation International.

Richards, A., 1939, *Land, Labour and Diet: An Economic Study of the Bemba Tribe.* Oxford University Press.

Richards, P., 1996/98, *Fighting for the Rain Forest: War, Youth and Resources in Sierra Leone.* Oxford: James Currey (Reprinted with additional material 1998).

Richards, P.W. 1996/1999. *The Tropical Rainforest.* Cambridge: Cambridge University Press.

Report on Forestry in Trinidad and Tobago by the Conservator of Forests. *Trinidad and Tobago Council Paper* 8, 1926, 5–6.

Rivière, C., 1969, 'Fétichisme et démystification: l'exemple guinéen', *Afrique Documents*, 102–3: 131–168.

1971, *Mutations Sociales en Guinée*, Paris: Editions Marcel Rivière et Cie.

1974, 'Les partis politiques guinéens avant l'indépendance', *Révue Française d'Etudes Politiques Africaines*, 107: 61–82.

Robertson, R. 1992, *Globalization: Social Theory and Global Culture.* London: Sage.

Robinson, R.L., 1926, Report on Forestry in Trinidad and Tobago by Captain R.C. Marshall. In Forests: Despatch from the Secretary of State for the Colonies, 22/12/1925.

Roe, E., 1991, '"Development narratives" or making the best of blueprint development', *World Development* 19 (4): 287–300.

Root, M. 1993, *The Philosophy of the Social Sciences.* Oxford: Blackwell.

Rose, H., 2000, 'Risk, trust and scepticism in the age of the new genetics', in B. Adam *et al.* (eds), 2000, *The Risk Society and Beyond: Critical Issues for Social Theory*, 63–77. London, Thousand Oaks and New Delhi: Sage Publications.

Rosenau, J., 1990, *Turbulence in World Politics.* Princeton University Press.

Sabatier, P., 1988, 'An advocacy coalition framework of policy change and the role of policy-oriented learning therein', *Policy Sciences* 29: 129–168.

Sachs, W. (eds), 1992, *The Development Dictionary: A Guide to Knowledge as Power.* London: Zed Books.

Sayer, J.A., 1995, 'Science and international nature conservation', *CIFOR Occasional Paper* No. 4. Bogor, Indonesia: CIFOR.

Schmidt, Corsitto, 1998, *Analyse des plans d'aménagement des forêts classées Ziama et Diecke du point de vue de la participation des populations.* Nzerekore: Projet de Gestion des Ressources Rurales (PGRR), GTZ and DNFF.

Schnell, R., 1949, 'Essai de synthèse biogéographique sur la région forestière d'Afrique occidentale', *Notes Africaines*, October: 29–35.

1952, *Végétation et flore de la région montagneuse du Nimba (Afrique occidentale française)*, Memoires de l'Institut Francais d'Afrique Noire, 22. Paris: IFAN.

Schrum, W. and Y. Shenhav, 1995, 'Science and technology in less developed countries', in S. Jasanoff *et al.* (eds), *Handbook of Science and Technology Studies*, 627–651. Thousand Oaks, London and New Delhi: Sage Publications.

Scoones, I., 1996, 'Paradigms, polemics and pastures', in M. Leach and R. Mearns (eds) *The Lie of the Land: Challenging Received Wisdom on the African Environment*. London: James Currey and New York: Heinemann.

1999, 'New ecology and the social sciences: what prospects for a fruitful engagement?' *Annual Review of Anthropology* 28: 479–507.

Scoones, I. and J. Thompson, 1994, 'Knowledge, power and agriculture: towards a theoretical understanding', in I. Scoones and J. Thompson (eds) *Beyond Farmer First*, 16–31. London: IT Publications.

Scott, J., 1998, *Seeing Like a State: How Certain Schemes to Improve the Human Condition Have Failed*. New Haven and London: Yale University Press.

Schwartzman, Simon, 1991, *A Space for Science: The Development of the Scientific Community in Brazil*. University Park: Pennsylvania State University.

Shackley, S. and B. Wynne, 1995, 'Global climate change: the mutual construction of an emergent science-policy domain', *Science and Public Policy* 22.

Shand, E., S. Kacal, F. Homer, R. Cross, C. Smart, 1993, 'Protected areas in Trinidad and Tobago' in Stanfield, D. and N. Singer (eds.) *Land Tenure and the Management of Natural Resources in Trinidad and Tobago (Part 1, Land Tenure)*, Land Tenure Center, University of Wisconsin-Madison, LTC Research Paper 115, July 1993.

Shapin, S. and S. Schaffer, 1985, *Leviathan and the Air Pump: Hobbes, Boyle and the Experimental Life*. Princeton University Press.

Shore, C. and Wright, S., (eds), 1997, *Anthropology of Policy: Critical Perspectives on Governance and Power*. London: Routledge.

Shore, C., and S. Wright, 1997, 'Policy: a new field of anthropology', in C. Shore and S. Wright (eds) *Anthropology of Policy: Critical Perspectives on Governance and Power*, 3–39. London: Routledge.

Shrum, W. and Y. Shenhav, 1995, 'Science and technology in less developed countries', in S. Jasanoff *et al.* (eds), *Handbook of Science and Technology Studies*, 627–651. Thousand Oaks, London and New Delhi: Sage Publications.

Shrum, W., C. Bankston and D.D. Voss, 1993, *Science and Technology in Less Developed Countries: An Annotated Bibliography*, 1976–1992. Metuchen, NJ: Scarecrow.

Simmula, M. and I. Oy, 1999, Certification of forest management and labelling of forest products: Discussion note on main issues. Paper prepared for the World Bank Group Forest Policy Implementation Review and Strategy Development: Analytical Studies. Washington DC: World Bank.

Sivaramakrishnan, K. and A. Agrawal, 1998, 'Regional modernities in stories and practices of development', Paper presented at Crossing Borders Initiative conference, Yale University, February 1998.

Skinner, E.C., 1990, 'Mass media in Trinidad and Tobago', in S.H. Surlin and W.C. Soderlund (eds), *Mass Media and the Caribbean*. New York and London: Gordon and Breach.

Solberg, B., 1997, 'The interface between research and policy-making in forestry: needs and improvement possibilities', Paper presented to the World Forestry Congress, Turkey, 1997.

Soulé, M. and J. Terborgh (eds), 1999, *Continental Conservation: Scientific Foundations of Regional Reserve Networks*. Washington, DC: Island Press.

Soumah, M., 1976, Etude pharmacognosique et chimique du *Vernonia colorata* utilisé en médicine populaire dans la traitement de la gale. Memoire de diplome de fin d'etudes superieures, Institut Polytechnique Gamal Abdel Nasser, Conakry.

Southgate, D., 1998, *Tropical Forest Conservation. An Economic Assessment of the Alternatives in Latin America*. Oxford University Press: New York.

Souvannovong, O., 2000, 'Activities of FAO in support to forestry research with special reference to Sub-Saharan Africa', in *Report of the Meeting of Heads of Forestry Research in Eastern Africa*, 14–16 December 1999. Rome: Food and Agriculture Organisation.

Spitulnik, D., 1993, 'Anthropology and mass media', *Annual Review of Anthropology* 22: 293–315.

Sprugel, D.G., 1991, 'Disturbance, Equilibrium, and Environmental Variability: What is 'natural' vegetation in a changing environment?' *Biological Conservation* 58, 1–18.

Stattersfield, A.J., M.J. Crosby, A.J. Long and D.C. Wege, 1998, *Endemic Bird Areas of the World: Priorities for Biodiversity Conservation*. Birdlife Conservation Series 7. Cambridge: Birdlife International.

Stieglitz, F.V., 1990, 'Exploitation forestière rurale et réhabilitation des forêts: Premiers résultats d'un projet de recherche interdisciplinaire en Haute-Guinée', manuscript, Berlin.

Sutton, P., 1983, 'Black power in Trinidad and Tobago: the 'crisis' of 1970', *Journal of Commonwealth and Comparative Politics* 21(2): 115–132.

Sutton, R., 1999, *Policy Processes: A Review*. London: Overseas Development Institute.

Sylla, A.S., 1976, Etude pharmacognosique et chimique de *Ocimum viride* utilisée en médicine populaire comme antihistaminique et antihémorroidaire, mise au point d'une forme pharmaceutique stable et diffusible. Memoire de diplome de fin d'etudes superieures, Institut Polytechnique Gamal Abdel Nasser, Conakry.

Symes, G.A., 1991, Report on Forest Policy and Forest Management. National Forestry Action Programme. Port of Spain: FAO/Forestry Division.

Synnott, T., 1989, 'South America and the Caribbean', in D. Poore (eds), *No Timber Without Trees: Sustainability in the Tropical Forest*, 75–116. London: Earthscan.

Tansley, A.G. and T.F. Chipp, 1926, *Aims and Methods in the Study of Vegetation*. London: British Empire/Vegetation Committee (Crown Agents for the Colonies).

Tardy, C., 1998, Paleoincendies naturels, feux anthropiques et environnements forestiers de Guyane Française du Tardiglaciaire à l'holocene recent: approches chronologique et anthracologique. Thesis, University of Montpellier II.

Taylor, C., 1988, 'Introduction and Commentary', in Hoskins, W.G. and A. Butler. *The Making of the English Landscape*. London: Guild Publishing (1988 edition of a 1955 work).

Taylor, P. and F. Buttel, 1992, 'How do we know we have global environmental problems? Science and the globalisation of environmental discourse', *Geoforum* 23: 405–416.

Taylor, L. and A. Willis, 1999, *Media Studies: Texts, Institutions and Audiences*. Oxford: Blackwell Publishers.

Terborgh, J., 1999, *Requiem for Nature*. Washington, DC: Island Press.

Thelen, K.D. and Faizool, S., 1980. *Policy for the Establishment and Management of a National Parks System in Trinidad and Tobago*. Port of Spain: Forestry Division, Ministry of Agriculture, Lands and Fisheries.

Thrupp, L.A., 1989, 'Legitimizing local knowledge: from displacement to empowerment for Third World people', *Agriculture and Human Values* 3: 13–25.

TIDCO 1996, Tourism Management Plan (1996). Port of Spain: Tourism Industry Development Corporation.

Toppin-Allahar, C., 1991, *National Forestry Action Programme Report on National Parks*. FAO/CARICOM/TFAP Country Mission Team to Trinidad and Tobago. Forestry Division, Ministry of the Environment and National Service and FAO.

Trinidad and Tobago, 1934a, Report on an investigation into the uses and marketing of forest products in Trinidad and Tobago. *Trinidad and Tobago Council Paper* 100, 1934. Port of Spain: Government Printing Office.

1934b, The Forest types of Trinidad and their principal species. *Forestry Pamphlet* 2, For teachers. Port of Spain: Government Printing Office.

1934c, Report of the Committee appointed to consider and report on the Report of the Conservator of Forests on Forestry in Trinidad and Tobago. *Trinidad and Tobago Council Paper* 56, 1924. Port of Spain: Government Printing Office.

Troup, R.S., 1926, Note on Captain R.C. Marshall's Report on Forestry in Trinidad and Tobago. In Forests: Despatch from the Secretary of State for the Colonies, 22/12/1925, relating to the Report on Forestry in Trinidad and Tobago by the Conservator of Forests. *Trinidad and Tobago Council Paper* 8, 1926, 3–5.

Truman, D., 1951, *The Governmental Process: Political Interests and Public Opinion*. New York: Knopf.

Tylor, E.B., 1871, *Primitive Culture: Researches into the Development of Mythology, Philosophy, Religion, Language, Art and Customs*. London: J. Murray.

UNBIO, 1999, *Monographie Nationale sur la Diversité Biologique*. Unité Nationale pour la Diversité Biologique. Conakry: Direction Nationale de l'Environnement, Ministère des Travaux Publics et de l'Environnement, Republic of Guinea.

UNDP, 2000, *Human Development Report*. New York: UNDP.

UNESCO/UNEP, 1989, Atelier national d'élaboration de stratégie d'éducation environnementale en République de Guinée. Conakry, 27–30 December 1989.

Vogler, J. and A. Jordan, 2003, 'Governance and the environment', in F. Berkhout, M. Leach and I. Scoones (eds), *Negotiating Environmental Change*, 137–158. Cheltenham, UK: Edward Elgar.

WCFSD 1999, *Our Forests, Our Future*. Report of the World Commission on Forests and Sustainable Development. Cambridge: Cambridge University Press.

WWF, 1997, *Global 200 Ecoregions* (map). Washington DC: World Wildlife Fund.

1999, *Ecoregional-Based Conservation: A User's Guide*. Draft 6 December 1999. Gland, Switzerland: WWF.

Wade, R., 1982, 'The system of political and administrative corruption: canal irrigation in South India', *Journal of Development Studies* 18(3).

1997, 'Greening the Bank: the struggle over the environment, 1970–85', in D. Kapur, J. Lewis and R. Webb (eds), *The World Bank: Its First Fifty Years*. Washington: Brookings Institution Press.

Wade, J. and R. Bickram, 1981, Proposed Legislation for a System of National Parks and Equivalent Reserves in Trinidad and Tobago. Draft, Forestry Division/OAS Project August 1981. Mimeo. Port of Spain: Forestry Division.

Warren, D.M., L.J. Slikkerveer and D. Brokensha (eds), 1995, *The Cultural Dimension of Development: Indigenous Knowledge Systems*. London: IT.

Wells, M., K. Brandon and L. Hannah, 1992, *People and Parks: Linking Protected Area Management with Local Communities*. Washington DC: World Bank.

Western, D., M. Wright and S. Strum (eds), 1994, *Natural Connections: Perspectives in Community-Based Conservation*, Washington DC: Island Press.

Whitmore, T., 2000, 'Biodiversity', Letter to the Editor, *New Scientist*, 11 March.

Willard, C.A., 1996, *Liberalism and the Problem of Knowledge: A New Rhetoric for Modern Democracy*. University of Chicago Press.

Wilson, P., 1973, *Crab Antics: The Social Anthropology of English Speaking Negro Societies of the Caribbean*, New Haven: Yale University Press.

Wood, G. (eds), 1985, *Labelling in Development Policy*. London: Sage.

World Bank, 1991, *The Forest Sector: A World Bank Policy Paper*. Washington DC: World Bank.

Worster, D., 1994, 'Nature and the disorder of history', *Environmental History Review* 18(2): 1–16.

Wynne, B., 1992a, 'Misunderstood misunderstanding: social identities and public uptake of science', *Public Understanding of Science* 1: 281–304.

1992b, 'Uncertainty and environmental learning: reconceiving science and policy in the preventive paradigm', *Global Environmental Change* 2(2): 111–127.

1995, 'Public understanding of science', in S. Jasanoff *et al.* (eds), *Handbook of Science and Technology Studies*, 361–388. Thousand Oaks, London and New Delhi: Sage Publications.

1996, 'May the sheep safely graze? A reflexive view of the expert-lay knowledge divide', in S. Lash, B. Szerszynski and B. Wynne (eds) *Risk, Environment and Modernity*. London: Sage.

Yearley, S., 1988, *Science, Technology and Social Change*. London: Unwin Hyman.

Yelvington, K.A., 1993, 'Introduction: Trinidad ethnicity', in K.A. Yelvington (eds), *Trinidad Ethnicity*, 1–32. Tennessee University Press.

Zeroki, B., 1990, Etude relative au feu auprès des populations des bassins versants types du Haut Niger. Conakry: European Union.

Index